Marian Pallister has worked as a feature writer and commentator, covering social issues in Scotland and round the world, particularly in disaster and war zones. She previously lectured in journalism at Napier University and has taught English subjects at Argyll College. She also founded the charity ZamScotEd, which supports the education of vulnerable young people in Zambia. Her previous books include *Argyll Curiosities*, *Yesterday Was Summer: The Marion Campbell Story*, *Lost Argyll*, *Cruachan: The Hollow Mountain* and *The Crinan Canal*.

NOT A PLACK
THE RICHER
ARGYLL'S MINING STORY

Marian Pallister

BIRLINN

First published in 2018 by
Birlinn Limited
West Newington House
10 Newington Road
Edinburgh
EH9 1QS

www.birlinn.co.uk

ISBN: 978 1 78027 504 8

British Library Cataloguing-in-Publication Data
A catalogue record for this book is available from the British Library

Typeset by Initial Typesetting Services, Edinburgh
Printed and bound by Clays Ltd, Elcograf S.p.A.

To miners and their families,
past and present

Contents

List of Illustrations   ix

Prologue   xi

1   A layman's look at the world of minerals   1

2   Mines of Morvern and Ardnamurchan   11

3   The Munchausen factor   38

4   The coal of Kintyre   57

5   Digging for profit   88

6   The Inveraray mines   103

7   Life, work and the changing world   151

8   Inveraray Metal – a stitch-up and the wind down of the Inveraray mines   164

9   The men behind the Islay mines   183

10   Lochaline and Strontian – mines for the future   194

Epilogue   215

Acknowledgements   219

Bibliography   223

Index   227

List of Illustrations

Alexander Bruce's 1733 plan of the mining development at Loch Sunart

Section of Bruce's plan showing elevations of the Strontian mine buildings and a new quay for shipping lead

The Strontian mines in the Ardnamurchan hills

Bruce's 1733 plan showing the 'Liedges Dale' (Liddesdale) lead mines and quay built by the Morvern company

The pithead at Drumlemble

Memorial in Kilkivan cemetery for Donald and Daniel McPhail

The pithead at Machrihanish

Argyll Colliery miners, Kintyre

Miners who attended the NCB Mechanisation Training Centre, Sheffield

Working for the National Coal Board at the Argyll Colliery

A plan of the Craignure copper mine in the hills west of Auchindrain

Plan of proposed extensions to the Craignure mine, June 1843

Plan of an adit (entrance) into the Craignure mine

The Forestry sign at the remains of a Craignure adit

Another Craignure adit

Receipt for ten casks of copper ore sent by the Duke of Argyll in October 1840 on the steamer *Commodore*

Mines around Inveraray, 1896

Plan of the Coillebraid mine, 1855

The Rolling Tube and Wire Mills in Birmingham bought Inveraray ore

Argyll Estates gamekeeper Tom Kirsop investigates remains of an adit to Coille-Bhraghad

An entrance to the Kilmartin copper mine

Remains of a storehouse and spoil heap at Kilmartin mine

The geological layering at the entrance to Kilmartin copper mine

The mines to the north of Lochgilphead

The landscape around Castleton, shaped by mining ventures of the past

The South Knapdale hills, pock-marked with lead mines

Miners at the the Morvern silica mine

Silica at Lochaline quay

Setting explosives at Lochaline

A flooded mine tunnel showing the dangers every mine can present

Alistair Scoular, who worked in the Lochaline mine in the 1950s

A 'pug' loaded with sand emerges from Lochaline mine

Prologue

Robert Moody was born in 1797. He was baptised on 30 July that year in the parish of Tanfield, County Durham. He was the son of John Moody, or Mewdey, of Kip Hill, another hamlet a mile or so distant. Robert seems to have grown up in the district but perhaps didn't go to school because, when he married Ann Leonard in that same church where he had been baptised, both he and Ann 'made their mark', rather than signing the register. A miner at Beamish Colliery, Robert was 24 years old when he married Ann on 2 June 1821. By 1827, he was a widower and, on 11 August 1827, he was married again, this time to Mary Brown. It was Mary who answered the knock on the door on 7 March 1832, the day a 'melancholy occurrence took place at Beamish Colliery', according to *Local Records or Historical Register of Remarkable Events* by John Sykes, published in 1833.

It probably wasn't that much of a surprise. Pit accidents were two a penny and lives like that of Robert Moody were cheap. But Mary was looking after four children (surely not all her own in just five years of marriage) and was 'far advanced in pregnancy'. The news was that Robert was one of three men caught underground by 'an unexpected rush of water'. Robert was with the colliery viewer or agent – a man named William Millar – and the two of them drowned. A third man managed to escape 'with difficulty'. It was sixteen long days before the bodies were recovered. The water was drawn off and the bodies, according to the report by John Sykes, were 'in a most shocking condition'. Sykes adds, 'On taking the shoes from Moody, his feet separated with them.' The bodies were buried the following day, 24 March 1832.

Flooding, explosions, rockfalls – all in a day's work in the mines of these islands. For those today who think that health and safety regulations have 'gone mad', the litany of past disasters is a harsh reminder of the horrible deaths and injuries suffered because of the lack of safety measures.

By the time Robert Moody drowned in the darkness of Beamish Colliery's coal seams – today Beamish is the site of a thriving and fascinating museum commemorating the mining industry of the area – safety was on the agenda, even if few measures were actually taken. In Volume 15 of *Transactions of the North of England Institute of Mining Engineers*, John Bedlington, a colliery viewer at Sheriff Hill Colliery, is reported to have made an address to the proprietors of collieries on 13 September 1814. Mr Bedlington, a man whose family seems to have been employed as viewers, told the pit owners:

I now beg leave to revert to the lack of attention in those viewers who are said to inspect two or more (even to the number of six) collieries; any one of which requires their sole and not divided attention, as they seldom, if ever, from observation, know the actual state of any one of them. The information they possess is chiefly from the reports of their under-viewers, and in many collieries they are very worthy, intelligent men, but why are they consigned to that situation, when it would be more to your interest were no such men as upper-viewers known? I am convinced, to have a resident sole viewer of ability, unshackled by those whose knowledge of the colliery must be greatly inferior to his own, is the first step towards a total emancipation from the chaos in which the management of collieries seems to be enveloped.

In other words, the man who died alongside Robert Moody may well have had little knowledge of the pit in which the two of them died such hideous deaths because Mr Millar was perhaps required to 'view' and report on up to half a dozen pits and perhaps, as viewer of many pits, he was master of none.

Why tell the story of Robert Moody? Because he was my three times great-grandfather and, as a purveyor of social history, it bothers me greatly to think of lives being so cheap that decades could pass before measures were taken to ensure that men, women and children working in an increasingly industrialised world could be safeguarded.

It was a year after Mr Bedlington's address to the mine owners that Sir Humphry Davy visited the collieries near Newcastle to investigate the types of gases produced in them. A couple of months later, in October 1815, the first safety lamp (invented by Dr William Reid Clanny of Sunderland) was tried out and found to be too unwieldy to be of any use. Whether George Stephenson or Sir Humphry Davy then produced the first useful lamp is hard to pinpoint but Davy, of course, has the credit in the name 'Davy lamp' that came down through generations of miners in all manner of mines.

It is not recorded what Robert Moody and William Millar carried with them to light their way in Beamish Colliery some 17 years after a safety lamp was invented. Suffice to say that three and four decades after that invention, miners in Argyll were carrying candles to light their way in dank, water-filled tunnels in their search for lead, copper, silver, gold and nickel. And it is perhaps even more appalling that, during the years of the Second World War, men working in the tunnels of the silica mine at Lochaline in Morvern had no protection against dust inhalation, resulting in lung disease, and the only issue of 'equipment' was a pair of Welly boots.

The injustices were not limited to safety. Tennessee Ernie Williams sang a song in 1947 called 'Sixteen Tons'. The American singer had a major hit with this number which was, in effect, about bonded labour. 'I owe my soul to the company store' was a reference to the truck system, which members of the British Parliament had tried to regulate as far back as 1831. The song was written and first recorded by Merle Travis in 1946 – not about the historic Klondike gold miners of the 19th century but about contemporary injustices in the Kentucky coal mines that his brother John had written to him about.

These injustices were ancient and very firmly embedded in certain industries – particularly the mining industry. Under what was known as the truck system, employers paid their workmen in goods or tokens, which could be exchanged only at shops owned by the employers. In Britain, the Truck Act of 1831 tried to rescue workers from this form of bonded labour. The Act listed many trades in which the payment of wages would henceforth have to be made in coins. The Truck Act was discussed in Parliament a number of times over the following decades and, in 1871, the commissioners appointed to examine the workings of the Act reported in favour of lead mines being incorporated into its scope. This should have protected miners in Argyll, where numerous lead mines had operated for centuries. But the wheels of progress grind exceedingly slow, particularly when it comes to progress that safeguards workers' rights and costs proprietors money. To recap – commissioners had said in 1871 that it would be a good idea to make sure lead miners were paid in cash rather than loading sixteen tons only to find themselves 'another day older and deeper in debt', to quote Mr Travis's song.

Thirteen years later, a Mr Chappel asked the procurator fiscal at Inveraray to put the Truck Act into force for the protection of lead miners on the island of Islay. It was 1884 but the procurator fiscal had to tell Mr Chappel that 'although the Act applies to an iron or coal miner, it does not appear to apply to a lead miner. I am therefore unable to do anything in the matter.'

Sir Donald Macfarlane, MP for Carlow and then, from 1885, for Argyll, asked in Parliament whether this was a 'true exposition of the Law' and, if it were, then whether steps would be taken to amend it. The Lord Advocate had to tell him that, despite the 1871 suggestion that lead miners be paid in cash as other sorts of miners were under the Truck Act, this amendment had still not been incorporated into law. Hansard for 21 July 1884 records that the Lord Advocate said he would 'inquire into the particulars . . . with a view to considering as to legislation'.

Three years later – and if a week is a long time in politics, think how long three years must have seemed in the life of a lead miner – the Truck Act was amended in 1887 to cover almost all manual workers. In 1896, a further Act regulated the amounts that could be deducted from wages for bad workmanship.

Such measures may seem to apply only superficially to Argyll. Yes, the lead mines of Islay are well documented and lead was mined successfully around Tyndrum. There was a coal mine at Drumlemble that gave Kintyre its only railway – and what else? Surely this writer's indignation should be directed elsewhere in Scotland, where mining created the livelihoods of great swathes of the population?

But let's scratch the surface of this geologically diverse edge of Scotland. Let's look at the old maps and delve into the archives. We then find that Argyll and its islands are pockmarked with the remains of mines of every type. Our forests – today's industry – have grown over the dozens of 'adits' – or horizontal entrances – and shafts that took men underground to exploit yesterday's mining industry and, in turn, sometimes to be exploited themselves.

The threads of silver and gold, copper and nickel, lead and coal have all too often proved illusive. The economic ups and downs of the past 300 years have opened and closed (and sometimes opened again) many potential sources of a dizzying range of minerals. The 1715 and '45 uprisings, intended solutions to the forfeited lands situation, a legally acceptable system of unpaid bonded mining labour that was halted at the start of the 19th century, some questionable 19th-century company legislation and some more than questionable 'engineers' and 'mineralogists' have left a patchwork of deserted workings. But there also remains a thriving mining industry that has emerged from the mistakes and misapprehensions of the past to create a very valuable present in an area of Scotland that most people identify as a rural idyll rather than an industrial heartland.

My family has shifted somewhat over the past two centuries and so, while this is written in respectful memory of a man so cruelly parted from his shoes (note that they weren't even boots, let alone steel-toed safety boots), Robert Moody's great-great-great-great-granddaughter has immersed herself in the mining history of Argyll, not County Durham.

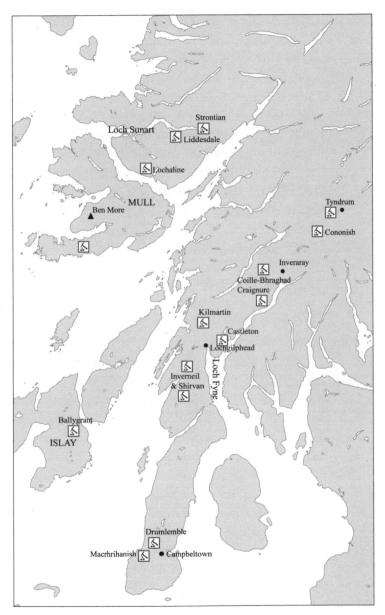

Location of mines in Argyll

1

A layman's look at the world of minerals

The way that minerals have been used throughout the millennia in some ways presents us with a history of man's social and intellectual progress. Moving on from the use of stone and flints to facilitate contemporary living must have seemed as revolutionary as the invention of the steam engine, the mechanical loom or electricity. Stone had enabled the sourcing and preparation of food and had provided protection against intruders. The discovery of metals that could be sharpened into more efficient tools and weapons was a major step forward. In time, such metals would also provide coins as currencies replaced a barter system.

The International Lead Association tells us that lead has been used for millennia not only for 'useful purposes' but also to create artistic or perhaps religious artefacts. The oldest known lead artefact was discovered in Turkey and is more than 8,000 years old. Later, the pharaohs filled their ceremonial spaces (for the living and the dead) with lead figurines and used lead in a process to glaze pottery. The Romans, always practical, used lead for water pipes, aqueducts, tank linings, wine vats and cooking pots. It was a soft, plastic metal and rust resistant. Early scientists used it in paints, pigments and cosmetics – which with hindsight we know was not such a good idea in terms of human health. Even the Romans themselves began to suspect that some of their illnesses might have been caused by lead. Not convinced, later generations continued to use the metal for all manner of purposes. There was even a compound known as 'sugar of lead' (lead acetate), which was used to sweeten wine and food.

The Romans called lead *plumbum*, which gave us the English word for a plumber – the skilled person who fitted lead pipes before the advent of plastic. By the Middle Ages, lead was the turn-to metal for everything from roofs to coffins. Water tanks were made from lead and it was used in churches in the stained glass windows that taught Bible stories to the illiterate. It was the preferred metal for knuckle-dusters and, from Caxton's time, for printing machines. Easy to assume, then, that, when the Norsemen came to Argyll and the Isles, they would have been keen to exploit the lead mines of Islay, although there is no proof that this was the island's main attraction.

Copper has at least as long and almost as diverse a history. Like lead, some of its first uses seem to have been to decorate its finders – a copper pendant found in the area of today's northern Iraq was dated to 8700 BC. Around the globe, man seemed to like this attractive metal – Mesopotamians had organised a proper industry by 4500 BC. The Egyptians weren't far behind. The Chinese were producing copper by 2500 BC, although it was well into the Christian era before the peoples of Central America and Africa began to work with the metal.

At first, it was used decoratively. It was, like lead, a soft metal and so no use in its virgin state for weapons or tools.

Then the Mesopotamians started to experiment. They had cracked the difficulties of extracting copper from ore by 3000 BC. They then invented ways to create an alloy of copper and tin – bronze – that could be forged, hammered and hardened or melted and moulded.

From this emerged new crafts and professions, including metalsmiths who made pots, trays, saucers and drinking vessels. The tools it was now possible to manufacture included razors, harpoons, arrows, spearheads and chisels – 3000 BC found man able to shave, shape a house and make his quarrels much more unpleasant.

It is clear from analysis of the bronze alloys from Mesopotamia in 3000 BC (87 per cent copper, 10–11 per cent tin and small amounts of iron, nickel, lead, arsenic and antimony) that the composition of the hills and glens of Argyll and its islands bears strong similarities to those in the Middle East. However, to paraphrase comedian Eric Morecambe's riposte to conductor André Previn's critique of his piano playing, 'all the right metals but not necessarily in the right order'. But we will come to that.

In the third century BC, the Greeks began to use coins instead of a bartering system and copper became essential in their monetary structure. The Romans, of course, developed that system further, as well as exploiting new mining methods and iron smelting to advance all manner of uses for all manner of metals. At the peak of the Roman Empire's industrial reach, it exploited copper mines in Turkey, Spain and Anglesey which, according to online magazine *The Balance*, produced up to 15,000 tons of refined copper every year.

Copper works best when alloyed with other metals, such as tin and nickel. Used with nickel it has been applied to the hulls of ships because it does not corrode in seawater and it repels shellfish such as barnacles. That makes ships travel faster (and in modern times increases fuel efficiency). The process was first used on ships of the British Navy in 1761 and, 20 years later, according to *The London Magazine*, all the Royal Navy's ships would be given the copper-bottom treatment. Admiral Keppel said that copper-bottomed ships gave additional strength to the navy, giving rise to the idea that 'copper-bottomed' equates with total resistance to failure. The phrase 'copper-bottomed' should really be 'copper and nickel alloy bottomed' but that is less than catchy and doesn't quite carry the same feeling of thorough reliability.

Today, copper (having been through financial doldrums in the 20th century) has again found favour as one of a range of minerals used in mobile phones, tablets, computer systems and space technologies. The entrepreneurs of the 19th century often struggled to find a profitable market for their ore. Since the beginning of the 21st century, however, copper and other metals used in communication technologies have seen a 25 per cent rise in demand. Markets fluctuate for many reasons and those dabbling in mining for metals in 18th- and 19th-century Argyll had already begun to fall victim to discoveries of huge quantities of a range of minerals in every corner of the world – and every corner of the world was becoming not only accessible (possibly much more accessible than Argyll's nooks and crannies) but also under the control of colonial powers.

For landowners and those who leased mines, keeping production costs low and identifying the swiftest and cheapest forms of transport for their product were of paramount importance. Before legislation could put the building blocks of workers' protection into place, this led to very questionable practices. The lead miner in Morvern in the early 1700s was paid in oatmeal – a pittance enough for his hard work. The 19th-century copper miner in central Africa may not have been so privileged. Exploitation was global.

Nickel may not have had a name until 1751, when the Swedish chemist Axel Cronstedt first identified and isolated it as an element, but clearly from the analyses made of the alloys used in ancient times, it was known and valued. It had been known as 'Devil's Copper' because the miners of the 15th century were convinced that the red-brown ore that looked so much like copper was poisoning them. Cronstedt's naming of Element 28 could have been playful, if we allow that scientists can be so, because the German word 'nickel' has a meaning similar to our 'Old Nick'. At that time, nickel was left firmly in the ground – mainly because it was so difficult to extract rather than out of respect for the health of the miners. It would be many generations before it was acknowledged that it was the arsenic in the ore that poisoned the workers.

In the 19th century, nickel was used in alloys, one of which was created from Argyll minerals, in the great search for lighter, more efficient weaponry. It became very valuable during the Crimean War and the American Civil War but, after these conflicts were resolved, the price dropped, leaving mine owners struggling to find a home for their ore.

Copper and lead were the first of the minerals to be found in Argyll and it seems from the records that, whenever a new mine was contemplated, it was to search for seams of one or other. Sometimes this met with success, sometimes not. Silver, gold and nickel have also been mined with varying degrees of success and gold is still on the mining agenda in the Tyndrum area. Coal was at the heart of one of Argyll's oldest mines – the Drumlemble colliery in Kintyre, which originally provided coal for work in lead mines. The records show that the Constable of Tarbert bought coal in 1326 for smelting but how much further back can a commercial mining interest be traced?

During that period between the 9th and 13th centuries when the Vikings ruled 'all they could sail round' on the western seaboard of Scotland, lead, copper and silver were certainly mined on the island of Islay and, as R.M. Callender and J. Macaulay point out in *The Ancient Metal Mines of the Isle of Islay, Argyll*, one of the surviving Norse names, Balulive, is the name of a lead mine. Callender and Macaulay are, however, also at pains to point out that '[t]here is no evidence other than a volume of opinion that the Norse invaders of the ninth century mined for metal on the Island of Islay'. The Vikings certainly used metals of all sorts for helmets, weapons, tools and agricultural implements, not to mention their very beautiful jewellery, but it is more likely that they extracted Islay minerals from the locals as a tax rather than that their young migrant men extracted them physically from the ground.

Further north and on the mainland, mining for lead and coal in Morvern and Ardnamurchan was also an ancient adjunct to crofting. Methods were crude but production sufficient to class lead mining as 'one of the staple industries of the county', according to the lawyer Duncan Clerk, who produced a report on Argyll in 1878 for the Highland and Agricultural Society of Scotland. He noted that several mines in the area around Strontian had 'been wrought for a period of 150 years previous to the year 1855' – in other words, from 1705. On a very elaborate plan produced by Alexander Bruce in 1733, mining in the Loch Sunart area was declared to have 'become famous by this the greatest national improvement this age has produced'. Mr Clerk explained that, by 1748, the White Smith Mine in that district had employed over 500 men and boys. After 1855, most of the mines in the area closed 'for want of capital, and on account of their distance from a proper shipping place'.

It is heartening, therefore, that, while lead is no longer 'one of the staple industries of the county', the metal strontium is still mined in the Loch Sunart area. Strontium was discovered in 1790 by two scientists – Adair Crawford and William Cruikshank – who were analysing the local lead ore. In 1791, it was identified as a new element. Humphry Davy then isolated the metal in 1808 using the brand-new process of electrolysis. Like copper, the metal has found its uses in modern technology. For a while in the 20th century, it was in huge demand for the glass of cathode ray tubes for televisions. Today, the world's most accurate atomic clock, accurate to one second in 200 million years, has been developed using strontium atoms. It has more mundane uses, of course, from the crimson colour that strontium salts add to flares and fireworks to the strontium chloride used in toothpaste for sensitive teeth.

There were also lead mines south of Loch Sunart in the Morvern peninsula (and a smidgeon of coal was found there, too). But it is the finest quality sand that created a viable industry at Lochaline from the start of World War II. The seam of silica sand was identified in 1895 and, in 1923, an Edinburgh Geological Survey showed the sand to be one of the purest deposits in the world. Because it is almost free of iron, it is ideal for producing high quality glass. However, silica sand was a cheap import at the time and this pure deposit was ignored because of the inaccessibility of Lochaline (such a familiar story for all Argyll's mines throughout the centuries).

When war broke out and the supply of sand for high quality glass to make periscopes and gunsights was threatened because of blockades that prevented imports from elsewhere, Lochaline came into its own. With a short break after the financial collapse of 2008, the silica mine has continued to produce this fine sand that was preserved under layers of lava from the volcanic eruptions on the island of Mull some 50–60 million years ago.

Geologists say that the most northerly known outcrop of carboniferous rocks in Britain is at Inninmore Bay in Morvern. A poor seam was also found on Mull. This reminds us that the area was, hundreds of millions of years ago, a tropical swampy area. When the giant plants and ferns from those swamp forests died, they formed layers at the bottom of the swamps. The plant remains were flooded, sealed in by another layer of vegetation and then, during the following millennia, pressure and heat would have built up on top of the plant remains, subjecting them to chemical and physical changes. As the oxygen was pushed out, the drowned forests metamorphosed into coal. The higher the pressure and the longer the process was allowed to go on undisturbed, the better the quality of the coal. While this is clearly what happened in areas such as the Fife coalfields, in Morvern and Mull the end product was poor.

Even those of us with the most rudimentary knowledge of geology can see that the west of Scotland literally has a volcanic history. The Ardnamurchan peninsula, for example, has a 55-million-years-old underground volcanic complex. Mull has a volcanic past. The BBC News Science and Environment website reported that, according to the eminent Scottish geologist Professor Iain Stewart, 'All along what is now the western shores of Scotland, huge volcanic centres erupted colossal quantities of magma. The islands of Arran, Mull and Skye are among the remains of a chain of volcanoes that draped much of northern Britain and Ireland in enormous amounts of lava and volcanic ash.'

Minerals were formed when rocks melted as the earth's crust formed. Liquid copper, lead, silver, gold and zinc would have flowed into the cracks between larger molten rocks as they slowly cooled. The fluid minerals would then have crystallised and solidified. Copper solidifies later than the other minerals within larger rocks, creating a higher concentration in the deposits. When the upper layers of rocks erode, that's when the minerals are exposed and can be mined. The movement of the earth's crust caused by volcanic eruptions and earthquakes in the intervening millions of years means that seams of minerals are frequently irregular, fractured and downright puzzling to those attempting to mine them.

Thus it proved for those who attempted to mine among the remains of the 'huge volcanic centres' along the western shores of Scotland – all too often frustrating those who sought financial success from their mining forays. The Inveraray-born writer Neil Munro employed artistic licence in his novel *John Splendid* by moving the discovery of mines around the Clan Campbell capital back a century or two. In a dedication written in 1898 to introduce the novel, Munro said, 'You may wonder, too, that the Silver Mines of Coillebhraid, discovered at the time of your great-grandfather, should have been so strangely anticipated in the age of Gillesbeg Gruamach. Let not those chronological divergences perturb you.' His fictionalised Marquis of Argyll, however, spoke a fundamental truth about the returns any landowner or lease-holder could expect from the fractured seams of minerals in this county. In a courtroom scene in which the circumstances of a stabbing are investigated, the Marquis asks a witness what his trade is. 'I'm at the Coillebhraid silver-mines,' the man tells him, adding, 'We had a little too much to drink, or these MacLachlan gentlemen and I had never come to variance.'

The Marquis expresses his frustration by banging his fist on the table and saying, 'Damn those silver-mines . . . they breed more trouble in this town of mine than I'm willing to thole. If they put a penny in my purse it might not be so irksome, but they plague me sleeping and waking, and I'm not a plack the richer.' In Scotland, in the 15th and 16th centuries, a plack was a four-penny-piece copper coin.

Illusive seams, injudicious investment, unstable work forces, jittery markets and the sheer remoteness of Argyll meant few were ever 'a plack the richer'.

2

Mines of Morvern and Ardnamurchan

Jim Blair held out the kind of wee boulder you might add to a suburban rockery. 'Have you ever held a piece of lead?' he asked. The answer had to be 'Not to my knowledge' because this wee boulder looked like so many others to the untutored eye. Jim's eye, however, is highly practised. He is the chairman of Lochaber Geopark, a fascinating not-for-profit project based in Fort William. The geology of Lochaber (which includes parts of historic Argyll) is his lifeblood and we met in the Geopark premises in Fort William High Street — a treasure house displaying masses of minerals hewn from the surrounding mountains and glens.

Some of those minerals glitter and sparkle in their glass showcases. The dull slab balanced in Jim's two palms held no such charms. I held up my hands to receive it, but Jim lowered his hands until I had no choice but to put mine on the table. Wise move. The mass of this chunk of ore was, well, yes — a lead weight. We use that expression so unthinkingly but this simple demonstration illustrated clearly that it is no idle idiom. Lead really is very heavy — 11.34 grams per cubic centimetre or, in pre-decimal terms, a cubic inch of lead weighs almost half a pound.

As my hands registered why criminals get rid of surplus bodies by wrapping them in lead overcoats or giving them lead boots, I couldn't imagine how hard it must have been to extract lead ore in the primitive mines of Argyll in the 17th and 18th centuries. As Jim explained, throughout the years up to as late as 1850 when the Morvern and Ardnamurchan mines were still active, the men brought the ore out in buckets, then washed it and roasted it on site. Their biggest problem was the depth of the tunnels they were working in and how much water they could pump out. Thomas Newcomen's engine was in use from 1711 (one Newcomen engine could do the work of the equivalent of 500 horses – horsepower that had previously been the only method of pumping out water from a depth of 150 feet). James Watt improved on this enormously in 1765 by fitting a condenser and over the next decade made further improvements. With his partner Matthew Boulton, Watt manufactured pumps for the Cornish mines and other major engineering works, such as canal construction but the remote Highland mines were still operating with a bucket system well into the 19th century.

The sheer physical effort of working in such conditions – and in the relentless Argyll weather that could close a mine for weeks in winter because of the cold and flood it in the 'summer' with an excess of rain – is hard to imagine. Even harder when we read a snippet from a rent book in the archives at Dunollie Museum near Oban: 'Strontian, 1728 – Robert Frazer, miner, payments in meal.' Robert Frazer and his fellow workers were required to bring out the ore containing this heavy metal, working in waterlogged tunnels, and were paid so little that their rent could only be rendered in oatmeal. The miners were not alone in paying rent in meal, of course. That same rent book lists a carter, a chapman, a mason, a wright, a servant and many others, all paying in the same way to Sir Alexander Murray's estate. But judging from the weight of this lump of lead, mining must surely have been the hardest occupation, and the conditions in this part of the country perhaps more difficult than elsewhere.

We have seen from Duncan Clerk's report that mining had been up and running in the area around Strontian since 1705. It is perhaps timely to remember what was happening at that time in Scotland. The civil wars that had raged throughout the 17th century had left the people of Morvern and Ardnamurchan impoverished and insecure. Much of Scotland was still feudal, at least in concept if not in practice. Historically, the MacLeans of Duart had been the feudal overlords of this part of the mainland but, in 1670, the 9th Earl of Argyll led an armed invasion and took over two-thirds of Morvern as well as much of the rest of the Duart estates.

The complex allegiances that the Earl and his late father, the Marquess of Argyll, had made during the civil wars meant that he knew what the inside of a prison looked like and what it was like to be under threat of execution (the Marquess himself had been executed). He was, however, given a renewed charter on lands and offices of state by Charles II and was seen in the years of the Restoration as a moderate member of the Privy Council of Scotland. The Highlands were in a parlous state and his role included persecution of the Covenanters, even though the records suggest this went against his personal convictions.

Argyll's fortunes fluctuated wildly as the nationwide political situation seesawed. In the 1680s, he was in exile in Europe at the time of Charles II's death and he conspired to invade Scotland from Holland in support of the Duke of

Monmouth's claim to the throne. The attempted coup was a failure and the Earl was executed as his father before him had been. His successor attempted fruitlessly to recover his estates by currying favour with James VII of Scotland, II of England. His next step was to switch his support and aid William and Mary of Orange (Mary being the daughter of James II) in their bid for the throne. Their accession in 1689 may have led to a superficially peaceful period of history but in the Highlands all was far from settled.

Scotland's aristocracy found itself deeply in debt – which, of course, meant the 'ordinary' people would also struggle mightily. Living in a range of castles on a limited income may have been tough for the likes of the 1st Duke of Argyll but how much tougher for the miner in his employ? The 1st Duke's estates were returned to him, and there is evidence that his successor would consider agricultural reforms to improve the lot of crofters (and increase his own income, of course) in Morvern, but the restrictions placed on how a man could worship, where and how he could work and who he should owe allegiance to unsettled too many in this remote area of the Highlands.

It wasn't only the civil wars that left the people of the Highlands wanting. There had been a seven-year famine in the 1690s that hit crofters hard. Indirectly, the madness of the Darien scheme added to the uncertain financial state of the country as a whole. In trying to recoup their losses and turn Scotland into a trading nation and colonial power like England, the aristocratic members of Scottish Parliament approved not only a charter establishing the Bank of Scotland in 1695 but also the Company of Scotland, which was to raise subscriptions to create capital capable of trading with Africa and the Indies. So desperate were Scotland's great and good (or not so good) to prove the country a financial force to be reckoned with that they managed within a few weeks to raise £400,000 sterling, which today would be worth around £47 million. That was around a fifth of Scotland's total wealth and, in 1698, an expedition set off for the Isthmus of Panama. There were 1,200 potential settlers on board the ships that headed for the Bay of Darien and, while we can mock now at the inappropriateness of the goods taken to trade with, the tragedy was that the tropical climate wiped out three-quarters of those who had travelled with hope in their hearts of a new personal future and a new future for Scotland. Still more tragic was that the people at home didn't know any of this and a thousand more would-be colonists sailed in a second expedition in 1699.

The words 'Darien scheme' have become a byword for failure and over 300 years later heads are still shaken over the foolishness of it all (not to mention the piracy, dirty dealing, tropical fever and unspeakable violence). The Scottish aristocracy and merchant elite had only added to their penury by dabbling in this unfortunate project and, to save their own skins, many pushed for a union of the parliaments that they hoped would create a bigger nation capable of successful international trade in which they would have a share. There was a petition to the English parliament to cancel Scotland's national debt before the country went bankrupt. Instead, Article 15 of the 1707 Acts of Union that joined the parliaments of Scotland and England, granted Scotland £398,085 10s in an effort to prevent a knock-on economic disaster in the English economy.

The families of Morven and Ardnamurchan would, of course, have known next to nothing of the Acts of Union or the implications. Edinburgh might as well have been

St Petersburg in terms of them being able to reach the city overland. Even in 1753, when the Rev. Mr Lauchlan Campbell signed an abstract minute (now held in the archives at Inveraray Castle) of the Synod of the United Parishes of Ardnamurchan and Glenfinan and the adjacent Bounds in the West Highlands, the accessibility of Morvern by land was described as almost non-existent. These parishes, Mr Campbell recorded, were the most extensive in Scotland, consisting of 'five countries viz Ardnamurchan, Sunart, Moidart, Arisaig and South Morar'. They were 'very unaccessible' (*sic*). Travellers could go no further than five miles on horseback in the 32-mile stretch of the Ardnamurchan peninsula or the 16 miles of the Morvern peninsula which by then bounded the Argyll properties.

In the first two decades of the 18th century, the people of Morvern and Ardnamurchan were tenants of the man who put down the first Jacobite uprising in 1715. It was the Hanoverian forces under the command of the Duke of Argyll that, with some ups and downs and near misses, contributed to the Jacobite defeats at Sheriffmuir and Preston. The Jacobites were, of course, Catholic. The civil wars had also left a strong Episcopalian following scattered throughout the Highlands (the modern idea that the Scottish Episcopal Church is the Church of England with a Scottish accent ignores a long and sometimes bitter history based much more on theology than the marital problems of a monarch). Moidart, as Mr Campbell noted in his Synod minute, was 'where the Young Pretender first raised his standard in 1745', noting that the whole population of Moidart, 'except one old woman', was Roman Catholic, as was Arisaig and South Morar. East Sunart, he wrote, was altogether inhabited by followers of the Protestant Jacobite Mr John

MacLachlan, a 'non-juring clergyman of the Episcopal persuasion' who had 'attended the Pretender in the late [1745]
rebellion'.

After 1722, Ardnamurchan had become the property of Sir
Alexander Murray and, although his lead mines had provided
a place of employment from 1705, the miners continued to
be paid a pittance. The local population did not adhere to
the religious persuasion required by law, and centuries-old
clan loyalties and allegiance to the idea of a Jacobite on the
throne could not have been wiped out by changes of land
ownership. It has to be suggested, therefore, that the area had
been an uprising waiting to happen in 1715 when the Old
Pretender made his bid to regain the Stuart ascendancy a year
after the House of Hanover succeeded to the British throne.
Perhaps feelings intensified even more when, in 1745, the
Young Pretender actually landed on their shores.

After the 1715 Jacobite uprising, of course, there were
harsh measures taken to 'tame' the rebellious Highlanders.
It is clear that attempts to eradicate the Gaelic language and
to impose Presbyterianism in Catholic and Episcopalian
areas were not successful – certainly not in Morvern and
Ardnamurchan – but the presence of armed soldiers must
have been as intimidating then as under any modern military
occupation. Garrisons were installed at Fort William, Fort
Augustus, Fort George, Inverness and elsewhere.

General George Wade was sent to Scotland (or 'North
Britain' as it was now called in an attempt to quell ideas of
nationalism) in 1724 as commander-in-chief, and he remained
until 1740. He is the man whose name is connected with so
many military roads, as well as being mentioned in a stanza of
the national anthem:

Lord grant that Marshal Wade
May by thy mighty aid
Victory bring.
May he sedition hush,
And like a torrent rush,
Rebellious Scots to crush.
God save the King!

Wade was ordered to make sure the law to disarm Highlanders was enforced and, in an early report from the North British front, he warned that the Highlanders were able and willing to bear arms against the Crown. But to whatever degree his road- and fort-building duties and peacekeeping efforts kept him busy, General Wade also took time to enhance his substantial personal fortune. When he died in 1748, aged 75, he left £100,000 from his many investments, including part ownership of the lead mines at Strontian.

Who were his partners? One of them was Sir Alexander Murray, a former Member of Parliament and a man who had been imprisoned for his support of the 1715 Jacobite uprising but who had subsequently sworn allegiance to the Hanoverian monarchy. Even so, if tenants were ever privy to the private affairs of their lairds, the people of Ardnamurchan would have had good cause to think that this new man in their lives shared their political views. He had maintained his links with the Pretender. When he moved to Ardnamurchan at the beginning of the 1720s to the property his father had just bought, George Lockhart MP (another closet Jacobite) recommended him to the Pretender as a secret agent in the Highlands. This was hardly a candidate for partnership with the North British embodiment of the Hanoverian regime, General George Wade.

Murray, however, had other ideas. For one thing, the family estate was (like so many others) in need of care and attention. The Ardnamurchan lands had been bought (no doubt at a knock-down price as part of the sale of forfeited lands programme) with cash from the sale of much more valuable lands in Peeblesshire. Young Sir Alexander (or 'Sandy Murray' as he was referred to by some of the Pretender's aides) had paternal instructions to develop Ardnamurchan's agricultural and mining enterprises as part of a general reconstruction of the family's estate. And, of course, he was only too well aware that he had Wade breathing down his neck.

On a visit back to the Lowlands in 1726, he had an interview with George Lockhart, whose extensive private papers give us a fascinating insight into the machinations of the day. Having been quizzed by Lockhart about the allegiances of the local clan chiefs he was now living and working alongside in the Highlands, Murray accused Lockhart 'with some sort of emotion' of trying to draw him back into the Jacobite struggle. He could not deny that his heart was still a Jacobite heart and that he considered the Pretender to be the true king, but he could have left Lockhart in no doubt of his intentions when he told him:

My dear Mr Lockhart, you do me justice in believing the little I could ever do was from such motives, but I am now a new man. I like the King and my country as well as ever I did, and I will draw my sword whenever there is to be a general effort for restoring the King and his kingdom of Scotland, but in the interim my head and heart are set upon improving the Highlands estate I have purchased, and bringing the mines to perfection (which will be a service

done my country) and I will think upon and undertake no
other business of any kind.

And indeed, in the same way that the Duke of Argyll
had begun to modernise the agricultural methods used
in Morvern, so Murray had already set about introducing
up-to-date irrigation and drainage systems in Ardnamurchan.
He built harbours for better access to the area, re-ordered
the leases on agricultural land so that one tenant would farm
an area previously worked by four or five families but, most
significantly in terms of the political influences now shaping
his plans, he improved the mines where lead deposits had
been worked for several decades and, in 1729, leased the
Strontian mines to the York Buildings Company. This was
the company set up to acquire lands that had been forfeited
in Scotland after the 1715 uprising (its history to the modern
eye has a rather shady element, emerging as it did from a
waterworks on the Thames). In that time of confusion and
increasing financial disorder, creditors (often bogus) tried to
claim debts from forfeited properties. The bizarre situation
of tenants continuing to pay their rents to their former, now
landless, lairds went on for years, while the clergy had no way
of being paid their stipends, which were the responsibility of
landowners who were now in a financial limbo.

When a number of estates were finally made legally ready
for sale in 1719 and 1720, the problem was – who would
buy? Hardly anyone in Scotland had the cash and no one
wanted a repeat of the investment disaster of the Darien
scheme. The government in London, therefore, was looking
for a company that would get it out of its Scottish estates difficulties and, while it seems from this distance to hold no logic,
the York Buildings Company, which provided businesses

and householders in London with water pumped from the Thames, was chosen as that company. Its senior partner at that time was Edward, Duke of Norfolk, and as it bought into the assortment of forfeited Scottish estates or into their industrial concerns, other new landowners and investors with an eye on the main chance became shareholders in its various ventures. And those shareholders by the end of the 1720s included Sir Alexander Murray and General George Wade.

When the company leased the Strontian mines in 1729, they were worked opencast and then developed commercially by sinking shafts and driving levels into the hillsides but the local workers remained poor. As shareholders, General Wade and Sir Alexander Murray may have prospered for a few years on the profits from the mines but that record book at Dunollie Castle showed poor Robert Frazer paying the rent in meal the year before the lease agreement came into force. The lead may have been processed and sold in a more profitable manner because of the improvements Murray and his new best friends then put into practice but, instead of employing more local workers at a living wage, miners were imported from elsewhere and few local people benefited from leasing the works to this national company with dukes and generals on its board.

The fact that the lead mines were doing well enough to line the pockets of Wade and the York Buildings Company shareholders offers up the distressing thought that, however improved the times, workers were still exploited. Although provision of houses and stores was made for the incoming miners, the truck system must have operated if men were not paid in cash.

General Wade is referred to in glowing terms on an intricate map of the Sunart mines that Alexander Bruce drew up in

1733. Bruce is described in several records as 'captain' of the Strontian mines but elsewhere he is described as Lieutenant Bruce and Sir Alexander Murray, rather than Bruce, is said to have been responsible for the copious notes on the map. One of the groups of dwellings for workers was named New York, a name found throughout Scotland wherever the York Buildings Company bought into some industrial venture or other.

This map, with many elaborate scrolls depicted around its border, is entitled 'A Plan of Loch Sunart &ct: become famous by the greatest national improvement this age has produced'. The central title of the plan reads, 'To His Excellence George Wade Esq., Lieutenant General & Commander in Chief of His Majesty's Forces in North Britain. This Plan is most Humbly Dedicated.' Are these Bruce's words or Murray's? Either way, the sycophantic inscription must surely have curried some favour with the military commander of 'North Britain'. George II was 'His Majesty' by this time and, as we have seen, not everyone in the area of Sunart – in either the Argyll-owned Morvern or the Murray-owned Ardnamurchan peninsulas – would have raised a dram to him were they to have had access to an illicit still in the surrounding hills.

Bruce undertakes not only to offer a cartographer's-eye view of the area but also to pen in drawings of mine buildings, crofts, houses, castles and ships. The verbal descriptions (whether written by Bruce or Murray) of the area and this 'greatest national improvement' that the age had produced are presented in what can best be described in modern terms as caption bubbles. These bubbles refer to the 'great undertaking' under Wade's direction of building roads and bridges with the intention of 'civilising and enriching the country'. The mines, it is suggested, would add to that intention. Wade's 'prudent and steady conduct' is praised to the heavens and referred to as both 'moderate' and 'clement'. Wade, the plan is at pains to point out, had even been charitable to 'several families and people in Scotland', contributing to the 'peace, profit and pleasure of these parts'.

Elsewhere, history has presented Wade as a much tougher commander than this and, perhaps to appease his critics, one of the bubbles suggests that even those who found themselves in less than harmony with General Wade on all matters agreed 'that from such good beginning, and surprising progress, it is presumed a speedy & happy period may be put to so great a work by the same hand'.

Because neither Murray nor Bruce were native to the area and therefore not Gaelic speakers, some of the names on the map are questionable but, under what is labelled on the map as '64 improved acres – Achnaha', the narrative of the mines of Strontian begins, 'The barony of Ardnamurchan and Sunart (the privileged bounds of York Buildings Company for raising mines and minerals) is ye property of Sir Alex Murray of Stanhope, who first discovered ye lead mines of Strontian'. This is akin to saying that David Livingstone 'discovered' the Victoria Falls in Zambia. Well known to the locals, the Strontian mines– like the Victoria Falls – were new only to those who had just come upon them.

The mines are described as lying West North West and East South East 'at three miles gradual ascent from Strontian at ye head of Loch Sunart, and are rank't among ye richest of their kind in Europe'. Murray, the plan stipulates, had leased the mines to the late Duke of Norfolk and Company in 1729, reserving for himself a sixth part of the ore that would be raised. The narrative of the plan suggests that infrastructure and industry were to win the hearts and minds of those who would peruse this map (and, as it turned out, Murray was desperate for investment in what he punted as the Sunart mining miracle). The hearts and minds of the miners and crofters were harder to win.

It might have been assumed that local labour, albeit poorly paid, would have benefited from such progress. In fact, the 500 men eventually employed by the company were brought from mining areas in England for their expertise and the village of New York was erected to house them. These dwellings were quite futuristic, constructed as they were of timber frames. But, yet again, it was not local people who profited from the construction and erection of the miners' quarters. The frames were made in London and shipped north. That does perhaps pay compliment to the new harbours that had been built but is akin to sending groups of enthusiastic volunteers to build houses in African villages today – diminishing the self-worth of the local people by assuming they don't have the skills required to carry out the tasks themselves.

The lead was worked opencast at first. A smelting 'miln' with four hearths was built, a bridge across the river was constructed with 'oaken piles', a 'handsome house for their manager, clerks and office' went up, as well as stores. The drawings of these buildings – some two and three storeys high and one with what looks like a bogey track leading to the embarkation point on the loch side – on the 1733 Sunart plan suggest a bustling mining community. As well as the industrial buildings, which included a malt barn and kiln, stables, work-houses, peat barns, timber and coal yards, several 'biggings', or buildings, for smiths, carpenters and other craftsmen, there were also roads built to get the ore to the smelting milns and furnaces. These, according to the 1733 plan, were constructed 'at a great labour and expense'. They were not rough tracks but levelled and either paved or laid with gravel.

Today, the access to this stunningly beautiful area of Scotland, which shows little evidence of its mining past, is made possible by roads that swoop and bend around the hillsides. The origins of those roads facilitated the extraction of lead and there are some visitors unused to single-track travel who may feel they are time travelling back to 1733. The area in the early 1730s had become, the Bruce plan proclaimed, 'wholesome and pleasant', despite the intense industry that clawed lead from 'the bowels of the earth'. And, as the infrastructure developed, so too did the work in the mine. As the expert workforce dug deeper, sinking shafts and sumps and driving drifts, as the plan explains, they came to richer seams of ore, in some places three and a half yards wide. In other places, there were '38 inches of solid ore bedded in the stiff loam'. With around 500 men working constantly at the mine, everyone seemed confident that the expenditure of 'several thousand pounds' on all of this infrastructure was a very good investment.

Gardens were enclosed for the workers (which would presumably have augmented the meagre diet their wages of meal could provide), ship owners were being employed to transport the lead and there are elaborate detailed instructions of how to enter Loch Sunart safely – so Loch Sunart, as the plan declared, had indeed 'become famous' by this 'greatest national improvement this age has produced'. The plan shows 'several appearances of lead veins in the hills which have never been worked', as well as giving details of the lead mines on the land retained by the Duke of Argyll to the south of Loch Sunart in Morvern. There is a claim that Sir Alexander Murray also discovered Glendon lead mines 'some time after his having obtained a lease of them which he afterwards made over for a premium to some gentlemen in partnership'. The partnership was called the Morvern Company and both lead and copper were found but, in 1733, had not 'been hitherto worked with that vigour requisite for more complete discoveries'. Some lead had been exported but no ancillary buildings, such as smelting furnaces, had yet been built. First things first: 'They have built a handsome dwelling house for their manager, clerks and office at Liedgesdale beside a key (*sic*) with compleat stone house upon it, two warehouses, lodging houses for workmen, two large stables and as many barns, a malt kiln and smith's shop, and work house, beside several biggings at Glendon.'

Here, too, a paved road had been built. The settlement now had streets and passageways – quite revolutionary in an area that saw no roads connecting with what could really be described as the 'mainland' for another few decades to come – and all the surrounding land had been brought into use for village hay, pasture and gardens. The elevations shown on the map depict two two-storey buildings at 'Liedgesdale' (Liddesdale), a number of single-storey buildings, some dwelling cottages and a bridge over the river.

There are some fascinating scraps of information contained in smaller 'bubbles' here and there on the plan. One tells us that, in 1730 and 1732, Captain Jacob Roe had found some Spanish gold and silver coins while he was fishing over the wreck of a ship lost when the Spanish Armada fled up the west coast to escape Elizabeth I's fleet. Another is the more sinister reminder that, until 1715, there had been a garrison posted at Castle Tioram which controlled the entrance to Loch Shiel. The castle was the traditional seat of Clan Ranald and had been seized in 1692 by government forces. Clan Ranald was allied with the Jacobite Court in France and, during the 1715 Jacobite uprising, government forces attacked and burned the castle. The inclusion of this snippet emphasised that General Wade was now in charge and the area was no longer a clan stronghold but 'North Britain'.

Tragically, this was all bluff and sales talk. For all this fanfare about 'the greatest national improvement this age has produced', Murray was struggling. The 'considerable expense' of all the buildings and the technical improvements overstretched him and the company and in the background was an acrimonious divorce that bled him dry financially. The fancy paved roads led only to bankruptcy and, by 1740, the York Buildings Company had given up the lease. Even in 1733, as Bruce and Murray were drawing up their elaborate map, Murray had had to sign over his whole estate to his brother to keep property from going to his ex-wife and, in turn, his brother was bankrupted in 1738. Just a decade after he clearly tried to attract investment in the mines through the publication of the Loch Sunart Plan, Murray was dead, his whole family's fortunes were gone and the welfare of the mineworkers was in jeopardy. No one was a plack the richer.

Despite the divorce (and possibly his over-enthusiastic development of the Sunart mines) having ruined the family fortunes, a eulogy found in the Murray papers granted that he had an 'ingenious head' that could instruct on 'intricate and perplexed affairs'. His final years had been stressful: he sailed very close to the Jacobite wind while supping with General Wade; he poured too much money into the infrastructure of the Loch Sunart mines without any real knowledge of the possible returns there might be; and he must have been only too well aware that the end result of his divorce was that Argyll miners would end up struggling to survive.

His nephew inherited not only what was left of the family property but also Alexander Murray's political views and,

two years after 'Sandy' Murray's death, the nephew supported the 1745 Uprising. Not surprisingly, he died in exile.
Meanwhile, back in Ardnamurchan during the '45 Uprising
(it must be assumed bravely and boldly under the nose of the
still-present troops garrisoned in the Highlands), gunpowder
was stolen from the lead mines around Strontian to aid the
Young Pretender's invasion in nearby Moidart. The horrific
outcome of that incident was that the miners were deliber-
ately starved to death when the government troops created a
blockade that prevented food and supplies being taken from
Loch Sunart up into the hills where the mines were located.

In August 1749, a gentleman who signed as M. O'Connor
submitted a report 'on the state and condition of the mines
of Glendhu in Morvin (*sic*)' to the Duke of Argyll. This
described the mines as 'very favourably situated with respect
to carriage and navigation, being within three miles of
Lithsdale (*sic*) on Lough Swinort (*sic*)'. Substantial ships, Mr
O'Connor explained, could harbour in Loch Sunart in safety.
The mines were also conveniently within seven miles of the
'rich mines' of Strontian and there was plenty of water for
'buddling, washing and dressing the ore'. However, provisions such as timber, coal, candles, gunpowder, iron, steel,
and cordage had to be 'drawn from distant markets'.

The Glendhu mine at this stage had two parallel veins up
the centre of the hillside running for about half a mile. The
principal vein was three yards wide. Samples of the ore were
sent to the Duke with the report. There had been several
previous trials but Mr O'Connor saw no reason why there
would be a body of ore near the surface and advised going
deeper, suggesting that 'the skilful miner' stood a fair chance
of getting 'ore in plenty'. He surmised that previous work had
been carried out by unskilled workers, leaving shafts fallen in,

the smithy, storehouse and workers' cabins demolished and razed to the ground, and the drifts, sumps and levels choked with rubbish and flooded with water. Skilled workers could produce good ore but he reckoned that £1,000 was needed to 'erect, repair, clear up and put the whole into a good working posture'. It is likely that in 1745, just four years previous to this report, government troops destroyed the infrastructure of the mine following the theft of the gunpowder, rather than its state being the responsibility of unskilled workers.

This was not Mr O'Connor's concern. He told the Duke that he had been informed that another lead mine had been discovered on the estate in the neighbourhood of Glendhu and he had also been told about a copper mine by men who had worked it but who said it 'proved a poor adventure and that everything at that place was under water'. Mr O'Connor 'declined visiting this mine'.

The Riddell family bought the Ardnamurchan lands in 1767 and a range of small companies leased the mining in the area of the Strontian River, continuing to extract ore at Bellsgrove, Corrantee and Whitesmith until 1815, albeit using a drastically reduced workforce. In 1794, just 46 miners and 30 labourers were employed. The lead was used for bullets during the Napoleonic Wars, which perhaps accounts for the closure of the mines in 1815 when that conflict came to an end and demand for lead slumped. Ironically, even while that war effort was going on, it wasn't local people who benefited from the brief boom in the demand for lead – it was French prisoners of war who were employed to work the mines.

From 1817 to 1836, the mines were worked intermittently on a philanthropic basis – for the first time in history, the welfare of the workers being the main concern of the land-owners. The records from 1847 to 1871 show wildly varying quantities of ore being extracted from Bellsgrove – from as little as 16 tons to as much as 310 tons. The Strontian Mining Company had taken the lease in 1846 but they had given up by 1850. More small companies came in and out of the equation, until the early 1870s when the price of lead crashed. An attempt to reopen Bellsgrove Mine, started in 1901, failed before any ore was raised.

Conditions for the workers never seemed to improve whoever was in charge and the only consolation can be that, in time, mine owners were taken to court when accidents happened, leading eventually to the formulation of health and safety legislation. In 1851, a miner named Duncan Cameron was killed by a rockfall in a lead mine at Strontian. The inquiry into the death took place in Tobermory on the island of Mull and witnesses told the procurator fiscal that the workings were unsafe and there was no protection for the miners. James Floyd, superintendent of the mines, had to answer a charge of culpable homicide and the case came in the wake of numerous complaints made to the laird, Sir James Riddell, the mine owner of the day. Perhaps the frequent changes of leaseholders contributed to the lack of safety. In evidence, it was heard that, three years previously, a former leaseholder at the mine had removed pit props that had supported partitions in the mine. Some men had quit their jobs because they were afraid of falling rock but one man told the court, 'I knew this myself but I had either to submit to work there or starve – Necessity with me had no law – The other mines in which I had wrought are worked in a different, safer, principle and more attention paid to the security of the lives of the workmen.'

The precognitions taken from the men make tragic reading. Clearly they were experienced miners and they had warned

James Floyd time and again of the danger of one particular rock – warnings that he ignored and even laughed off.

On 9 August 1851, a statement about the death of Cameron was made for the Tobermory court by Alexander Lowrie, a 48-year-old residing at Anyheilt in the parish of Ardnamurchan. Lowrie had 25 years' experience as a miner in both lead and coal mines in Leadhills in Lanarkshire, Tyndrum, Kirkudbright and elsewhere and had been working, from time to time, in the Strontian lead mines for the previous 12 years. He had been out of work for a couple of years after being injured in a rockfall in a mine elsewhere. He had recently asked for work from James Barrett the manager of the lead mines at Strontian and was working for 20 pence a day (when 240 pence made one pound). As many miners did, he came to an arrangement to carry out a particular piece of work over a set period of time – known as a 'bargain'. He was one of 18 men who would carry out blasting in the mine over a period of six weeks. He had then refused to work in a particular area until a dangerous road was repaired but James Floyd laid him off for having allegedly complained to mine owner Sir James Riddell. Because the miners were paid 'once every two months', Lowrie was going to have to wait for a month before being paid wages due, despite being legally entitled to be paid immediately because he had been laid off. Lowrie told Barrett he would 'take him to law', to which Barrett replied that he could do so if he liked.

Floyd had given Lowrie occasional odd jobs, but in April 1851, Lowrie started work again, this time with Duncan Cameron, Alexander McPhee and Alexander McMaster. This team was blasting in the middle level of Bellsgrove from the April until July. Floyd said they were to be paid at the rate of £2 10s per fathom. Lowrie testified: 'Before we began our operations we complained to Mr Floyd that a large stone which was loose at the top and on its east side but fixed at its base and on the west side was dangerous & ought to be removed . . . The Stone was about 8 or 9 feet high and about 12 feet broad . . . It was hanging about 18 Inches to the fathom off the plumb.' The team was to work from the base of this stone, following the vein of lead. They were to make an opening four or five feet broad and to make a shaft of three fathoms. Floyd told them he would take the stone down 'so soon as he had made a place for it' and to have no fear of it. The men did fear, however, and, although they began working, several of them spoke to Floyd and warned him that their lives were in danger. And of course, as they worked, the stone loosened but, despite seeing the state of the stone every day, Floyd 'invariably told us that there was no fear of the stone'. Lowrie stressed, 'I told him that the stone was dangerous and that I and the others were afraid it would fall on us & kill us − I offered more than once to take the stone down on the payment of 4 shillings which he refused with a laugh.'

Then, on Thursday 7 August, the men were to start work at 3 p.m. and Lowrie questioned Floyd about the price on the work they were doing because rumours had been flying about the rate. Floyd said the rate was £2 2s a fathom (this to be shared by the team), which Lowrie complained was under the rate and told his boss that he could 'never submit to work at under wages', adding 'I will work out the shift of this day but no more.' But of equal concern was whether the stone had been removed. It hadn't, of course, and, although Lowrie threatened to walk off the job, he in fact went to work with Duncan Cameron. They had met Alexander McMaster coming out of the mine, who told them to take care of themselves 'with that stone', saying that it was 'exceedingly dangerous to our lives'. McMaster and his work partner McPhee had already quarrelled that day with Floyd about its removal. Floyd told them they could take it down but, as they were not to be paid to do so, it remained there as Lowrie and Cameron went to work at about 4 p.m.

Their first job was to make a bore in the vein and to charge it with powder for a blasting. This hole, Lowrie testified, was close to the bottom of the stone and, after boring the hole about 22 inches deep, Duncan Cameron charged it with the powder and stemmed it. Lowrie said:

> During the time we were preparing the hole, Cameron and I talked of the stone . . . I remarked 'Duncan, if that stone falls it will kill us' . . . He answered 'It will' . . . and before the blast was fired off I touched the face of the stone with the hammer as I had done before we began our work . . . It was hanging over us in a measure and very considerably off the plumb . . . Duncan Cameron afterwards applied the lighted match to the blast and we mounted the ladder to a place of safety. We had remained at this place about three minutes when a report announced that the blast had exploded . . . Cameron went down first & I followed. Before we had reached the bottom Cameron stood still and said the smoke is coming up too thick wait till it clears away . . . I replied no, the smoke will clear from the bottom before we get down.

The men went down, each carrying a candle to light their way. It took them five minutes or so and they then waited until the smoke and rubble cleared. The first thing Lowrie then did was to check the stone, which still seemed secure in its place. They began then to work on the shaft but, after quarter of an hour, Lowrie heard a rumbling noise. '[B]efore I could rise or speak the large stone already alluded to came down and buried us both under it. I cried to Duncan McPherson who was working above us to come to our aid . . . I heard Cameron cry out once 'Oh Christ there is no help for me' . . . I heard him cry repeatedly but as I was in despair myself and as I fainted under the stone I can't describe anything else that he said.' The stone struck the side of the shaft and broke in pieces. Both Lowrie and Cameron were buried under those pieces but Cameron was lying with the edge of the stone concentrating the whole weight on his body. Lowrie was able to drag himself out, although he couldn't stand because of his injuries, and could only shout 'at the pitch of [his] voice to Duncan McPherson to come and that Duncan Cameron was killed'.

The management had clearly been warned time and again that this tragedy was waiting to happen. The refusal of the men to move the stone themselves is understandable when we consider that they were either paid a pittance of a wage or, in the case of the 17 men who made the 'bargain' with Floyd, were paid for piecework. If they didn't fulfil the task they were paid for, they would get no payment and so, understandably, no one would take time out to make the tunnels safe. Some of the men who gave evidence in the case against James Floyd in 1851 were angry enough by 1854 to try to raise a legal action against the mining company. There was no sympathy for them and the Sheriff Substitute ruled the action out of order. The court costs of £4 15s must have eaten a huge hole in the men's meagre income.

Strontian lives on (as does mining in the area) as the name of an element identified in 1790 by Dr Adair Crawford. It was named 'strontites' in 1793 by Professor Thomas Hope at the University of Glasgow and eventually isolated by Sir Humphry Davy in 1808, when he changed its name to 'strontium', the only element named after a place in the UK.

We will hear more of the modern mining in Strontian and in Morvern later but, before we take a closer look at the bizarre shenanigans that surrounded the mining industry in Argyll in the late 1700s, a word about the mines to the south of Loch Sunart in Morvern that were on lands owned by the Dukes of Argyll.

The main lead mine was the one that Mr O'Connor reported on in 1749, when the Duke seems to have intended to take a greater control. Sir Alexander Murray had formed the Morvern Company and leased the Lurga mine in Glendhu from the Duke of Argyll. The rent paid to the Duke in 1737 was £41 17s 7½d. The Morvern Company also built a pier at Liddesdale to export the ore excavated from the mine. It was on the north side of Glen Dubh, a quarter of a mile up a small burn, some five miles from Liddesdale. It was reached by a packhorse track. The vein was at first worked opencast. Lead and zinc were also found around half a mile from Glensanda Castle.

In the *First Statistical Account* of 1790, Rev. Norman MacLeod wrote, 'At the head of Loch Alin [sic] Bay, there is a very flattering appearance of coal; to work which, a feeble attempt has been made, and a few tons of good quality found; but, not being persecuted with vigour, it has not succeeded. This is the more to be regretted, as the mine lies close by the shore of this good and commodious harbour.' In other words, contrary to the huge efforts to be endured transporting lead from the Lurga mine in the hills above Loch Sunart, the coal was almost in the boats and ready to be exported, if only someone had come along and invested in the mine. Several thin seams of coal had been exposed around Loch Aline and, in the 18th century, the seam at Inninmore Bay was worked using an opencast system. In the early 19th century, three adits were created in the hillside. Modern geologists disagree with the idea of a 'flattering' appearance of coal as, like that found in Mull, it seems to have been of a poor quality.

Norman MacLeod also recorded that an attempt had been made a few years previously to mine lead on a farm called *Lurgbhuidh* without much success. This may have been the Gaelic name translated by Murray as 'Lurga' and certainly, by the 1790s, it is difficult to know what state mining was in there. However, in the *Second Statistical Account* of 1845, Rev. John McLeod says that ore from the Lurga lead mine in Glen Dubh was of 'a considerable richness'. This suggests that the mine was still in operation over a century after Sir Alexander Murray took out the lease from the Duke of Argyll, although it did few favours for that failed entrepreneur. John McLeod's report also mentions copper mines at Ternate on the Ardtornish Estate, which he believed had been in operation since quite ancient times. There were, he wrote, 'still, in the neighbourhood, favourable appearances of this very valuable material'.

Jim Blair of Lochaber's Geopark suggests that, as on the isle of Islay, the proliferation of potential mineral excavations would have been encouraged by landowners desperate for funds to run their estates both in the area and elsewhere – properties in London or Edinburgh had enormous upkeeps. Shepherds and crofters would come across 'threads' of ore and report them to the likes of Sir James Riddell's factor or the Argyll chamberlain for the area for a paltry reward. Sometimes, that thread would be followed up and exploratory excavations made.

There were, however, charlatans of the mining world who made a far better living than the poor shepherds rewarded with a coin for showing the source of a lump of lead ore to the factor. The mineralogists' trick was try to convince landowners of the viability of old workings or suggest that their expertise had identified a new vein of coal, copper or lead. One man was spectacularly brazen in this field in the late 18th century – Rudolph Erich Raspe.

3

The Munchausen factor

Few of us have read the original *Baron Munchausen's Narrative of his Marvellous Travels and Campaigns in Russia*, penned by Rudolph Erich Raspe in 1785. More probably we have seen or heard of interpretations of the character in comics, stage and radio plays or movies such as *The Adventures of Baron Munchausen*, the 1988 version of these wild stories co-written and directed by Monty Python star Terry Gilliam. Raspe based his humorous 'narrative' on the tales told by the real life German officer Baron von Munchausen, a contemporary of his who had been ridiculed in society because of his wildly embellished wartime tales. The psychiatric condition known as Munchausen Syndrome is named after the Baron – or perhaps more accurately after the cruelly comic version of the Baron portrayed by Raspe.

The book was a runaway success from the outset, yet the name of Raspe has not gone down in history as one of Germany's leading writers. Instead, he is linked with shady activities in the fields of geology and mining and his presence in Argyll, recorded in detail in reports preserved in the Argyll Archives at Inveraray, leads us to see him as the 'rogue' his biographer describes. Able to spin his own embellished stories, this was a man who painted Argyll as a Klondike waiting to happen. But just how did he insinuate himself into the service of the Duke of Argyll?

Rudolph Erich Raspe was born in March 1737 in Hanover, Germany. He studied law and jurisprudence at Göttingen and Leipzig and worked as a librarian for the university of Göttingen. In the 1760s, he worked in university libraries and became known as a scholar specialising in natural history and antiquities. He wrote poetry, taught and began to write on a wide range of subjects, which led to him becoming an honorary member of the Royal Society in London. Employed in the 1770s to improve the curio collection of Frederick II of Hesse, he blotted his copybook when he sold some of the curios and pocketed the cash.

Under a cloud, he left for London, where he went into publishing and translated a number of books from the German. The English art historian Horace Walpole mentions Raspe as 'a Dutch savant'. Walpole seems to have supported him financially for a while and helped him to publish *An Essay on the Origin of Oil Painting* in 1781. However, he was dropped from the Royal Society and we next find him in a somewhat different field altogether.

Matthew Boulton, who by this time was well established in his partnership with the Scottish engineer James Watt in their Birmingham engineering and manufacturing company, employed Raspe as assay master and storekeeper in the Dolcoath mine in Cornwall. Raspe began writing books about geology (as well as keeping his options open with books on art history) and developed an interest in tungsten, which was identified and named by Spanish chemists in 1783. Tungsten has the highest melting point and lowest vapour pressure of all metals, and at temperatures over 1650°C has the highest tensile strength. An ingot of the metal was found in

2003 and identified as the 150-year-old 'Trewhiddle Ingot'. Some have speculated that it was produced by Raspe during a visit to Happy-Union mine at St Austell, because he had shown a deal of knowledge about the metal and its properties – and that therefore *he* was responsible for the earliest known smelting of tungsten, ahead of the Spanish.

I am no scientist, no geologist and have had no access to the papers that have led to mining expert Colin Bristow suggesting the link. What I do know is that, in the late 1780s and early 1790s, Raspe was touring around Scotland trying to persuade a number of landowners, including the Duke of Argyll, to reinvest in old mine workings or start up new mining ventures and that the Duke was a lucky man to escape without being defrauded.

When Raspe travelled to Caithness, he convinced Sir John Sinclair that his estates were a treasure trove of potential mines. He planted ore he had brought from Cornwall to 'prove' his point that there were valuable veins of gold and silver to be worked and, when his ruse was about to be exposed, he did the same disappearing trick he had effected when he pocketed the cash from his sale of Frederick II's curio collection.

His interest in minerals by the 1770s seems to have had more to do with potential personal gain than with the pursuit of science. As early as 1776, he had asked Captain James Cook to let him go on the voyage to Tahiti because he 'knew' that he would find both gold and diamonds in the volcanic ash there. Captain Cook turned him down. But we may well wonder how so many were so easily duped. Sir John Sinclair was an MP, president of the Board of Agriculture, a campaigner on a range of important agricultural issues and compiler of the *First Statistical Account of Scotland* and yet he was almost taken in by Raspe's fool's gold, shipped up from Cornwall and buried on the Caithness estate. He had entertained Raspe at Thurso Castle, enjoyed the German's Midas-style machinations that seemed to turn iron into gold (Raspe evidently did Paul Daniels-style tricks with metals) and was even well enough disposed towards Raspe (despite the exposed confidence trick with the Cornish ore) that he sent him away with a substantial sum of money in his pocket.

The extensive correspondence from Raspe to the Duke of Argyll suggests he may have planned another elaborate sting prior to the one he almost pulled off in Caithness. The Duke, like Captain Cook, did not take up Herr Raspe on his recommendations but it has to be said that Raspe was certainly willing to lay elaborate groundwork for his potential swindling activities.

The man described by biographer John Carswell as 'a rogue' spent the July and August of 1789 travelling around the Duke of Argyll's extensive lands and properties. Raspe reported on the marble quarries of Tiree and Iona, the slate quarries of Easdale and the mineral mines from Loch Sunart to the southern most of the Duke's estates. He spoke of 'speculation and industry' and of 'abundance', almost everywhere he went. He wrote extensive accounts on this apparent tour of inspection and, according to his glowing reports of the potential fortunes that the Duke might expect to reap were he to sow as advised by this self-styled mineralogist, Argyll and its people should have been industrially enriched to this day.

This was a time of development – the new castle at Inveraray was finally completed in 1789 for John, 5th Duke of Argyll and his wife, Elizabeth, and the planned new town, begun in the 1740s, was coming to fruition. In that year, George Langlands was employed by the Duke to draw up maps and plans of many of the estate farms and other surveys of the properties had been carried out in the previous decade so, at face value, a survey of the mines and quarries seems to fit with the Duke's improvement projects.

Raspe arrived in Inveraray in very early July and he met with the Duke's tacksmen, presumably to get an overview of the situation. There was a visit to the quarry at St Catherine's on the opposite side of Loch Fyne on 3 July that set the tone for his reports – here there was 'an abundance for many years to come'. His suggestions for the use of the stone (chimney-pieces, ovens, chemical laboratories, canisters for tea, tobacco and snuff) and its profitability (the 'cheapness of raising and working this excellent stone give it a run in these markets') imply that this was not just a man who knew his minerals but an entrepreneur, a man with connections, a man who understood markets and trends.

Careful not to spread his fairy dust on every project visited – the 'black sooty substance' delivered to him from Glen Aray was identified not as coal but 'phlogisticated lime and magnesia mixed with a little iron'. As a noun (he seems to have been a little free with language, although we must remember that German was his native tongue), 'phlogiston' is a hypothetical component of combustible substances. With cynical hindsight there is a hint that Raspe just wants to blind with science.

After a couple of days exploring more quarries around Inveraray, he visited 'two mines said to have been found in the brook at Essachlaibh, a little north west of and under Tombreak and above the sawmill in the park at a place called Altriochan near a weir and another brook'. If this is an anglicising (or an understanding with a German ear) of the name *Allt Eas A' Chosain* (meaning 'a waterfall' and often written as 'Essichossen'), then this became an active lead and then nickel mine, also going under the name of *Coille-Bhraghad* (and written as 'Coillebraid'). Between 1854 and 1867, more than 400 tons of nickel ore was produced.

Herr Raspe, however, wrote that near 'a very romantic waterfall' where a drift mine had been tried, he 'found nothing in it but a few sparks of Munwick or sulphurated iron, which to all appearances have been mistaken for copper ore'. He added, 'Not one speck of lead or other ore remained or was to be seen and further trials by longer drift or upon deeper levels seem to me hardly advisable.' Further investigation would be 'a lottery', as was the case, he said, at Altriochan above the sawmill.

It is perhaps a misrepresentation of Raspe's intentions but it seems that, the further he went from Inveraray, the more positive he became about the possibilities of the mining and quarrying projects he was shown. While correspondence held in the archives at Inveraray suggests that this Duke and others could be hands-on, especially when a project held particular personal interest for them, Raspe would probably have counted on the fact that, with chamberlains in strategic areas dealing with the day-to-day running of the estates, the Duke was unlikely to do much personal checking on his activities. If he had employed Raspe to look at mines and quarries, then he would read his reports and act accordingly. So, off Raspe went to the Garvellachs (the tiny islands lying between Mull and Jura in the Firth of Lorn, once home to St Brendan, who founded a monastic settlement on the largest island, *Eileach an Naoimh* – 'isle of the saints' – in 542 AD). Raspe wrote in the report, begun at Easdale (centre of the slate industry) on 30 July and 'finished and sent off from Aros on Mull' on 6 August 1789, that these islands could supply all the Highlands with lime as befitting 'Your Grace's patriotic and paternal intentions'. The 6th-century beehive monastic cells are still in evidence today. Ironically, had Raspe's advice been followed, they would have been obliterated in the rush to quarry the lime yet, when he reached Iona, he could not 'suppress an humble request that Your Grace would please to protect . . . against future dilapidation and decay' the ruins of the monastery and abbey there. There was, Raspe said in this report, lead on Iona and coal on Mull 'in the Ardtun cliffs . . . or rather in Loch Scrivan' and he drew the Duke's attention to the various qualities of marble in Tiree.

Nothing but thorough in laying out his bear traps, Raspe followed up the Aros report with one from Ardtornish in Morvern on 9 August and then there were a further 19 pages of report-cum-letter on 20 August from Fort William. In this tome, he sold himself well. 'I am perhaps too warm and sanguine in my wishes and hopes to see these remote parts enlivened by useful industry; but the growing opulence, taste and luxury of these united Kingdoms seems to justify almost any speculation and it will be my duty on my return to London to blow the spirit of adventure into a flame, and to divert it towards the Highlands.'

At the start of the 18th century, Scotland had joined England in the hope of kindling prosperity for both countries. Throughout the century, the traditional lairds and aristocrats had struggled to keep their heads above water but they had also bought into the 'growing opulence, taste and luxury' of the era. The Enlightenment still dwelt and breathed in urban Scotland. Adam Smith was still living, David Hume's light had been extinguished only in the previous decade. Inveraray new town was first designed by William Adam and completed by Edinburgh-born Robert Mylne. The 5th Duke employed Mylne (founder of the Architects' Club, collaborator on

St Paul's Cathedral and founder member with John Smeaton of the Society of Civil Engineers) to create some of the castle's neoclassical rooms. Raspe knew the buttons he was pushing.

So what adventures did he plan to fan into flame? On 25 July 1789, he had visited Ardtun 'to examine a coal mine upon Your Grace's estate'. Even at a distance of two miles, he claimed, he could see significant clues. He confessed that, until that day, he had trusted the commonly held mineralogists' view that coal could not be found under a layer of volcanic material. Then – 'ocular proof'! He had seen extinct volcanoes in Germany, described them in pamphlets (one of which had been plagiarised, he claimed, so respected was his view). Yet now, he was to 'recant previous ideas' and say instead that fire and heat would have no effect on coal underground. '[T]his bed or seam of the Ardtun kennel coal, so far from being destroyed by the heat of a running lava was rather produced by the same and . . . impregnated and saturated with petroleum'. 'Kennel' or 'cannel' (candle) coal is coal that can be ignited with a match to burn with a bright flame and local people said that coal was present on the island in several different places. In the *First Statistical Account of Scotland*, Rev. Mr Dugal Campbell of the parish of Kilfinichen and Kilviceuen in the Presbytery of Mull described the towering Ben More and the Ardtun cliffs fringing the Ross of Mull. Mr Campbell was sceptical about the idea that Ben More was a volcanic mountain (today we know that the lava from this mountain flowed across to Morvern in the east and well beyond Ardtun in the west) but explained that the cliffs of Ardtun in south-west Mull had similar, if not so elegant, basaltic pillars as the island of Staffa and that they were interspersed with seams of coal. Campbell claimed there was a seam 'about three feet thick in a hill called Bein-an-Ini' and recalled that, early in the century, Sir Alexander Murray of Stanhope (Ardnamurchan and Morvern are, of course, just across the water from Mull) had bought this hill 'for the sake of the coals'. He had begun to work a mine there but 'his affairs getting into disorder', according to Mr Campbell, 'he was obliged to stop the work'. When Sir James Riddell bought the Ardnamurchan estates, he too made a trial at this site 'but after some coals were dug, he also gave up the work'.

Mull was an island in need of employment. The herring had been over-fished, the price of kelp was dependent on market forces and the salt tax was crippling. Mr Campbell would have been anxious for any industry to succeed but, although since Riddell had stopped work at Bein-an-Ini a number of people had taken a look at it, he only knew that locally, the coal was considered good. Mr Campbell also wrote about a seam of coal 'about 18 inches thick' on the sea coast of Ross, the property of the Duke of Argyll. It seems likely that he encountered Raspe because he said in the *Statistical Account* in the 1790s that 'His Grace sent a skilful person to view it'. Some coals had been dug and they burned very well but no trial had subsequently been made. The minister also reported on coal on the property of Captain McLean of Kinlochalvin, 'at Brolass and Gribun'.

As reported in the *Geological Conservation Review*, geologists have concluded that the bottom layer of what is now know as the Ardtun Leaf Beds is coal but that is not to say that Raspe was entirely accurate when he wrote that the coal he found in the second stratum of the Ardtun cliffs was 'very black' and the 'floor of the coal'. The coal, he wrote in his report, lay between four and six feet above high water and he had found a 10-inch-thick seam of 'rich good coal' that formed within itself a seam of about four inches thick of 'the richest and light jetty kennel coal'. He added that the seam was excellent coal and safe to work because of the firm and safe roof under the cliff.

Driving in adits from the shore would be too expensive to allow a mine to pay for itself but, once again, Raspe knew how to couch issues in language aimed to get results. 'The great want of coal in this part of the Highlands' would justify such expense. It wasn't just worth having a go here – he also recommended that another two sites in Mull should be trialled. 'For the purpose of connecting Your Grace's ideas upon the means and methods of discovering coals in the Highlands', Raspe flagged up more 'coal' he claimed to have discovered on 27 July on the south coast of the island. On the property of Mr Macgilvray of Bennigoil, 'under whose astonishing and romantic basalt cliffs', Raspe claimed there was a bed or seam of very bad sulphurous and mouldering coal, and rock formations near Carsaig also gave 'proof' of a coal bed. Again, modern geologists have noted carboniferous deposits in the Carsaig area – but enough to create a mining industry? They don't think so.

In 1844, the then Duke wrote a letter home from a trip to Italy that seems to prove the geologists wrong and Raspe to a degree right. The Duke had been told that this coal was 'equal to the best Glasgow coal and I am in great hopes that it will be good enough to warm me'. He also hoped that, on this island where peat had to be cut all summer to warm people in winter, the coal would make a difference to lives 'without wasting the best weather of summer in preparing for the winter'. A Mull Coal Company was set up but this was never to become an industry – Raspe's enthusiasm had indeed been overkill.

He was next to be found in Morvern, on 6 August, where he was pleased once again to air his new 'discovery' that coal could be found under a layer of volcanic material. He claimed a dazzling range of exploitable commodities throughout the peninsula. There was, he said, an abundance of iron, gypsum, pozzolana, coal, lead and copper. Pozzolana is the volcanic material that creates a watertight cement – a material usually imported from southern Italy and which was in such short supply during the Napoleonic Wars that adequate repairs to the newly built Crinan Canal were never carried out. Had there been a supply in Morvern, so many problems would have been solved.

Raspe said that herdsmen had discovered a seam of coal many years previously and that a short adit had been driven into it. The *Statistical Account* confirms this but, again, Raspe paints the possibilities in over-positive terms. When he visited on 8 August, he found it overgrown with brambles and 'filled up to the knees with water'. Boldly, he waded the full 48 feet of the level and said he found a seam of coal 14 inches thick. He suggested there could be more coal in the cliff and, although what he took out was of inferior quality, he felt it was his duty to recommend a further trial by lengthening the level under the cliff. The seam, he said, could become thicker and of better quality and boring could uncover another seam. There could also be further seams on the property of Mr Allan Maclean of Drimnin, where he saw two seams of 'excellent caking and kennel coal'. Because of a very rapid stream running under these, they were 'inaccessible and impractical' but 'more than one seam' could be found by pile driving.

There is a pattern running through the copious notes that Raspe sent to the Duke: what you can see is not that good or, if you can see it and it is good, it is not accessible right now – but with investment, all the beautiful things in the world could be yours. The modern advertising methods of selling a lifestyle rather than a product were second nature to Raspe more than two centuries ago.

In a further eight pages sent on 29 August from Fort William, Raspe talked about a copper mine six miles from Ardtornish, about a mile and a half beyond Loch Ternate. The ore was in granite similar to that found at Strontian (the implication being that Strontian was a success so this should be too). There was no lead but there was a sulphurated yellow copper ore, which he estimated was worth between £9 and £10 a ton. 'In my opinion,' he said, this 'justifies reasonable hopes of success.' He pointed out that Cornish copper ore, 'upon which so many thousands depend for their subsistence', sold at an average of £7 a ton but that Anglesey ore was hardly worth £4. This higher quality ore, therefore, if there were plenty of it, would not only rake in a fortune but also could provide employment on a major scale. Could the Duke look at past records to see how much ore had been lifted from this mine in the past? Was there a previous survey with details of the depth, length and connexions within the mine and what its state was when work was ended there? Raspe's list of questions was logical and convincing.

These details would be important if the work were to resume, he said, but he had been unable to get satisfactory information from 'some very old men' who had only vague memories of the mine. 'They expressed the depth of shafts and lengths of levels not in foot or fathoms but by the years and months that several workmen had been employed upon them, which hardly conveys any idea,' Raspe wrote petulantly. Clearly Raspe had never been subjected to those sums which began, 'If nine men worked six weeks', or he might have computed the information he needed.

The old men also had no real memories of whether the five shafts sunk in different places had ever been connected underground by drifts or levels. One piece of information Raspe felt he could rely on was that, in a sudden flood, the workmen had lost £150 worth of tools in one of the shafts. It was also clear that, because these old men remembered that hand winches had been used to bring buckets of water from the deepest parts of the mine, these works could 'not have been of any considerable depth or as Alex Bruce in his plan of Loch Sunart published in 1733 expresses it, not to have been carried on with vigour required for complete discoveries'.

Raspe is scathing and accusatory about the way the mine had been left. With scant evidence, he declared, 'These works were carried on with unpardonable neglect and ignorance on the part of the adventurers.' He suggested that their 'overseer, captain or manager' had drowned the works 'with premeditated malice or a fraudulent intention to prevent control and enquiry'. One of the shafts was sunk where the first heavy rain or winter flood would fill it with water. This was the cause of the flooding that lost the £150 worth of tools, he surmised, adding, 'A similar abomination I have never seen anywhere.' His indignation brings the word 'evil' into play and he brings on the safety of men who might work there in the future, the generous patronage of the Duke, the fact that it would of course be an expense to resuscitate the mine but that a careful survey and proper pumps could secure the faulty shaft and all would be well. His connections with Matthew Boulton and James Watt would have been convincing in terms of this recommendation.

On 10 August, he had visited the 'Glendon lead mines or grooves'. Glendon was the name given to the Glendhu mine by Alexander Bruce in his 1733 plan and, as we have seen, there had been successful mining (despite the unconscion-able trek to take ore to Liddesdale for shipping) followed by tragedy for the miners. All that Raspe says is that he 'found nothing but hard quartz spar veins without any spark of lead, yet in the form of a regular vein, which as it were crosses both mountains and the intermediate glen'. Perhaps there was no more lead. Perhaps the walk over the hills was too much for the 53-year-old and he may have felt he had put enough work into setting a sting for the Duke of Argyll.

What the Duke's response was to the lengthy reports he received from Raspe is not evident in the archives. If he paid the German for a couple of months' 'surveying' and Raspe saw a bit of Scotland, perhaps the 'rogue' was content. The Duke certainly did not fall for any tricks Raspe may have planned – or perhaps this was a practice run for the real sting carried out on Sir John Sinclair in Caithness two years later. Sarah Tindal Kareem, in her 2014 book *Eighteenth-Century Fiction and the Reinvention of Wonder*, suggests that Sir John could not 'turn Raspe away in anger because he realised that the man who puts his trust in fool's gold can only blame himself'. In the world of Raspe, nothing was as it seemed.

After the Caithness sting, he went to Ireland and ended up managing a copper mine on the Herbert Estate in Killarney, County Kerry, where he died in November 1794 of typhoid. When he arrived in Inveraray in 1789, he had already written *Baron Munchausen's Narrative of his Marvellous Travels and Campaigns in Russia*, although few were aware that he was the author. While he was not shy in publishing his treatises on everything from wild flowers and high art to minerals and volcanoes, he was smart enough to realise that this book could see him in the law courts on charges of libel. The true authorship was not revealed until after Raspe died.

Our German 'rogue' had intended this as a political satire on the exploits of the real Baron Munchausen who, after retiring from the Russian army, dined out in German aristocratic salons on the outrageously tall tales he told about his military career. Raspe wrote it for laughs and the stories, told in the first person, become ever more ridiculous as the fictional Baron Munchausen describes his prowess as a sportsman, soldier, world traveller and solver of international problems. The book upset the real Munchausen but delighted audiences. Raspe, of course, lost control of it, other writers added many new tales (to this day, new versions in every medium are still being produced) and there were translations into many languages.

The paradox of it all is that, had Raspe given Baron Munchausen a different name, his skills as a teller of tall stories could have won him real fame and fortune. Instead, he chose to tell tall stories of a different kind to Scotland's landowners and was chased for his pains. While he died in sad circumstances in Ireland and is rarely remembered, his Baron Munchausen character lives on and earns fortunes for 21st-century writers, actors, comedians and the creators of cartoons.

The final sting in the tail for poor Raspe is that Sir Walter Scott used him as a model for a character in one of his own fictions. Herman Dousterswivel, the German mining swindler in *The Antiquary*, which Scott published in 1816, was based on Raspe's Scottish adventures in the late 1700s. Scott wrote in a preface to the novel that, while Dousterswivel might seem a 'forced and improbable' character, 'the reader may be assured that this part of the narrative is founded on a fact of actual occurrence'. The Duke of Argyll seems to have thought that Raspe's mining reports were 'forced and improbable' and sent him on his way. Sir John Sinclair should have read 'Munchausen' for 'Raspe' and he wouldn't have ended up sharing double billing in a Walter Scott novel. Sir Walter Scott found Sir John a bore and probably created his character Dousterswivel as much to poke fun at Sir John as to expose the rascal Raspe.

If this account – in common with Sir Walter Scott's fictional summation of Raspe – seems harsh, it must be tempered with some biographical detail that suggests he did, in fact, make some valuable contributions to what at the time was an embryonic range of sciences. Geology, palaeontology, archaeology, even biology, scarcely had labels, let alone developed theories in Raspe's day. The origins of the world and all species dwelling in it were deemed by the majority to be as described in the Book of Genesis. Some today see Raspe's work on basalt as a major contribution to the development of the sciences of geology and palaeontology.

Following his studies in Göttingen and Leipzig, he worked at various levels in the library in Hanover from 1761. This clearly gave him access to a huge range of material and he was able to deduce from his reading a plausible geological hypothesis that moved the science on from the idea of the world being created by God in seven days to one that considered the effects of natural phenomena such as volcanic eruptions. He was to some extent inspired to follow this line of inquiry by a major earthquake in Lisbon in 1755 but he also unearthed forgotten groundwork carried out by the English polymath Robert Hooke who, in the previous century, had produced *Lectures and Discourses of Earthquakes and Subterranean Eruptions*. This explored the idea of connecting the origins of mountains and islands to such phenomena. Raspe also took on board some of the discoveries of the

French geologist Nicolas Desmarest. In 1763, Desmarest had considered, during explorations in the Auvergne, that the prismatic basalts there were old lava streams. He compared them to the columns of the Giant's Causeway in Ireland and linked them to the activity of now-extinct volcanoes.

Raspe launched his own theories in various papers – his first geological publication, *Specimen Historiae Naturalis Globi Terraquei* published in 1763, was a compendium of such hypotheses. Later, there was a periodical called *The Cassel Spectator* (which came out briefly in 1772) that also established his credentials in the field of basalts or volcanic rock. In his reports to the Duke of Argyll on the mineralogy of Mull, Morven and Ardnamurchan, he refers back to these publications. The idea that layers of volcanic ash could create or protect matter of commercial value (such as the layers of coal subsumed but shielded intact by the lava produced by volcanic activity on Mull) was a valid and valuable one. This and his work on the origins of the Habichtswald range of mountains in the German area of Hesse were, in part, what allowed him to be elected to the Royal Society on 1 June 1769.

Like Hooke before him, he seemed destined to prove himself as a polymath. He wrote about the ancient literature of England and Germany. He seemed learned in matters of art and antiques and his research and publications led him to network with contemporary scholars such as Benjamin Franklin (one of the founding fathers of the United States and a renowned polymath), John Pringle (President of the Royal Society), the art historian Johann Joachim Winckelmann, Georg Christoph Lichtenberg, the German scientist and satirist who dedicated himself to experimental physics, and Johann Gottfried Herder, another fellow German whose range covered philosophy, theology, poetry and literary criticism. These were not lightweights and they seem to have at least given Raspe the time of day.

If only he had stuck to this route of scientific research or to his explorations of ancient poetry or art. He had managed to secure in 1767 what, from this distance, seems a prestigious contract cataloguing the art collection of General Johann Ludwig von Wallmoden-Gimborn, an Austrian cavalry officer reputed to be an illegitimate son of Britain's George II by his mistress Amalie von Wallmoden. The general then got him the job of curating the Kassel art galleries in Hesse. Johann Wolfgang von Goethe (then a disciple and friend of Winckelmann), who would become Germany's most esteemed writer of the modern age, sought Raspe's help to find good plaster casts of ancient sculptures for his growing collection. He was appointed professor of antiquities at Germany's first college of technology. What more could the man want? Evidently, more money. Trusted to buy items of art in Italy for Frederick II, ruler of Hesse-Kassel, he instead sold some of Frederick's valuable items and pocketed the cash.

All his appointments and his links to prestigious acquaintances were blown out of the water, along with his membership of the Royal Society, from which (according to the Royal Society's records for 7 December 1775) he was expelled because of 'breaches of trust'. It is intriguing in view of this incident and later revelations of Raspe's deviousness to learn that Desmarest did not publish an essay on his Auvergne research until 1774, when he noted the succession of volcanic outbursts and the changes the rocks had undergone through weathering and erosion. Did Raspe have access to the research done in the 1760s and use it to enhance his own reputation? That is the problem when we come to evaluate Raspe's true value to the development of geology. Could a man capable of profiting from the sale of the property of others and of 'planting' ore with a view to fooling a Scottish landowner about the mining possibilities on his land be trusted as a serious scientist?

It is why we have to treat with suspicion the speculation that the Trewhiddle Ingot – that lump of tungsten found in Cornwall during Raspe's period of working there for Mathew Boulton – was produced by him ahead of known methods of smelting the metal. Boulton, who of course is famous for his collaboration with James Watt on producing the steam engine that revolutionised mining by providing pumps to prevent mines flooding, employed Raspe between 1782 and 1788 as assay master and storekeeper in the Dolcoath mine in Cornwall. It was this connection, this apparently lowly appointment, that seems to have given Raspe sufficient clout to be considered a candidate to survey the Duke of Argyll's mines and quarries and, subsequently, those in Sutherland. The modern employer might have looked at Raspe's curriculum vitae and surmised he was a chancer. But a man who could name-drop such a cast of acquaintances as Raspe had at his fingertips and could flaunt so many publications must have seemed plausible in the mining world of the 18th century – a world that was beginning to overflow with characters equally brazen but less well connected.

4

The coal of Kintyre

Lead and copper were minerals that, in quantity and of appropriate quality, could make fortunes but, in Argyll, coal was the potential life-changer that the crofter and the fisherman never had in his home. The record of it being used to fire furnaces for smelting ore that appears in the account books of Tarbert Castle in the 1400s shows that it was available and available in large amounts – but to have been able to access coal at an affordable price would have made life in the Western Highlands and Islands so very, very different.

The Duke of Argyll, who wrote in 1844 that he hoped the new-found coal in Mull would help crofters to live 'without wasting the best weather of summer in preparing for the winter', at least understood the harshness of a life heated only by peat. Yes, we love the smell of a peat fire but the modern notion of that peat fire is nothing but a romantic fantasy. Without the backbreaking, time-consuming peat cutting of the summer (when as much time as possible should have been devoted to nurturing crops and animals), there could be no fire in the winter. It was a family task and, if a woman lived alone, she had to hope that her neighbours would help out. In Norman MacCaig's poem 'Aunt Julia', the narrator recalls with affection and awe his Gaelic-speaking auntie who lived alone and tackled every job on the croft. He says with admiration:

> I can see her strong foot
> stained with peat.

Once the peats were cut, they had to be stacked to dry. The beautiful lush green scenery of Argyll is engendered by a high rainfall, so drying anything in Argyll is achieved with difficulty and the end result of such intensive labour was a smouldering fire that radiated little except that sweetly perfumed smoke. Coal, however, was for centuries an expensive import. Despite the long history of mining, the technology had not made much progress by the 1700s.

Better quality coal was usually deeper in the ground. In the English coalfields, some of the oldest pits reached depths of 300 feet. By the 1750s, some went down to a depth of 600 feet and by the 1820s some were as deep as 900 feet below the surface. That's just 100 feet short of The Shard, London's tallest building at the time of writing. The deeper the seam, the more costly it was to sink shafts and haul out the coal. There was also the question of pumping out water, as we have seen in the modest lead mines of Morvern. Even in the middle of the 20th century, haulage from the deepest of mines was still carried out by horsepower. In the 18th century, coal was brought out from one 600-foot deep mine using a gin powered by eight horses. The introduction of the Newcomen steam engine in the 1760s to drain mines of the water that regularly flooded them marginally reduced the cost of coal. But, for the consumer in Argyll and the islands, it wasn't just the cost of extracting coal that was the problem – problematic though that was. The tax imposed on the purchase price was as prohibitive as the tax on salt. Add to that the cost (and difficulty) of transportation and the crofter's peat fire was Hobson's choice.

'Ordinary people', therefore, never benefited from the coal mined in the south of the Kintyre peninsula in early times. Indeed, it seems almost to have been reserved for royal purposes from the days of Robert the Bruce, who used it for smelting during building and repair works on Tarbert Castle in the 1320s. In 1494, James IV visited Tarbert, Kilkerran and Dunaverty castles and sent a mining expert ('ain coll man') called John Davidson to survey the Kintyre mines. Mr Davidson was paid 18 shillings for the work and three shillings travelling expenses from Dumbarton by boat. It seems the coal was then used for works carried out at the various castles, particularly at Tarbert. The royal coal was transported by horse and cart from the first mine, which was to the south of Drumlemble on a ridge by Torchoillean.

On 9 April 1669, Archibald Campbell, 9th Earl of Argyll, granted a feu to Ronald McDonald of Sanda, for the old church lands of St Ninian and Ballygrigan, but reserved for himself 'all mines, minerals, coals and coal heughs that shall be found within the said lands, it being however lawful for the said Ronald to win coal for his own use'. Over the years, the Earl's descendants would ask their lawyers to pick over their rights to minerals with a very fine-toothed comb.

It was not until the latter part of the 17th century that the coal was used in industry, bringing together in 1678 two of the country's most expensive products – coal and salt. The saltpans at Machrihanish on the west coast of the peninsula needed coal to process the salt and it was fortuitous to have a coalmine on the doorstep. It was also about this time that whisky was gaining in popularity. The 9th Earl of Argyll, who then owned the whole of Kintyre, was sending friends gifts of a distillation made in the peninsula as early as 1667. Of course, once a tax was put on whisky, the stills took to the hills. The Scottish parliament introduced taxes first on malt and then on whisky itself at the end of the 17th century when the country's finances were devastated by the civil wars of the previous decades. After the Acts of Union with England in 1707, the English parliament set the bar even higher but, after three quarters of a century of illegal whisky production, eight distilleries were licensed in 1777. In 1782–3 and again in 1795–7, the Commissioners of Supply for Argyll banned the manufacture of whisky because of crop failures. When, in 1785, the Licence Duty was imposed, it made small-scale whisky production economically unviable. With the Excise Act of 1823, however, distillers could pay a licence fee of £163 10s and a set payment per gallon of proof spirit. This legislation laid the foundations for the Scotch whisky industry and led to Campbeltown, Kintyre's harbour town, having more than 30 distilleries and a huge appetite for coal to fire the distilling process.

By that time, the local coalmine was able to meet these demands. The Machrihanish coalfield is estimated to have been laid down more than 300 million years ago during the Westphalian Stage of the Carboniferous Period that shaped the geology of north-west Europe. It stretches across the Kintyre peninsula and, by the mid 1700s, two seams were being worked – a main one that was 17 feet thick and a shallower one in which the coal was of inferior quality. In 1749, the same Mr O'Connor who had, in August of that year, looked at the Morvern mines carried out a survey in Kintyre for the Duke of Argyll. A memorandum dated 30 September in the Argyll archives at Inveraray suggests that the methods being used to bring out the coal were fairly primitive. Water and flooding were major causes of concern, as was the threat of a collapse of sections of the works. In this 'question and answer' document, the Duke learned that the coal dipped one in five fathoms (a fathom measures six feet), although in some places it was even steeper. Of two seams, one was claimed by the miners to be 6ft 2ins thick, but the surveyor had measured just four feet. He had seen that coal was left in the roof of the mine but he didn't know what thickness it was and presumably, as there was no stone covering of the tunnel, to have removed this coal would have been disastrous.

The coal was a 'thin, slatey lying coal, not very black, nor has it much sulphur in it'. It was easily broken and burned well in chimneys but was 'not strong, nor does it last long'. The verdict was that it was 'not fit for furnaces' but it did sell for 2s 6d a ton, which was competitive in the Irish market – a market just 14 miles to the south across the water from Kintyre.

The lower seam was three feet thick and the coal was stronger, blacker and burned better. This seam lay 16 feet 'below the pavement of the upper coal'. However, the threads of this seam were at some distance from each other, creating extra costs for excavation. The coal would, the memorandum suggested, be more freely accessible towards the old works nearer the saltpans than in the direction of Campbeltown. In this seam the roof was good and a gin sink drawn by a total of eight horses was in place to bring out the water. Two horses worked two hours at a time, around the clock without stopping 'except in a drought in the summer time, when they might be idle'. They drew out 52 buckets of water an hour. There was uncertainty about the direction in which the mine should be developed but, 'about half an English mile from

Campbeltown', some 'black burnt-like stuff' was found that showed promise of a crop of coal.

Clearly many trials had been made in the surrounding area in attempts to find coal (or, indeed, to mine it illegally) but it wasn't thought wise to follow through on these because of the distance to both Campbeltown in the east and Machrihanish in the west on tracks that were not good. 'A prettie good road will be got there with some small expense,' Mr O'Connor suggested and his advice was that the best way forward would be to sink a trial on both sides of the old workings, one towards the north-west between the old workings and Kilkevan, the other towards the south-east between Drumleman (still the local name for Drumlemble to this day) and Campbeltown. As there was a dyke – a run of whinstone – near Drumleman it was advisable to test the quality of the coal first.

The difference in attitude towards ease of access regarding the mines in southern Kintyre and those in Ardnamurchan and Morvern is interesting from a 21st-century perspective. Today's roads in the majestic hills of the two northern peninsulas still give some small idea of the inaccessibility of these areas 275 years ago. The infrastructure between Campbeltown on the east of the Kintyre peninsula and Machrihanish in the west, however, gives a false impression of the ability to transport coal (and salt) in the 18th and 19th centuries. A canal and then a railway would improve the situation but the cost of such investment would render the pits financially vulnerable several times in their history.

Nor was transport the only investment to be considered. There were thoughts of introducing mid–18th-century technology in the form of an engine to draw water, which could be worked by water (there was plenty of it) or fire. Further advice to use a gin to keep the water out of the mine came in a report to the Duke of Argyll dated November 1752. The report, quoted by D.M. Seaman, M.I.M.E., C.ENG, in his document 'Coal Mining in Kintyre', said that a number of subscribers to the coalmine in Kintyre were looking for reassurance about its operation. They were concerned that there was 'a large body of coals still extant in the grounds of Drumlemill' in a seam six and a half feet thick that could 'in the summer season be easily kept free of water by a gin, but in the winter time it was with difficulty and a great expense the gin could keep it free'. These subscribers had themselves surveyed where the coal lay and suggested creating a reservoir to provide enough water to drive the pumps when most needed.

The unpredictability of water supplies in Argyll beset every engineering project. The Crinan Canal throughout the 19th century had either too much or too little water to operate its locks. Clearly the Kintyre mining operations faced similar problems. There was either too much water inside the mine tunnels to allow the work to proceed or not enough outside to operate pumps efficiently to remove that water. It was, of course, not a problem confined to this Kintyre coalmine but affected most of the lead, zinc and copper mines throughout the county.

The Drumlemble subscribers thought that, if the 'springs and rivulets in the hills above the coal works upon the lands of Kilchivan (*sic*) belonging to Mrs Forrester, the lands of Tirfergus belonging to Torquell (*sic*) McNeil and the lands of Ballegregar (*sic*) belonging to His Grace were collected together into a dam or reservoir which might be done at small expense, these might afford a large quantity of water for driving the pumps, and keeping the coal free of water'. There were two further rivers, they suggested, that could also be brought into play if necessary 'to keep a machine going all the year'.

They also had word of 'extraordinary good quality' coal to be had in the area that one of the subscribers, Baillie Watson, had used for his distillery and the report suggested that, if the Duke were to lease the mine to a company on reasonable terms, it would produce coal to rival that coming out of Saltcoats, Irvine and Ayr. Sadly, too many reports and comments made down the centuries contradict this brave assertion – most experts agreed that the Ayrshire coalfields yielded a superior product.

The Duke made a series of unsatisfactory deals with various potential investors but, by 1765, Charles McDowall of Crichen had sole management of the salt works at Machrihanish and was knocking on the current mine company's door for coal to operate them. Jobs at the saltpans were under threat and McDowall was surveying for his own coal, employing 15 men throughout the summer to carry out trials until the weather turned to rain and they had to be laid off. He was, however, determined to have the saltpans working by the following spring and that was coal dependent.

The solution was for McDowall to work both the coal-mine and the salt works and the Duke of Argyll agreed to lease him the Kintyre mines. McDowall wasn't only a saltpans owner but a Renfrewshire lawyer and politician with property aspirations and a history of legal negotiations in mining practices. When the tacksmen who had previously been running the mine (apparently into the ground in more ways that one) attempted to prevent the lease going to McDowall, it is easy to surmise that the smart lawyer was the better negotiator. In 1771, McDowall took a 27-year lease on the Campbeltown coal and salt works from the Duke and lost no time in having the mine surveyed with a view to making improvements he clearly already had in mind. Even before he signed the lease, he had contacted the Carron Company (Scotland's major ironworks, which had been established in 1759 near Falkirk on the River Carron) to see if they could manufacture mining equipment specifically for the Kintyre mine and, as soon as he had the lease in hand, he asked James Watt if he would make a survey of the Drumlemble mine. At the time, Watt was surveying possible sites for a new canal at Tarbert and between Loch Fyne and Loch Crinan and didn't get round to McDowall's survey until 1773, when he suggested a water supply for mine pumps, drainage of Loch Sanish, as well as the possible construction of a canal to transport the coal from the mine to Campbeltown.

When David Loch, merchant and general inspector of the fisheries in Scotland, visited the mine in 1778, the machinery was still basic. Loch, who made a tour of Scotland in that year and published his findings in *Essays on the Trade, Commerce, Manufactures and Fisheries of Scotland*, arrived in his hired sloop *Peggy* on Friday 24 April at 9 p.m., after a 13-hour sail from Rothesay. The next morning he went ashore at 5 a.m. and found most people still in bed. Perhaps that was because the herring were landed during the night – he wasn't to know. He found that, between 5 April 1777 and 5 April 1778, 10,847 barrels of herring and 213 hundredweight of dried fish were sent 'coastwise' to Greenock and Glasgow. Some 245 barrels of herring were retained for home consumption. The town was booming. Children were collectively paid £800 per annum to dress hemp, spin twine and knit nets for the herring 'busses' – there is no record of how many boys and girls were doing these jobs but Loch was very impressed at the figure expended on their industry.

On the afternoon of 25 April, Loch wrote, 'I accompanied Mr Charles McDowall, Sheriff of Renfrewshire, on a visit to his coal-works, four miles west of Campbeltown.' He added, 'The machinery being plain and simple, and consequently kept up at little expense, pleases me very much.' The mine was 'of infinite service to this part of the country, especially as no duty is paid on what they take away by land carriage'. The 'plain and simple' machinery may have been pleasing to Loch but the lack of more modern equipment disadvantaged the miners and their boss. Their work was harder and his profits must surely have been compromised when rain stopped play. In time, however, a waterwheel was installed and mine pumps operated at Machrihanish. James Watt designed improvements to water supplies for mills in Campbeltown, an upgrade of Campbeltown's harbour and, of course, plans were laid for the short canal that opened in 1791 to take coal from Drumlemble to Campbeltown, just ahead of work beginning on the Crinan Canal and the year that McDowall died.

Despite attempts to prevent it being constructed – in 1783 Campbeltown town council had applied for an interdict against McDowall when he started cutting the canal next to the mill dam – the coal canal was more or less successfully in operation until 1855 and, with a little bit of imaginative thinking, traces of it can be seen between the farms of Hillside and Gorton. An aqueduct was built across the Chiskan Water near a modern bridge on the Machrihanish road and the ghost of that can also be seen. There are few visible reminders of any of Argyll's mines – the above-ground evidence having being subsumed into forests, cannibalised for sheep fanks or enveloped in the moss that smothers much in this beautiful county. Skull and crossbone 'danger' signs beside forest tracks are often the only indication of the industry that once struggled there.

McDowall may have been too smart for his own good because there was a series of complaints against him as developments got underway. Drumlemble tenants James and William Ryburn and John Wilson, for example, sent a petition to Dugald Campbell, the Duke's chamberlain, seeking compensation for damage caused to houses and land by McDowall's coal works. Even so, McDowall certainly moved ahead with mine improvements and, between 1788 and 1791, coal output ranged between 31,000 and 41,000 loads at 6½d a load. According to the *First Statistical Account*, there were three cartloads to a ton and 40 carts of coal were consumed in Campbeltown a day. By 1798, the town was consuming 4,500 tons of coal a year.

In the years following McDowall's death, rents were increased, the coal company sought more land to provide milk for the miners and grazing for the horses and there was a dispute over unfair treatment of the men who provided the horses for the mine. When a beam of the engine broke and a new part had to be ordered from Greenock, the mine closed for six weeks. There is an edge to the correspondence of the time that suggests things fell apart after McDowall's demise and there were daily frictions that impeded production.

The Argyll estate received a tenth of the coal produced, as well as rent for the canal and the farm, which placed quite a burden on the coal company, especially at times when new equipment was installed. In 1801, funds were low and 'indulgence' for time to pay was sought from the Duke. The first decade of the new century brought technical troubles – the canal damaged neighbouring farms and mineshafts were in the wrong positions – but output was fairly steady. The flooding problems of the earliest years returned, however, in the 1830s and, from 1835 to 1837, there was a range of difficulties to contend with. The pit flooded in February 1835 and was closed for 16 months. A new pit opened in 1837 near the canal and a tram road was built to carry the coal 627 yards from the pit to canal. In 1837, the colliers went on strike in a bid to be paid on gross output. It sounds wholly unfair that the miners would have their pay reduced to reflect the net weight of the coal output rather than what their hard labour had actually produced. The company also had a dispute with the Duke over their dues at a time when the very position of the mine was shifting. In 1841, the pit manager John Howie died and the future of the pit seemed up in the air.

While the modern equipment certainly helped to increase coal production, it is easy to see that life was still harsh for the miners (supplies of fresh farm milk or not) and this didn't seem to improve much throughout the 19th century. One family, the McPhails, have traced their involvement with the mine back to the late 1700s. Hugh McPhail from Tirfergus was born in 1772 and grew up to be both a collier and a weaver, presumably needing two occupations to eke out an income enough to keep his family. He and his wife Mary, who came from Drumlemble, had sons and grandsons who also went down the mine, and sadly, at least two McPhails drowned in separate pit accidents at Drumlemble in the 1800s. One, Donald, died at the age of 33 and his son Daniel met the same fate in 1878 at the age of 29. In Kilkivan cemetery, there is a sad little corner where the headstones pay tribute to generations of coal mining McPhails.

What compounds that sadness is the number of graves in this ancient chapel's burial ground that commemorate tragically short lives. The deaths of children are somehow

expected in the 18th and 19th centuries – even at the start of
the 20th century, infant mortality was shockingly high. But,
on the bleak hillside at Kilkivan, surrounding the ruins of
chapels dating from the 6th century and medieval times, are
gravestones that mark the deaths of 19-year-olds, 20-year-
olds – youngsters who struggled on past the dangers of
childhood only to have their lives cut short as they entered
adulthood. Today, most of the gravestones themselves have
fallen and the same warning signs that keep us out of the old
adits and shafts of the disused mines the length and breadth
of Argyll tell us to keep our distance from the heavy toppling
stones. Poor families must have impoverished themselves still
further to erect such monuments to keep memories alive of
the brief flames that once burned in their communities. If
there was ever a doubt that mining offers a cruel life for those
who work in it and those who wait at home, this wind-
swept collection of graves overlooking the Atlantic puts it
to rest.

The talented Scottish filmmaker and activist Jan Nimmo,
whose outstanding documentary *The Road to Drumleman* tells
the more recent history of the Drumlemble mining community, was inspired to make the film because her own father
had been a miner there. After her father's death, she found
in his effects a poem by James MacMurchy, which was published in *Memories of Kintyre* in 1880. To have written out the
poem and kept it so safely suggests that it meant much to Jan's
father – and the knowledge that I too had a forebear who
drowned in the darkness of a coalmine offered me a poignant
connection. It is very Victorian but it tells a community's
story and expresses a community's pain.

Accident at Coalhill

July has come in wi' a sweet balmy gale,
To waft o'er the flowers on the mountains and dale,
And the wee smiling daisy wi' fragrance to fill;
But alas! It brought sorrow and grief to 'Coalhill'.

The miners just finished their labour below,
To the clear light of day, they hurriedly go,
When a noise, loud as thunder came fast to each ear,
Which caused all the miners to tremble with fear,

It's the 'waste' broken in, Hark! The waters now roar,
There are nine men below, we may see them no more,
May God them protect, who is mighty and wise,
And help them, for safety to flee to the 'rise'.

And Providence ordered the manager near
Descended the mine, braving danger and fear,
He reached the six men in their perilous cave,
And saved their lives from a watery grave,

Then down through the workings so wild,
Like a fond-hearted father, in search of his child.
But no sound of the three missing men could he hear,
But the wild roar of water, sae gloomy and drear.

Go back from the danger, your duty you've done,
The men are no more, their life's journey run.
But we hope they are safe on a happier shore,
When the struggle of life they'll encounter no more.

May the men who are safe give to God all their praise,
Who sent them relief, and lengthened their days.
May they trust in His bountiful Providence all,
For without His permission a sparrow can't fall.

James Todd left his home, just a short year before,
And his friends in Tollcross will see him no more,
When he came to Kintyre, how little thought he,
To die in the waters that flowed from the 'Ree',

Neil Smith, young and fair in his manhood and bloom,
And Donald McPhail shared his watery tomb,
Their friends and relations, now sadly do mourn
For the loved ones, that's gone and will never return.

MacMurchy, a poet, singer and preacher, was born in 1835, the son of a miner. Family records suggest that he began work at Drumlemble mine at the age of nine and he would not have been the only child working there, even though the 1842 Mines Act prohibited the employment underground of all females and all males under the age of ten. That Act had been passed when James was seven years old and, while the workings of the Drumlemble mine, although 270 feet deep, would not have been as complex and dangerous as conditions described by Friedrich Engels in his book *The Condition of the Working Class in England in 1844*, surely no work in a mine should have been carried out by children. Engels reported that tots as young as four were set to work, explaining that their job was either to take the coal or ore from where the miner loosened it to the main shaft or to watch the ventilation doors (a job that involved sitting for at least 12 hours in the dark, alone, with only a small candle). It is hard to decide which of these jobs would have been worse – the lonely, pitch black vigil over the ventilation doors or shoving heavy tubs without wheels over uneven terrain, sometimes on hands and knees. It was older children and 'half-grown girls' who did the heavy work, while the four- and five-year-olds were given the ventilation door watch, opening and shutting wooden doors to let air through the tunnels.

Perhaps because nine-year-old James MacMurchy started work after the Act was passed, he was given a job on the surface sorting coal. If that were the situation, at least he would have seen the daylight and breathed fresh air. In 1860, the age limit for boy miners was raised to 12 and, in 1900, to 13. But health and safety for children and adults alike was not a priority for many decades after that. As might be expected in a coalmine, it wasn't only flooding that put miners in mortal danger. On 25 July 1859, Donald Kerr and his son Alexander signalled to be taken up the shaft at 7 a.m. Mr J.L. Stewart, inspector of mines, said in his report of the accident that, when the two miners were about ten fathoms up the shaft, Donald apparently became tangled up in a broken belt wire and was dragged out of the bucket. He fell to the bottom of the shaft and was killed. The following year, on 22 December at Drumlemble, John McGechie, aged just 23, died when part of the roof and coal fell on him. By this time, accidents were at least being logged in the reports of the Inspector of Mines and Collieries. William Alexander was the inspector for the Western District of Scotland and often his reports placed the blame on the miners – careless use of machinery or explosives, for example – but here the cause is reported in just two words: 'Coal fall'.

There had been a more settled period for the mine in the 1840s. The miners were by then paid on gross output and mine inspections suggested it was well enough run. In 1847, the Duke gave permission for a change of access to a seam of coal. But, in the 1850s, when the Kilkivan pit was sunk around three-quarters of a mile to the west of the pit at Drumlemble, there were clearly financial difficulties and companies across Scotland made inquiries about taking on the coal works. A letter dated October 1854 to Peter Steven, the manager of Nitshill Colliery in Glasgow, suggested that whoever became tenant would have the right to sink shafts where they thought appropriate because the present pit was almost exhausted and producing just 9,000 tons of coal. This didn't meet the demands of Campbeltown. A farm, the canal and colliers' cottages were included in the price and Mr Steven was advised that he could not 'be on the ground soon enough' if he was really interested because a number of parties were also anxious to get their hands on this package.

This was a brave marketing pitch. There was a point in 1854 when no one (least of all the man who had been manager) knew who was actually managing the mines and the Duke was playing a hard game in terms of leasing to a new tenant. At the end of December 1854, the company bidding to take on the lease was almost begged by Mr Dalgleish, the Duke of Argyll's agent, to have a meeting to 'consider the offer so that I can let the colliers know whether the works are to carry on or not – they are now almost starving'. The idea of a 'number of parties' jostling over a lease on the mine was fiction – that miners were going hungry was stark fact.

A new lease was prepared but the tenant, Mr Steven, had not visited the works by October of 1855 and, unless a new shaft was sunk, production would have had to come to an end. In fact, Mr Steven gave up on the project and the company (Stewart and Watson) that had kept the show on the road during its troubles was left holding the baby. They had increased miners' wages but now, with no actual lease in force, they felt they were going to lose out if they tried to make improvements or even keep the place running. An inventory was taken in the November, an under manager, engineer and pit headman were put in charge to keep an eye on things and to 'raise coal for the use of the pumping engine' to keep the shafts and tunnels free of water. The cost of keeping the pit clear in this way was to be £7 a week while wages and supplies would be under £10 a week. A further dilemma was that the men got free coal, but someone would have to pay them for doing the work to bring the coal out. Meanwhile, the men were 'anxious to keep their houses on in the hope of the work restarting' but to put food on the tables in those houses, they planned to 'go to the Low Country meantime'.

What else could they do? The mine wasn't just limping along – it was disabled not by lack of coal but by lack of management. A Mr Smellie of Blackbraes Colliery near Glasgow showed some interest in December 1855 but, meanwhile, the bills for equipment kept coming in. The Duke gave notice to close the canal in 1856 because it did nothing but cost him money – doing so cost him a further £112 8s – and the farms were sold. Two years later a handful of men had been kept in employment and a new shaft yielded inferior coal. The Duke's tenants were now buying coal from elsewhere because it was cheaper. This sad spiral of diminishing demand compounding diminishing production was making any future for the mine look very bleak indeed. Without funding from the Duke, it was doubtful if the coal works could be let. 'Not a plack the richer' was certainly a phrase that must have been in the Duke's mind – and the miners were in dire straits.

Stewart and Watson (on rather shaky legal terms, it can be surmised) saved the mine from a £5,000 loss by 1858 but, in 1861, the company's Mr Stewart told the Duke he couldn't clear off the debt and he dreaded it going deeper. He warned the men of imminent closure and asked the Duke's permission to close the works, suggesting that, while it might be worked for another month, it was only going to cost more money and add to the debt. During their fortnight's notice, he deployed the men in raising the mining equipment. In 1863, all the Drumlemble pit's machinery went up for sale. But it wasn't the end of mining in Kintyre by any means. That same year, a company from Falkirk took a lease from the Duke and began boring behind the mansion house on Chiskan estate and, in 1866, Kilkivan mine was still in operation. And in 1872, J. Smellie and Son were recorded operating Drumlemble colliery and there are documents relating to coal sales from Drumlemble, Gig, Kilkivan, Trodigal and Gas in 1874.

This was a quite miraculous turnaround and, between 1874 and 1876, a light railway was built from Campbeltown to the Kilkivan Pit. In 1875, £5 shares were being sold in the Argyll Coal and Cannel (*sic*) Company, which had a stated capital of £50,000. David Smellie of Drumlemble, described as colliery proprietor and managing director, was provisionally director of this new company and the prospectus claimed that, due to the previous lack of capital, it had not been possible to exploit the pit's 'enormous resources'. Now, however, came the day and the hour. Potential investors were advised that the Duke of Argyll had leased 40,000 acres for 31 years, that 20 million tons of coal had already been extracted and that it was confidently assumed more valuable seams lay at lower depths. A new shaft was to be sunk and a railway was to run from the colliery to the harbour in Campbeltown. It was estimated that £30,000 would be needed for the necessary improvements, but on the plus side, new markets would open up. The boats bringing barley from France, for example, would take back Campbeltown coal (something that could never have been floated as a possible outlet in the 1790s and the early part of the 19th century when France and Britain were at each other's throats). There was also, the prospectus stressed, a huge market on the doorstep. By now, Campbeltown had 20 distilleries that burned 600 tons of coal a week to produce whisky. There were 8,000 people living in the town, using 1,700 tons of coal a week – and the coal from Glasgow cost six shillings more than coal from the local mine. The lease included 38 workmen's houses and a manager's house. What better way to invest a fiver or two than in the Argyll Coal and Canal Co. Ltd?

The Duke came on board to build the railway in 1876, the locomotives and tracks were due to be in place by June of that year, a new shaft had been sunk, opening up two new seams of coal nine feet and six feet thick and, meanwhile, a row of miners' houses was being built at Drumlemble. Work at Kilkivan also expanded but, in the world of mining, there is rarely a happy ever after. In 1878, water from the old workings at Kilkivan, abandoned half a century previously, burst through into the new mine area and flooded from over 160 feet below the surface to within 72 feet of the surface – a terrifying 90 feet of water. Terrible damage was done by the flood as the water's 'considerable force' raced through the tunnels and it is the fate of the miners that 140 years on still has the power to move us. The 'bottomer' was, by definition of his job title, working at the bottom of the pit and didn't stand a chance. Two miners were trapped and their bodies were later found near their place of work. Because the incident took place late in the shift, five workers in different parts of the mine were able to escape, presumably because they had already been making their way out by what was known as the 'blind' pit. Despite the pumps operating constantly, it took days to reach the body of the bottomer and four weeks passed before the bodies of the other men were reached. The distress of the families cannot be imagined.

This was described as a very unusual accident but the conditions and layout of any mine meant flooding, possibly with fatal consequences. Mr Stewart's report of the disaster suggested that 'the salutary provisions contained in Section 42 of the Statute, which provides that plans of abandoned mines shall be lodged with the Secretary of State within 3 months of the abandonment will in future tend to prevent such misfortune'.

It had been a public outcry over a mine-flooding incident that forced the tentative beginnings of a series of Acts that would eventually protect miners. There had been a freak accident at Huskar Colliery in Yorkshire in 1838 when a stream overflowed into the ventilation drift after violent thunderstorms. What shocked the public (and Queen Victoria herself) was that 26 children lost their lives. They included 11 girls, aged from 8 to 16, and 15 boys, between 9 and 12 years of age. Campaigners ranged from Friedrich Engels on the political far left to Anthony Ashley-Cooper, 7th Earl of Shaftesbury, on the right (the Earl, to his credit, also campaigned successfully for protection of child chimney sweeps). There was a Royal Commission report instigated by the Queen and the hastily cobbled Mines and Collieries Act of 1842 brought, as we have seen, changes governing the minimum age of children working in the mines.

Fortunately, the campaigning didn't stop there and politicians were forced to look at other elements of employment in the mines. The Coal Mines Inspection Act of 1850 introduced mines inspectors in an effort to reduce accidents but, as always, the fine-tuning took decades. The Coal Mines Regulation Act of 1860 improved safety rules and, as we have seen, raised the age limit for boys working in mines from 10 to 12. But there were still more than 1,000 lives lost each year in mining accidents and so, in 1872, the Coal Mines Regulation Act introduced the requirement for pit managers to be trained and state registered. Miners could appoint inspectors from among themselves. There was also a requirement to lodge plans of abandoned mines with the Secretary of State.

Was this an effective move? It became so in the future but, although there were plans of the old mine workings that Mr Stewart could refer to in his report after the Kilkivan mine catastrophe, whether or not they were registered with the Secretary of State would seem to have made no difference. The management knew of the derelict 50-year-old shafts and tunnels but still men drowned. It was not until the Mines Regulation Act of 1881 that the Home Secretary was empowered to hold inquiries into the causes of mine accidents – but those causes continued to exist.

On a more positive note, the Argyll Coal and Canal Company was throwing a wide net and exporting coal as far as Denmark, Norway, Sweden and Prussia and, when the Kilkivan seams were exhausted, there was enough cash in hand to extend the railway that had connected Kilkivan with a depot on the west side of Campbeltown to the Drumlemble mine in 1881. The company did not stay the course, however. As the 1880s progressed and a new seam was opened (called 'Wimbledon' because a local man won a shooting contest at Wimbledon and the new source of coal was also a cause for celebration), John Smellie, the man behind the Coal and Canal Company sold out to J. & L. Galloway, who took over the lease with the Duke of Argyll's agreement and, by the end of the century, it was the Campbeltown Coal Company that was issuing a prospectus. It had taken on the Argyll colliery with its four and a half miles of railway, its two locomotives, eight wagons and a market seeking 30,000 tons of coal a year. A new string was added to the bow – a bed of fireclay had been opened and, during the season the distillers were idle, the fireclay would be mined. According to the Mineral Planning Factsheet produced by the British Geological Survey, fireclay is found under almost all coal seams and it is used to make bricks or to line kilns and furnaces.

In the early years of the new century, the Campbeltown Coal Company wanted a lease that would allow them to mine for coal under the sea. Any such minerals were the property of the Crown but the Duke of Argyll wanted to ensure that he did not lose out. Between 1897 and 1903, output had increased from 10,483 tons to 25,610 tons. That was from the onshore pits. Now there was a suggestion that the company could mine under the sea and the Duke wanted to be clear about what he was entitled to and what he might have to pay in royalties. Legal experts Lindsay Howe were sent a letter on 4 August explaining the current situation. There was sufficient coal to last 'very many years' and the Duke would have been happy with that forecast but there were many other changes afoot at the start of this exciting new century. First, the undersea mining proposal and, secondly, an application to turn the workaday railway built to transport coal to Campbeltown into a narrow-gauge light railway running from Campbeltown to Machrihanish, linked with steamers and intended as a tourist venture as well as a local transport system, and with an extension to take coal straight to waiting ships instead of using carts from the depot to the quayside. This was also an opportunity for the Duke as proprietor, but with opportunities come responsibilities and those responsibilities dictated the caveats he laid before the proposed rail company. ·

The issue of this light railway was a little more urgent than the business of the undersea mineral rights because, earlier in the year, talks had taken place between the Galloways, who were the current colliery owners, Denny's the shipbuilders and other parties interested in this exciting business venture. The Argyll Railway Company had been formed to make an application for a Light Railway Order, which was granted in May 1904. On 22 July 1904, J. Lindsay Galloway of the Campbeltown Coal Company wrote to Mr Alfred E. Lowis, the Duke's chamberlain, seeking an extension of the company's lease so that they could recoup the 'large outlay' they would have to make extending the colliery if the Light Railway Order was to come through successfully. 'We rely upon His Grace assisting the promotions of the railway by granting the land on favourable terms,' Galloway told Lowis.

A meeting of the Light Railway Commissioners was scheduled for 28 September to hear objections and the case for the railway. The Duke's lawyers, Lindsay Howe, were told in August that he would only withdraw objections to the Campbeltown and Machrihanish Light Railway Order 1904 if compensation were guaranteed if things went wrong. Throughout that summer the atmosphere must have remained tense as letters were batted back and forth about the land the railway would cross, the effects on the seams of coal under the railway and how the Duke's royalties would be affected by the coal going straight from mine to ship. The Campbeltown Coal Company put in a request to buy the land from the Duke. Lindsay Howe told them of the complications – 'The Duke as Heir of Entail cannot voluntarily sell the land to the company or name the price which he will accept for it.'

The days when Dukes could pull rank (or cite complications of ancient land rights) were coming to an end, however. The Board of Trade passed the application for the railway, the Campbeltown and Machrihanish Light Railway Company came into being in May 1905 and the new company had the right to compulsorily purchase land and buildings that lay in the way of the railway extension, barred only from touching ten or more houses belonging to workers earning less than £1 10s a week. As Lindsay Howe had pointed out the previous summer, 'When the order is passed the company will have acquired right to take the land compulsorily and it will be necessary to have the price fixed by arbitration.' The Duke had laid out his conditions, offering to withdraw opposition if there was agreement on how the tenants would conduct themselves in relation to the colliery and that annual surveys would be made.

And, of course, the little railway went on to flourish. In the first three weeks of its existence, some 10,000 passengers had travelled on the train, most of them having come for the day from Glasgow on one of the company's new turbine steamers. But the railway's success was closely tied to the colliery's viability, the country's economic situation and to transport developments.

We will return to the fate of the railway, but what of the Duke's concerns about undersea mining? In December of 1904, he asked Lindsay Howe to check out his rights with the Crown authorities. His chamberlain had spent the previous months seeking evidence that the Crown authorities demanded. According to the authorities, the Crown Charters of the Barony of Kintyre contained 'no express grant of foreshore which is prima facie the property of the Crown'. Evidence was required 'of possession thereof for the prescriptive period duly connected with an habile title'. In relatively plain English, this means (according to Neil King's excellent online site set up to provide such information) that the Duke would have to have possessed unregistered land without legal challenge for at least ten years. To prove this possession, the Duke's staff collected a number of pre-cognitions, such as one from Hector MacNeal, who wrote that he had been proprietor of the Lossit Park Estate for the previous six years and that he, and his father before him, had always been charged for the removal of 'sea-ware, sand, and gravel from the foreshore of [his] property'. The family possession could be traced back 50 years to when the kelp industry was in full swing and 'all those who took part in this industry paid a royalty to the proprietor on the quan-tity of kelp they made'. A fossil bed had been found on the foreshore of the Lossit estate and the geological surveyor had been prevented from exploring without the appropriate authority.

This 'shore money' was confirmed by George Erskine Inglis, factor in Campbeltown for the previous 17 years, James McNeill, the Machrihanish wreck grieve of 30 years' standing, and Archibald Livingstone, described as a 'shop-keeper or grocer' of Pans, Lossit, who had been resident for 40 years – all to no avail. As the lawyers had pointed out, there was nothing in these precognitions to prejudice the Duke's case but, as it turned out, there was nothing in them to help the case either. A letter from the Commissioners of Woods, Forests and Land Revenues in Whitehall, London, told Lindsay Howe that the Board of Trade managed the sur-face of the Machrihanish foreshore and the Commissioners of Woods, Forests and Land Revenues had charge of the minerals under land and sea. On 23 December 1904, Lindsay Howe & Co wrote again to Mr Lowis confirming, 'We are afraid it is only too clear that the Duke has no rights to the minerals under the sea below low water mark, either under his Barony Title or under any Admiralty right belonging to him.' The lawyers cited a recent case – Lord Advocate v Wemyss 1899 – when it was decided that, under the law of Scotland, subsoils underlying the waters of the ocean, 'whether within the narrow seas or from the coast outward to the three-miles limit, and also the minerals beneath it, are vested in the Crown'.

The Duke clearly wanted to prove a point and had asked the lawyers to check out his Admiralty rights. These, according to Lindsay Howe, had been lost under the Forfeiture Act of James VII, restored to the then Earl and his children by William and Mary and, in 1904, the current Duke was indeed still holder of the office – but, even so, his rights did not extend 'beyond a right to unclaimed wrecks and to goods of flotsam, jetsam and lagan, ie, goods sunk, floating or attached to a float'. Certainly not to the coal under the sea at Machrihanish but, presumably, it had been worth a try. So, when the Campbeltown Coal Company began planning the undersea mining in September 1911, they worked under the restrictions that a barrier had to be left between the undersea and landward coal. The stoops (the pillars of coal left in place to support the roof of the seam) had to be approved in size by a neutral mining engineer – and the royalties had to go to the Crown.

This work began in earnest in 1913 but, in May 1914, the company gave notice that from the following May they were to give up the lease. In 1915, with the First World War well under way, the company sent out a letter to their customers asking them to support local coal. A third of the miners were now away at the war and, because of the uncertainties, those who remained could only work intermittently. Government policy was to keep all industries going and the 'practical way' to do that would be to buy Campbeltown coal. Before the end of the war, a new company had been set up but peace would not bring prosperity to the mine. The terrible economic plight in which the country found itself in the early 1920s didn't help a mine to keep going – and even before the General Strike of 1926, when the Trades Union Congress (TUC) supported Britain's miners in their battle with the mine owners, the Kintyre miners walked out. During that first strike in 1921, the mine flooded. A fire followed in 1925 that closed the main seam. The miners who had survived the 'war to end all wars', returning to the country they had fought for, found conditions only a little better than the trenches they had suffered in for four years.

In 1926, the miners were told their wages would be reduced by 13 per cent and their shifts increased from seven to eight hours. So who could blame them when they downed tools? The TUC support meant that workers from the road transport, bus, rail, docks, printing, gas and electricity, building, iron, steel, and chemical industries joined their strike and brought the country to a standstill. The Kintyre miners might not have had a workplace to walk out from if the Duke of Argyll had won his case against the company, which owed him for rent.

In this story of coal in Kintyre, the misfortunes seem to greatly outweigh the periods of success and yet, even when it seems nothing could get any worse, the records show that coal was being produced and the pits firing on all cylinders. A year after the General Strike, new management of the Campbeltown Coal Company reported an output of 25,000 tons of coal and 79 miners were employed. But high output goes before a fall and, a year later, an outfit called the Franco British Company took over the colliery with plans to produce coal gas. Trials seemed to be successful but, by 1933, when the Franco British Company had become the Coal Carbonisation Trust, Hansard of 14 February 1933 records that questions were being asked in Parliament about this organisation and its parent and associated companies, including Maisel's Petroleum Trust Company, that had attempted a coal-to-oil project and failed. Kilkivan mine was closed in June 1929 and, under a Ministry of Trade order, the Campbeltown and Machrihanish Light Railway Company was wound up in 1932.

During the Second World War, coal was clearly a priority for the national war effort and the Glasgow Iron and Steel Company Ltd was granted a licence to bore from September 1943 until November 1944. The results were positive enough for the company to open up two shafts for a new Argyll Colliery – just an eighth of a mile from the old pit – in February 1944. It was after the war concluded, however, that the pomp of an opening ceremony was staged. On 29 May 1946, Lady Lithgow (wife of Sir James Lithgow of the Glasgow shipbuilding company, Lithgows Ltd, who had a home in Argyll) declared the new colliery open. After the celebratory lunch, Frank Hodges, former general secretary of the Miners' Federation of Great Britain, announced that nationalisation was the future for mining. In 'Coal Mining in Kintyre', Jan Nimmo notes that, just a year later, Argyll Colliery was nationalised and became part of the National Coal Board. Perhaps after all the ups and downs during the preceding centuries created by a succession of leaseholders, this was the blessing the Kintyre coalfield had been waiting for. Certainly, the National Coal Board brought in all the latest equipment and modernised the operation completely. That isn't to say that there had been no new technology since electric light had been installed in 1905 but this was literally cutting-edge gear that sliced through the main 17-foot thick seam like a hot knife through butter. The coal went to the surface on a conveyor belt, perhaps watched over by the spirit of young James MacMurchy. By August 1950, production had increased to 280 tons per day.

But, of course, this is all about mining and mining and tragedy walk hand in hand. In February 1951, miner Donald Woodcock was killed by a fall of coal and his workmate Robert Hamilton was injured. Thankfully no lives were lost when a fire started in the mine in September 1958 but it raged for 17 days and, even when it was then decided to flood the mine, it took almost two months to get the fire under control. The conditions in the mine remained difficult into the next decade and there was also a drop in the demand for coal. The Clean Air Act of 1956 began to take effect by the 1960s as industries had to look for alternative energy sources. The oil and nuclear industries were rising forces and Old King Coal was no longer in charge of the energy market. There was even the discovery of oil in the North Sea in the 1960s – the death knell was beginning to toll. Many of the large coalmines closed down. These closures resulted in over 400,000 miners losing their jobs and, in Kintyre, where the payroll was already down to 200 men in 1960, a further 60 men were laid off in 1961. These numbers sound trifling in the face of the national situation but, in a small rural community, such job losses were catastrophic to the whole area.

Those clinging on to their jobs saw closure as inevitable. There was an increase in both water and running sand within the pit and, at times, 150 gallons of water a minute had to be pumped from the work face. Coupled with the dwindling market for coal, the only solution was for the National Coal Board to close up in March 1967, a year ahead of the next Clean Air Act.

Today, clean energy is the industry that is Kintyre's major employer. Wind turbines have been manufactured at Machrihanish for some time and, in 2016, Siemens invested £27 million in the factory, which is expected to treble the base's capacity and increase employment possibilities. Like all industries after the financial crash of 2008, there were difficulties but, in 2011, SSE and Highlands and Islands Enterprise took the existing company over. This was followed by a buy-out from the Korean firm CS Wind and the workforce increased to 170. Although the outcome of the UK's exit from Europe cannot fail to affect the plant, it is hoped that at least 300 people will be employed. Kintyre's tradition of providing energy looks set to continue well into the 21st century. And clean energy, rather than fossil fuel, seems to be making both investors and the local community 'a plack the richer'.

5

Digging for profit

The history of the coalmines in Kintyre in many ways reflects in microcosm the history of Scotland. The ownership of land, the Acts of Parliament needed to set up industrial ventures, the improvements (and otherwise) brought about by the industrial revolution, the new investors emerging from the growing new middle class – these developments that evolved from 18th- into 19th-century society prepared the way not only for the phenomenon generally known as 'railways mania' but also for a bit of a craze for mining.

Strict measures had been taken to avoid the financial disasters of the South Sea Bubble and the Darien Scheme of the early 1700s but, a century later, there was a relaxation of the limits on the formation of new businesses and on the number of separate investors (just five under the existing laws) who could be involved in joint stock companies. This 1825 measure allowed anyone to invest money in new companies with a view to getting a return on the investment. The invention of the steam engine, leading to the introduction of new-fangled railway networks, was exciting – and what could go wrong? The railways were promoted as 'foolproof' investments. In the 21st century, we fight shy of the word 'foolproof' because too much evidence weighs against the very possibility that something so described could indeed be successful. Two hundred years ago, 'foolproof' was too often an investment in 'fool's gold'

The burgeoning middle class of the 19th century, however, was innocent of such possibilities. In 1842, the Edinburgh and Glasgow Railway opened, with Queen Street Station delivering up passengers into Glasgow's growing business hub. In 1844, the Glasgow Stock Exchange opened. It became all too easy for companies to set up, sell themselves as a good bet and invite investment in company shares. It created a brief and beautiful bubble for the railways but bubbles burst and the railways had expanded so spectacularly on promised investments that the collapse was very public.

Less spectacular was the proliferation of small mining companies that also offered 'foolproof' investments for as little as £2 to £5 a share – worth around £200 to £500 today – and, all too often, these companies also went out of business. The possibilities of fortunes to be made in lead or copper threw up a breed of speculators who ranged from the serious expert in mining to the seriously dedicated charlatan – from the earnest miner trying to better himself to the fly-by-night prospectors who were almost literally here today, gone tomorrow, leaving a crude attempt at excavation in their wake. The dozens of such mines in mainland Argyll dot the Ordnance Survey Maps. To go in search of the 'disused mine', 'old silver mine' or 'lead mine' labelled on these maps is usually as unprofitable as the original search for the metals themselves. The lack of tangible remains of such short-lived ventures speaks volumes of their long-term success. Some did strike it lucky, however, and it is worth remembering that the Industrial Revolution was creating a huge market for minerals, particularly lead and tin.

The demand was so great that some kind of regulation of prices had to be devised and the London Metal Exchange was established. This was somewhat ironic, considering the lifting of company regulations that led to the proliferation of all-too-often valueless ventures. The exchange developed what we think of as the modern practice of 'futures' – putting a price on the metals that were mined in the increasing number of British colonies that wouldn't arrive by ship for at least three months. And this gives a clue to why a lot of the small mines in Argyll opened and closed in not much longer time than it took a load of copper to reach the UK from South America, Africa or Asia or for lead to arrive from America, Spain or Germany. These overseas mining ventures were often backed by British capital and expertise and were not, therefore, all about dodgy little fly-by-night companies. This meant the competition from abroad was crippling. However successful a mine in Argyll might be in terms of output, the transport from Morvern or Inveraray or Inverneil was never going to be easy. Railways were being constructed and boats were a boon if they could carry the weight of the freight but the ore from the tiny mine in Appin, Kilmartin or Inverneil faced a difficult and uneconomic trek across hills and glens to reach some central starting point. As the Irish would tell you, 'I wouldn't have started from here.' And then, when the complicated journey to Liverpool or Birmingham had been achieved, what profit was there in the effort? The appetite for lead was growing to meet the needs of burgeoning urban populations and the new industries setting up there. Lead was a ubiquitous element of roofing, piping, casting, building materials, lead shot, paint bases and glazing. But it was the metals pouring in from South America, mined by slave labour, that were able to compete better in terms of quantity and price.

That didn't stop both serious landowners and cavalier prospectors trying to get in on the act. In his updated *Gazetteer to the Metal Mines of Scotland* in 2014, Jeremy Landless made a comprehensive list of mines and identified many of the Argyll mining ventures – both the successful and those much less so. It says much about the working conditions faced by the 19th-century miners that some of the sites are where turbines are situated today – high on hillsides to gain maximum benefit from the wind. Imagine the trek on foot in all weathers to such exposed sites in bygone centuries.

An attempt at lead mining on Loch Fyne was made at Clachan Beag, and just over four miles south-south-west of Tarbert, Loch Fyne, was a lead mine at Coire Mhaim. Three copper mine sites have been identified on Meall Mor overlooking Loch Fyne south of Inverneil. Nearer the lochside was a zinc mine at Ardtilligan Burn. Above Inverneil itself, a lead mine was started at Achbraad, another at An Rudha, where there were three small workings that Jeremy Landless describes as being several metres apart, and workings are identified at Gleann Beag, Inverneil. Both copper and lead were mined to the north on Cruach Brenfield, between Inverneil and Lochgilphead and on Cruach Mheadhonach, where the modern road crosses from Loch Fyne to Achahoish. Cruach Mheadhonach stands some 741 feet high and offers beautiful views – but bleak working conditions for lead miners, especially as this mine was worked opencast. A number of trials for lead were carried out on the Shirvan estate that stretches across Knapdale to Loch Arail (Loch Errol) and around other lochans in the area between Ardrishaig and Achahoish. Near Achahoish itself, another lead mine operated at Allt Claigionnaich. Both lead and gold were sought in the Stronachullin Burn, 3.5 miles south of Ardrishaig, Loch Fyne.

Today, afforestation (and the natural mossing over of walls and buildings) has subsumed the evidence of such industry. Walking and cycling tracks are major tourist attractions that take visitors for pleasure to spots that were once reached only by hard effort, by men carrying the tools of their trade and the materials necessary to construct adits and shafts. The fruits of their labour had to be brought down hillsides now carved out for the daredevil mountain biker, the dedicated hiker and the dogged fell runner. It's doubtful that the most vivid imagination could have foreseen such transformation of purpose.

The Klondike effect might not have occurred until the 19th century but landowners had been trying to exploit their mineral wealth for hundreds of years before those company regulation changes. A.G. Rankine of Ardrishaig researched the background of southern Argyll's mines for The Natural History & Antiquarian Society of Mid-Argyll and notes that, in 1683, a German chemist resident in Edinburgh reported 'copper ore found in Cantyre (*sic*) in a hill the colour of gold'. A few decades later, prospecting began in the Inverneil area and, between 1745 and 1756, a Bristol company had excavated nine tons of copper and 19 tons 10cwt of lead from the Inverneil Mines. The prospectuses put out to attract investment went far and wide – a Derbyshire company took over these workings for a further two years and the Inverneil Estate map shows workings still active in 1776 before falling idle.

In September 1790, Sir Archibald Campbell, then owner of the Inverneil Estate, decided to develop his mineral resources and sent two teams of miners to assess the value of these old workings. The men leading the explorations both had previous knowledge of the estate mine workings. Neil McLarty was from Tarbert – a local man. But, more often, it wasn't the local population that benefited from mining operations. Men with mining experience in other parts of the country (or indeed in English or Irish mines) were more likely to be brought in to do the skilled work and the locals did the most menial labouring tasks. This didn't always lead to harmonious working conditions, especially if there were misunderstandings because of language or local custom. The Gaelic speakers of Argyll were sometimes seen in a poor light by men from elsewhere who did not appreciate their ways.

The second man Sir Archibald employed was Martin Freeman, who had come north from England in 1749 to work in the lead mines at Tyndrum and Morven. There, he met miners who had worked at Inverneil with the Clifton Company prior to 1749. By 1790, he was a mine manager in Islay. Freeman's report, dated 25 October 1790, gives a comprehensive account of the earlier mining activities on the estate and probably discouraged Sir Archibald from developing any further mineral work. Freeman pointed out that, while the original Clifton Company had extracted a 'considerable quantity of copper' at Inverneil and the Bristol firm had successfully worked the mines close to the Achahoish road, there was no reason to believe they were worth opening up again.

Although most of the evidence of the ancient workings has disappeared, giving way to the forestry and wind farm industries of 21st-century Argyll, a shaft and flooded adit have been identified on the south-west bank of the Inverneil Burn west-north-west of Achbraad. The Inverneil Burn and Allt nan Nathair, the burn that feeds into it, were revisited in the 19th century. By then, it was John Graham-Campbell who owned the Shirvan property and, on 3 January 1862, he leased the mining rights of Castleton, Strondoir and

Stronachullin to William Smith of Silvercraigs Lodge. Smith sublet the Castleton rights to the Castleton and Silvercraigs Mining Company, who began mining for copper. With a little imagination and a keen eye, it is possible to see an outline of this mine next to Lingerton Lodge, which stands close to the road heading south into Lochgilphead. In the 1860s, new shafts were opened up and the old spoil heaps were reworked. This was a common practice – new technologies often made this profitable and the lead works of one era often turned up newly identified metals at a later time. Nickel, for example, became the 'must-have' metal of the mid 1800s and was often found in the spoils of earlier excavations.

Just south of Inverneil on today's A83 is Stronachullin. There's a farm, fish farm and, up on the hills, wind turbines with all the buildings lower down the glen that a wind farm entails. But, in June 1862, the scene was a little different. This Strondoir–Stronachullin portion of the Shirvan estate had just been sublet by Mr Smith to the South Argyle (*sic*) Mining Company, which was floated with a capital of 25,000 £2 shares. Veins of copper and lead were identified there and worked from 1862. The company was on the valuation roll at Inverneil from 1863 to 1866 and seems to have reopened old mining sites in that time but begun no new ones. This seems typical of the here-today-gone-tomorrow companies of the day and it can only be surmised that those who invested in those £2 shares lost their money when the company wound up its operations.

There was a similar story with the Mount Erins Mining Company, which was mining zinc on the Inverneil Estate up the Ardtilligan Burn some two miles from the Tarbert Road. The South Argyle and Mount Erins companies had both folded by 1866. The Castleton and Silvercraigs Company had gone into liquidation in May 1865. The shareholders would have made the same from them as the estate owners – they would have been not a plack the richer. Despite all of this, lessons didn't seem to be learned. Geologist Patrick Doran was employed in 1865 to carry out yet another survey and he identified 18 separate mineral-bearing lodes, ranging from the Ardtilligan zinc lode in the east to Lochhead in the west. Living up to the extravagance of expression that so many mineralogists and geologists of the era indulged in, Doran described the lodes east of Loch Arail on the Achahoish Road as 'The Great Champion Lode' and said, 'I have every reason to believe if the sinkings are made to a proper depth that this lode will be found to be the richest in copper of any ever opened in Scotland or any part of Great Britain.'

Based on his report, in 1867 the Shirvan Copper Mining Company, with a capital of 20,000 shares at £5, was floated to mine on the Shirvan Estate. The outcome was no better than it had been for the Argyle and Silvercraigs companies. Poor Mr Smith, the original lessee of the mining rights, was in severe financial trouble by 1873 and the 'richest' seam of copper remained as much a pipe dream as the returns on the £5 shares were for the hopeful members of the public who had parted with their hard-earned cash.

I went in search of the Stronachullin workings, to discover what can be seen today. One, described in 1867 as a lead mine, on the south bank of the Stronachullin Burn had survived, according to a 1992 report by The Royal Commission on the Ancient and Historical Monuments of Scotland, into the 1980s and could be seen 'as an overgrown cleft' about 27 yards long in the north-facing hillside. There had been evidence there that spoil heaps to the north had been reworked and it has been suggested that this site was where small amounts of gold were identified in 1907. However, the work that has been carried out to establish the wind farm and some afforestation means that, by 2017, evidence of mining was lost – even to those who have lived all their lives on the property.

In the rekindled interest in mining that took place in Argyll in the first decade of the 20th century, the Shirvan Mining Company Ltd was set up in 1910 to mine the ore on the Graham-Campbell properties of Shirvan (a name that Castleton was also known by) and Stronachullin at Ardrishaig. The company employed local contractor James Carmichael to sink a 90-foot shaft on the Shirvan estate to test the quality of the copper. Had that proved a viable proposition, the Stronachullin site was to be developed. But new technologies could make this no more successful than earlier attempts in the 19th century and, two years after starting operations, the company folded.

The closure did not come before some feverish publicity circulated about the possibility of a gold mine at Stronachullin. In 1907, ore from the abandoned mine there was sent to Glasgow for analysis by the Tharsis Sulphur and Copper Company. This company had been set up in 1866 by Sir Charles Tennant to take over pyrite mines in southern Spain and he had become interested in metallurgical technology. The samples from Stronachullin were identified as gold, some samples yielding as much as 4oz to the ton, which is a rich mix. The *Argyllshire Herald* reported in September 1907, 'We understand that while several companies were prepared on the strength of reports by their mining engineers to take the matter up, Mr Darlington Simpson, a wealthy London gentleman, has definitely decided to sink a shaft and thoroughly test the value of the same.' More than a year later, there had been no movement although the newspaper was bravely declaring that, while the 'gold mine' had apparently not been abandoned, Darlington Simpson seemed to have lost interest.

At Creag Madaidh Mor, also known as the Kilmartin Mine, which sits beside the road from Upper Largie leading to Old Poltalloch, there was a copper mine that the rascal Raspe intended to visit in the late 1700s when he was also flirting with the mines owned by the Duke of Argyll. The Cornish mining entrepreneur Thomas Petherick did visit this mine in 1839 – Petherick seems to have been much less of a rogue than Raspe but did have his own best interests at heart. There were two adits leading into the mine which are still visible, a spoil heap and a drystone building, which was probably a smithy. Before the Campbells of Kilmartin fell upon hard times and sold out to the Malcolm family, they had this mine worked for a number of years in the 18th century. Although it is shown on an 1825 plan of the Kilmartin estate, it seems to have been abandoned before 1793. Indeed, a report in 1865 suggested it had not been worked for 100 years, which would mean it ceased operations as early as 1765. The local people on the Malcolm estate dated the mine as operational 'before the '45' – the 1745 Jacobite uprising being their most memorable timeline landmark.

A little further to the north on the Atlantic coast lies Loch Craignish, where the Barbreck estates had trialled for lead in 1762. To the south of the Crinan Canal, a trial for lead was made at Dunardry that same year by the same man – a Mr Lissington, employed by the Inverneil Estate. This man had been Martin Freeman's boss for a while and it seems his time was spent more in prospecting than mining. He revisited old workings and, as well as trials at Barbreck and Dunardry, he carried out exploratory trials at Strondoir and Silvercraigs, although Freeman reported that none of these brought much success and, with the benefit of hindsight, we can see from the failures of the 1860s companies that Freeman did a good job. Would that his 1790s report had been heeded 60 years on.

Cross over Loch Fyne to the Cowal peninsula and we find a flurry of copper mining and trials for copper around the Kilfinan area – at the farm of Inveryne, at Otter Mine, and at Tigh-an-Rathaid. There was also a lead mine at Blairmore. Back on the west coast of Argyll, north of Oban, a lead mine in Appin's Glen Creran, and to the north of Corran on Loch Linnhe at Inverscaddle, historically part of the Argyll estates, was another. To the west of Loch Linnhe was the copper mine at Allt An Doire Dharaich, north-east of Loch Tearnait, and, if we cross to the islands, there was a lead mine on Mull at Croggan and one on the lands of McLean at Crossapol on Coll, the 14-mile-long island that was also shared by the Duke of Argyll. The January 1798 edition of *The Scots Magazine* reported that lead 'was mined for some time' on Coll, suggesting it was worked out at that time. One of the county's oldest mines was in Glen Orchy and dates from 1422. And also in the east of 'old' Argyll there were lead mines around Tyndrum at Coire Thoin, Allt nan Sae, Crom Allt and Beinn Bheag, and Alt Eas Anie, a tributary of the River Cononish. Today, gold is being successfully mined in the Tyndrum area when the price of the mineral is right.

If you go looking for evidence of such mining activity, you must be careful. Where their remains have disappeared into the forests, the forestry authorities have often fenced off the entrances to shafts and adits – but not every mine has been identified and ancient shafts can be very deep. You may also be disappointed. Just as the ancient monuments of Argyll

– the burial cairns and standing stones – were stone-robbed
for centuries by farmers for walls and farm buildings, so too
the remains of mines have metamorphosed into sheep fanks
and byres.

Of course, many of the companies that set themselves
up and sought the support of people willing to invest their
precious savings in mining ventures had the most honest of
intentions. They employed managers who cared about the
welfare of the miners and they had the knowledge to mine
efficiently and profitably where the minerals proved to have
been generously laid down by nature in those early eons of
our planet's creation. It was unfortunate when first impres-
sions proved false and the quality or quantity of the mineral
meant the attempt had to be abandoned, bringing an end
to the hopes and dreams of both the company directors and
their investors.

But mining was a rough, tough industry. The manager and
foreman whose negligence led to the fatal accident in the
Bellsgrove mine may not have been the norm but they certainly were not so exceptional as to raise too many eyebrows.
The fact that the sheriff in Mull threw out the case when the
miners tried to claim against the management (despite the
foreman having been found guilty of manslaughter) suggests
a cavalier attitude towards the workers, but the whole business highlights the inherent bullying that characterised the
industry.

Sometimes the bullying wasn't directed at the miners but
at the landowners who proved reluctant to sign leases with
companies that were very much unknown quantities. Perhaps
the most bizarre correspondence on the mining front found
in the Argyll Archives comprises two unpromising letters
to James Robertson, the Duke of Argyll's chamberlain at

Inveraray. The first began 'My Lord', but Mr Robertson had not been elevated by anyone but Mr John Whitburn who wrote, on 28 August 1863, that he was planning to 'prosicute' his journey to Scotland 'amediateley' and wanted to know if His Grace could tell him about the availability of the Craignure mine and what the dues would be 'if wee think of working it'. He wanted Mr Robertson to know that he was 'quiet (*sic*) able to carry out any work [he] might approve of'. He wanted a speedy reply and a meeting was arranged between Mr Whitburn and his associates and the Duke's legal representative Mr Dalglish.

The second letter from Whitburn was written on 2 December 1863 and addressed from Shute Row, Redruth, Cornwall. On the envelope, there is the additional message: 'Sir Will you Oblidge (*sic*) me by sending the value of all the ores that has been returned out of the Craignure Mine.'

Mr Whitburn's spelling and grammar might be excused, as there was still a very fluid attitude towards that sort of thing in the mid 19th century. His lack of punctuality, general pushiness and complete lack of awareness of etiquette were perhaps much less easy to thole. An eight o'clock appointment had been made for Mr Whitburn and some of his colleagues to meet with the Duke's 'steward' at the Bedford Hotel in St George's Road, Glasgow, to discuss leasing one of the Inveraray mines. They turned up, Mr Whitburn claimed, 'at 8 clock persiselly (*sic*) and to our grait (*sic*) surprise he never come by wee waited on him all the following day hoping to have seen him but never had any upportunity (*sic*)'.

He 'sencearilly' hoped that no ill had befallen the steward but stressed that it was of 'searious importance' to him and his colleagues not to have the guarantee from His Grace that they had expected to arrange at the botched meeting. He had wanted to 'show [their] friends that they might have some confidence in laying out their monies in the Cragnure (*sic*) Mine in which they have all jointelly (*sic*) agreed to do according to the report that I have given them'. And then he became what at best can only be described as impertinent: 'I hope I have no need to remind you wat (*sic*) the duty of a steward is. You have long known that now. Dear Sir I hope that you will send me something as a grant as soon as possible and wat you charge for it wee are very willing to pay fearing you are unacquainted with drawing grants of mines. I wish for you to know the nature of it. Sometimes wee have a grant for six months and other times if necessary twelve months and 21 years at the end of eight months and the Lands Dues vary from 18 to 22.'

Considering that the 'steward' was in fact a lawyer employed by the Argyll Estate and that Mr Robertson had been running the estate and the local mines for longer than Mr Whitburn had been out of smocks, this tone was certainly not the way to win a contract for the Craignure Mine. Even though he concluded with his 'kind respects', he pushed his luck still further, with the cocky 'Pleased to answer this by return poast (*sic*).' We may smile at the cheek of it all at this distance but to receive such a letter must have made Mr Robertson see red. There is correspondence that allows us to know the outcome and there are no great surprises – except that Mr Whitburn thought he could meddle with the Duke of Argyll's representatives and win. James Dalglish, the Duke's Edinburgh-based lawyer, had in fact been at the Bedford Hotel ahead of the appointed hour and had waited until after 8 p.m. before leaving, 'having waited as long as [he] could consistent with reaching the railway station in time for the last train at 8.20'. Mr Whitburn was not to get the lease.

This was not the only curious correspondence in relation to the Inveraray mines – there were demands for information about ore, about the availability of leases and about sensitive details of the workings of the various mines – but it was certainly sent with the most audacity.

6

The Inveraray mines

Craignure

The mining correspondence explored at the Argyll Estates archives at Inveraray offers an insight into the industry in terms of the physical labour, the production and the sale of minerals. It ranges over legal niceties and scientific developments. It touches on drunken miners, delighted dukes, the triumphs and tragedies, successes and failures. As we have already seen, the succession of Earls and Dukes of Argyll blew hot and cold in their interest in mining – sometimes for financial reasons, sometimes because of personal passions in science or industry, sometimes because there were genuine hopes of development to provide for those living and working under a paternalistic system.

The vast tracts of land under the administration of the Argyll family in the 17th and 18th centuries meant that local chamberlains were employed to oversee agriculture and industry. Mines in Ardnamurchan and Morvern, Mull, Coll and in mainland Argyll as far south as the coal in Kintyre were all producing for the ultimate benefit of the Argyll Estates and a 'royalty' had to be paid to the estates by any company that leased a mine.

We have seen that some of the mines in the north of the properties were operational in the very early 1700s. In the vicinity of Inveraray, seat of the Earls and Dukes from ancient times, lead was being extracted from at least the middle of the 18th century. In 1747, a lead mine was in operation in Glen Aray, in the hills between Inveraray and Loch Awe, and, in the same year, the 3rd Duke of Argyll was in correspondence with his chamberlain in Inveraray about another lead mine in Glen Shira – in Gaelic, *Gleann Siara* or 'glen of the eternal river'. Today, this glen to the north-east of Inveraray is a Special Area of Conservation. After the 1715 Jacobite uprising, the 2nd Duke (who had led the government troops against the Jacobites at the Battle of Sheriffmuir) gave his support to the Jacobite Rob Roy MacGregor and negotiated an amnesty for him. This involved offering him a house in Glen Shira, where MacGregor lived for several years. The lead mine was near to this house but whether it was operational then is not known. By the time of the 1745 uprising, however, it certainly was being worked and the 3rd Duke's chamberlain employed one of the many experts from mines in Lanarkshire, Cumberland and Cornwall who would travel to Argyll over the coming century to advise on the viability of excavations. One named David Williamson courted danger by taking air pipes and candles down the Glen Shira mineshaft to enable him to make his report – but these were the only options open to him as the Davy safety lamp would not be invented for more than another half century.

In 1789, the German 'adventurer' Rudolf Raspe dismissed the idea that there was coal worth the digging in Glen Aray (due north of Inveraray) and, perhaps more significantly, he dismissed two mines in the close vicinity of Inveraray Castle. In his report to John, 5th Duke of Argyll, he wrote that there were two mines 'said to have been found in the brook at Essachlaibh, a little north west of and under Tombreak, and above the sawmill in the park at a place called Altriochan near a weir on another brook'. As he describes the first site as being 'near a very romantic waterfall', it is probable that this was at Allt Eas A' Chosain, or Essichossen as the mine came to be known, with the alternate name of Coille Bhraghad or Coillebraid Mine. On the maps, this is marked as a silver mine (a common catch-all). Raspe was taken there to identify copper but he reported that the 'few sparks of mundick or sulphurated iron' he saw had been mistaken for copper ore and that there was no lead, copper or other ore apparent. However, the Cornish word 'mundick' or 'mundic' means copper ore. Raspe would have picked up the word during his time working in Cornwall and, while he may have used it mistakenly in this instance, we have to suspect that he may have been trying to blind a Scottish duke with Cornish terms to suit his own purposes. Whatever was in Herr Raspe's somewhat manipulative mind, he told the Duke that it was 'inadvisable' to explore further. The 'Altriochan' site above the sawmill was, according to Raspe, equally unpromising following his tests for gold, silver and copper. Mr Hall, an overseer, showed Raspe 'some bright yellow pyrites' but Raspe dismissed this as 'only sulphur and iron'. As we shall see, Raspe was either not the 'expert' he purported to be or he had some other agenda – because throughout the next century, minerals would be mined successfully from Coille Bhraghad.

Just a decade or so after Raspe's visit, George Langlands, the surveyor and cartographer, would mark a copper mine on his 1801 map at Craignure, which lies up the hill from Auchindrain on the way over to Loch Awe. Today, Auchindrain is an outdoor farming museum. In Langland's time, the crofters' cottages and stables testified to the bustling farming community that is now a fascinating historical curiosity. There is a forestry road across the hills with stunning views across hills and lochs but then there was a footpath. This is some eight miles south of Inveraray and three-quarters of a mile south-west of Brenachoile. Just a few miles south on the modern A83 is Furnace, where by 1755, an iron furnace had been established and, although it closed in 1813, a gunpowder works was built on the same site. Furnace's position on Loch Fyne, with access to water transport, would become significant for the mining enterprises. By 1838, the Craignure copper mines were producing sufficient ore to stimulate correspondence between Robert Campbell, the then chamberlain at Inveraray, and Lord John Campbell, who was trying to preserve the interests of the estates in the face of his brother's profligacy. In July of that year, Robert Campbell was able to tell Lord John that he had put two large boxes of ore from Craignure of board the vessel the *Dunoon Castle*. The seam of ore from which this cargo had come was 'about 22 inches deep'.

Lord John seems to have been a hands-on proprietor, visiting Craignure regularly, even though he often stayed at the family's Glencaple residence in Helensburgh. In November of 1838, more ore was sent off for analysis by the steamer and, in his letter keeping Lord John informed of this, Robert Campbell begins to show himself as a remarkable steward. Sometimes letters deal solely with the mining concerns but many are weekly briefings that reveal he was involved with forestry, the running of the castle and its accounts. He was human resource manager, tour facilitator for the castle's guests and much, much more. Add into this equation his almost daily visits to Craignure, descending into the mine to see what the veins of ore were really like, how difficult the rock-cutting exercises were likely to be and selecting the samples of ore to send off for analysis, and one begins to wonder how many hours there were in Mr Campbell's day.

In February 1839, a letter came from the British and Foreign Copper Company that advised caution. The ore of the quality sent in the samples was worth around £25 a ton but making decisions about extending operations based on the value of an isolated specimen was not recommended. Guidance was now sought from a range of experts (real ones, not rapscallions – or Raspe-scallions). Following seams of ore was never easy and sometimes a man with long years in mining was needed to explain that instinct was needed to judge where next copper might appear. The tools that would make this a science were still a long way into the future. Robert Campbell had men in place to continue excavating at a lower level at Craignure, and they were given firm instructions to carefully keep iron ore separate from copper ore. One such expert, a Mr Taylor from a well-known Cornish mining family, advised that Lord John should employ 'some miners who understand the business that they could work it cheaper and turn it to better account'. Mr Taylor seemed anxious to lease the mine for 15 or 19 years and offered the same level of 'lordship' (percentage of profit) that was usual in England.

At this time, the Cornish 'mining captain' or agent Thomas Petherick from Tywardreath had come north with his associate Taylor and they were in consultation with Sir James Riddell in Strontian about leasing one of the mines there. Petherick was an expert in developing mining machinery and, in 1830, had patented a mechanised method, called 'jigging', for separating the finer-sized copper, lead and other ores from the waste. He also seems to some extent to have had the welfare of the workers at heart, having become involved in the rather violent politics of Cornish mining during the 1820s, claiming that the working of the mines was 'considerably impeded by the scarcity of miners, owing principally to the want of dwelling houses in the neighbourhood'. Now Taylor suggested he visit Craignure on his way south. On 8 March, Robert Campbell was able to tell Lord John that Petherick had indeed returned to Inveraray and given some basic advice about the Craignure venture that Campbell seems to have immediately put into practice. He evidently had a good opinion of the mine, said he'd send one of his own men to help the local workers and recommended a new tunnel be started.

While he went off to visit the Malcolm-owned mine at Kilmartin, he left a list of the kind of tools which Robert Campbell needed to tackle the hard granite the men would encounter in digging the new tunnel. Campbell told Lord John he would buy these for when Petherick's man arrived. Petherick also communicated directly with Lord John, sending him a plan of the Craignure copper mine, and explained that, if he could in fact get two 'steady and proper men', he would send them to begin the tunnel driving, which would be some 18 fathoms long.

He told Lord John, 'After repeated examination of the strata, I can form no satisfactory estimate of the time of performing this work as the ground will probably be found very variable, and some of it perhaps very hard.' Modern geologists will confirm that this is Argyll rock through and through. Cut a stick of it and the wording will read 'Difficult'. Petherick also shared with Lord John that, at Kilmartin, 'the copper raised was from some old workings made, it is said, immediately before the '45. I have recommended to Mr Malcolm having these workings cleared up and examined. They consist of two levels driven on the vein into rising ground and a sink below the upper one . . . where the ore was probably found.'

The men who Petherick identified for Craignure were working at that time at the Knockeenahone Mine in Waterford, Ireland, and he was waiting for Robert Campbell to give the go-ahead to send them to Argyll. He was also able to tell Lord John that his 'treaty for the Strontian Mines' was drawing satisfactorily to a close. This efficiency in identifying the Irish miners and the apparently positive deal with Sir James Riddell must have given him clout in terms of the Craignure mine and, at the end of March, Robert Campbell wrote to Petherick to send the men from Ireland to Argyll. He was anxious to learn how to proceed with the tunnelling as he now knew that there was 8 per cent copper in the ore from Craignure and, with deductions for freight charges to Swansea (where the ore was to be sent), smelting and other processes, this would bring £6 8s 6d a ton.

Petherick clearly was a respected mining consultant of his day. He had associates in London, Cornwall, Wales, Ireland and Germany and seemed to travel between each area regularly from the datelines on his letters. One of the partners in the intended Strontian venture was a Mr Rennie of the London and Westminster Bank, who also had interests in the Cornish mines and asked Petherick to go and inspect them. Before returning to Inveraray, Petherick was therefore off to the south-west of England. This information reached Inveraray on 8 March 1839 and Petherick intended to be there himself around 1 May. Considering the modes of transport available in the late 1830s (bad roads, inadequate boats), this was surely ambitious. But, then, Mr Petherick was an ambitious and persistent man. In a tone much more suitable for such a request than that adopted by the Cornish opportunist John Whitburn nearly a quarter of a century later, Petherick wrote, 'I hope your Lordship will not consider me intrusive in observing that as you propose to work the mine on your own account instead of granting a lease of it (which I repeat I should be disposed to take upon reasonable terms as to royalty fees) I shall be glad to assist your Lordship's views therein, in any way in which I may be able to promote them, from my intended residence in the north, any benefit to myself being rendered dependent upon the success of the undertaking, which would be the most agreeable arrangement to me.'

Petherick was going to lease the Strontian mine and clearly would have preferred to lease the Craignure mine. He was instead, however, to be paid as an adviser and he was wise enough to include a list of people who would vouch for both his character and his mining qualifications. These included John Rundle, MP for Tavistock, and Sir John Guest, MP for Merthyr Tydfil, as well as Cornish businessmen and a copper merchant in London.

As a copper mine, Craignure was never going to make much money. The reports from the start about the quality of the ore were always questionable. There were difficulties over receiving even the basic necessities for proceeding with the work at the mine. On 6 April 1839, Lord John was advised that the transportation of gunpowder for Craignure was a problem because 'if the steamer's people knew that the packages contained powder they would reject them'. Suggestions as to how the packages of 'powder' could be got on to the *Rothesay Castle* steamer included using a 'box with a padlock that would go back and forth the same as family bread boxes which the steamers are taking constantly'. One would be kept in Glasgow, one at the mine. If Lord John paid cash and got

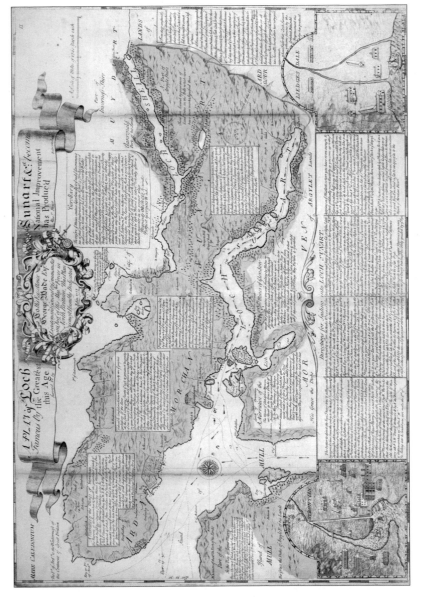

Alexander Bruce's 1733 elaborate plan of the mining development at Loch Sunart, probably prepared as a prospectus for potential investors. (© National Records of Scotland)

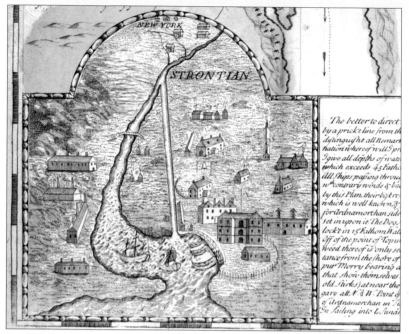

Section of Bruce's plan showing elevations of the Strontian mine buildings, and a new quay for shipping lead. (© National Records of Scotland)

The Strontian mines in the Ardnamurchan hills. They were worked for lead in the 18th century and strontium to the 21st century. (© British Geological Survey Survey/NERC)

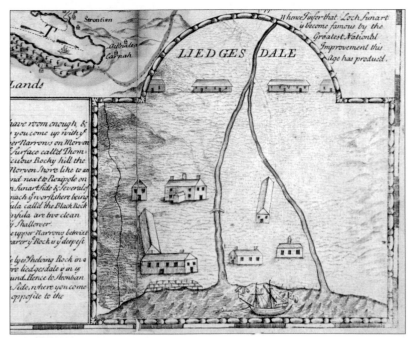

Bruce's 1733 plan showed the 'Liedges Dale' (Liddesdale) lead mines and quay built by the Morvern Company. (© National Records of Scotland)

The pithead at Drumlemble, in the Kintyre coal field. A canal, then a railway, took the coal to Campbeltown. (MacGrory Collection)

Right. A mother's memorial in Kilkivan cemetery for husband Donald and son Daniel McPhail, who drowned in Drumlemble pit. (Author's collection)

Below. The pithead at Machrihanish. Saltpans flourished when the coal industry developed. The railway crossed the Kintyre peninsula. (Campbeltown Heritage Centre)

The Kintyre coal industry survived to the 1960s. These are Argyll Collicry miners. (Courtesy of Catherine Harvey, whose father Archie McLean is centre front)

The Kintyre coal mines saw many tragic accidents down the centuries. Under National Coal Board ownership, however, men received professional training. (Jan Nimmo collection)

Above. Working for the National Coal Board at the Argyll Colliery, when the Kintyre coal field experienced some years of prosperity (Catherine Harvey collection)

Right. A plan of the Craignure copper mine in the hills west of Auchindrain. (Argyll Estates Archive)

Section,

across the Copper Vein, at

CRAIGNURE.

Scale, a quarter of an inch to a foot, horizontal
one eighth do do vertical.

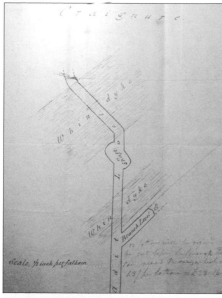

Plan of proposed extensions to the Craignure mine, drawn up in June 1843. Flooding was a constant problem in all Argyll mines. (Argyll Estates Archive)

Plan of an adit (entrance) into the Craignure mine. Twelve fathoms were to be cut at a cost of £28.16s. (Argyll Estates Archive)

The Forestry sign at the remains of a Craignure adit. Overgrown, the entrance to deep shafts is a danger zone today. (Author's collection)

Another Craignure adit. Afforestation has subsumed evidence of this site, where men worked for a century extracting copper then nickel. (Author's collection)

Receipt for ten casks of copper ore sent by the Duke of Argyll in October 1840 on the steamer *Commodore*. (Courtesy Argyll Estates Archive)

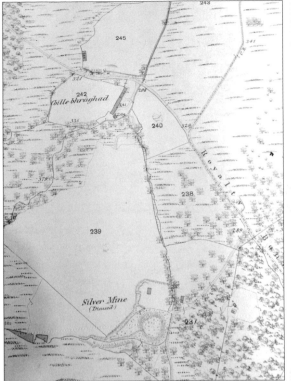

1896: mines around Inveraray. The Coille-Bhraghad (Coillebraid) mine was most successful, producing copper then nickel. (National Library of Scotland)

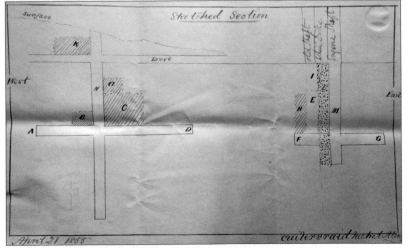

This April 1855 plan of the Coillebraid mine shows it was already producing nickel. 'Inveraray Metal' became a by-product. (Argyll Estates Archive)

Above. The Rolling
Tube and Wire Mills in
Birmingham bought
Inveraray ore, but the
industrial revolution
created a fickle market.
(Argyll Estates Archive)

Right. Argyll Estates
gamekeeper Tom Kirsop
investigates remains of an
adit to Coille-Bhraghad.
Miners had to work in
difficult, cramped
conditions. (Author's
collection)

An entrance to the Kilmartin copper mine, leading to a deep shaft. Miners had to trek high into the hills to reach the mine before starting work. (Author's collection)

Remains of a storehouse and spoil heap at Kilmartin mine. Elsewhere, spoil heaps were later worked over for nickel. (Author's collection)

Miners starting a 12-hour shift no doubt ignored the beautiful geological layering at the entrance to Kilmartin copper mine. (Rosemary Neagle collection)

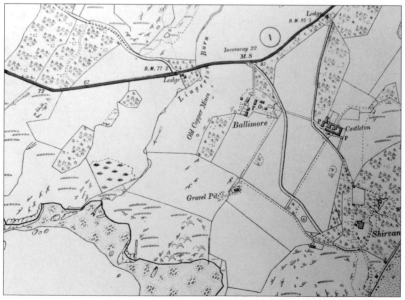

The mines to the north of Lochgilphead. Silver, lead and copper were extracted down the centuries. OS 1899. (National Library of Scotland)

The landscape around Castleton to the north east of Lochgilphead has been shaped by the mining ventures of the past. (Author's collection)

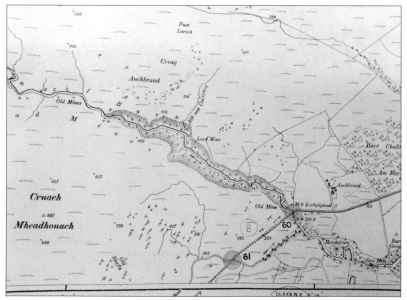

The South Knapdale hills were pock-marked with lead mines, some operating to the late 1800s. OS 1872-73 (National Library of Scotland)

The Morvern silica mine became vital in World War II. Work continued in peacetime (miners pictured in late 1940s). (Morvern Heritage Society collection)

The silica, loaded from Lochaline quay, was used for wartime navigational aids. Today it is used in high quality glass. (Lochaline Quartz Mine collection)

In early years, safety was not today's high priority. These men wore no protective clothing working with explosives at Lochaline. (Morvern Heritage Society collection)

This awe-inspiring tunnel belies the dangers every mine can present. Health and safety regulations can never 'go mad'. (Morvern Heritage Society collection)

Right. Alistair Scoular, who worked in the Lochaline mine in the 1950s, shows the extent of the mine in those early days. (Author's collection)

Below. A 'pug' loaded with sand emerges from Lochaline mine. Today, the latest machinery makes this a mine for the future. (George King collection)

a discount for his 'bread boxes', he would pay 45 shillings net based on 'a large quantity exclusive of the box carrying it'. An invoice dated 26 April 1839 addressed to Lord Campbell details 'Craignure copper mine, 1.⅛ cask F. Powder 6s 3d'.

There were also wages to be paid. One account of payment by Robert Campbell 'to work people at Craignure mine 1ˢᵗ March 1839 to 1ˢᵗ June 1840' was listed thus:

Alexander Campbell for driving perpendicular shaft at Craignure mine

John Douglass, cartwright for jobbing

Alex [?] for safety fuze

Alexander Campbell for the last part of driving shaft as contracted

John O'Neill – account for powder

Malcolm Munro for work as contracted for piece-work at the mine

The Strontian men employed at mine as per account and receipts

Peter McCallum for carrying tools to and from the smithy as per account . . .

Gillies for 3 days work

Archibald Campbell, blacksmith for work done for the miners from 25ᵗʰ April 1838 to 3ʳᵈ June 1840

John Robertson for powder

John Buchanan

Malcolm Clark for building and thatching house for
lodging people at Brenchoille

James MacLean for candles and paper

Peter MacIntyre for [?] and plenishing house for
lodging miners

Malcolm Munro for twelve days work with horse and
cart taking down powder casks from Inveraray to the
mine

More detailed accounts show that six months' costs for
miners' time and wages amounted to £30 0s 2½. Martin
Clark was paid £4 11s for quarrying, Malcolm Munro
received £1 9s 4d for quarrying, Robert Buntain, the smith
at Inveraray, was paid £63s 4½d and the cartwright John
McDonald received £1 17s. These are clearly external jobs
and miners' wages were still to be negotiated. In May of 1839,
Petherick was on his way to Germany but wrote to Lord John
that he had sent to Cornwall for a pattern for dressing tools to
prepare the ores for smelting and for a supply of safety fuses –
all necessary but adding to the mine's financial outgoings.

And, although Robert Campbell would stoically write
time and again to Lord John that things were progressing
well at the mine, what he was labelling 'progress' was to
have pushed forward by seven yards in as many weeks, with
'a much harder seam of rock' ahead. And all too often he
had to add the rider 'They have not come to any ore yet'.
Meanwhile, a house had been built for the men who came
from Ireland and the two of them had spent a week putting a
roof on it. Campbell was at a loss where to find thatch in May
and was worried that sending to 'the low country for wheat
straw' would be very pricey.

Petherick's plans included safety measures of which the Argyll folk were clearly innocent (witness smuggling gunpowder in bread bins) but, again, these must have added to the cost. He wrote from Germany that, if the safety fuses hadn't arrived from Cornwall, then the smith could be given instructions to make a 'shutting [shooting] nail' and from the stock of copper bolts he had left at Port Glasgow, a stem could be made for the blasting process that was 'much safer than iron'.

He was unimpressed with the progress the miners were making but hoped that before long that 'if the mine prove successful, the native labour will be able to perform most of the various operations, as I consider that the temporary inconvenience of training them will be amply compensated by the ultimate result'. This of course would have been an ideal situation all round – employing local men would have been of huge benefit to the economy. But Bob Clark, manager of the Auchindrain Township Museum, says this never became the situation at Auchindrain, the nearest source of potential labour for Craignure. The skilled workers always came from Leadhills, the Pennines or Cornwall and, while some would settle in the area, others would simply move on to the next job – like Alexander Lowrie, the miner in Strontian who gave evidence after the fatal accident at Bellsgrove, whose CV read like a map of Scotland. Only the haulage contractor in Auchindrain benefited in any long-term sense from Craignure and indeed the other Inveraray mines, and the size of the stables there is testimony to the need for big horses and big carts to transport the ore.

While Thomas Petherick seems to have successfully transported himself around Europe to a timetable he was able to predict with confidence, mine essentials seemed to go missing with annoying regularity. Those fuses (the box marked 'patent safety fuze (*sic*)' contained 40 coils, each of 24 feet, so it wasn't a small item) and the box of patterns, dressing tools and other materials Petherick had ordered ('two sledges for breaking the larger pieces of ore into sizes which the miners in the adit will explain . . . one cobbling hammer for breaking still smaller and selecting the inferior ore . . . 1 breaking hammer for reducing the above ore . . . 1 bunking plate – a bed of cast iron for placing the ore on to be broken by the breaking hammer . . . 1 riddle – an iron sieve for sifting the molten ores') had all been sent from Cornwall by schooner to Liverpool and should then have been forwarded to Robert Campbell to be picked up at Greenock. Petherick wrote, 'I presume it must have reached him before this' but the implication is that he didn't trust the delivery service.

By late July 1839, with Petherick heading back to Inveraray to consult with Lord John, Robert Campbell said the men had dug a 33-foot tunnel through extremely hard rock. About three tons of ore had been turned out. This progress pleased Petherick and he set two of the men to 'select the saleable ore of the rock'. He left Campbell to go to Strontian for a week and Campbell suggested letting the cutting of the tunnel to the men – in other words, a 'bargain' would be made at a certain price for the rest of the work. As luck would have it, the next stretch of ground was the easiest to date and, by the end of August, there was a 54-foot tunnel. Petherick planned to bring some of the experienced miners back from Strontian to Craignure, enabling a perpendicular shaft to be sunk to meet the tunnel. He was planning ahead to have shelters built for the men to work outside sorting the ore once it was extracted and Campbell asked Lord John if he could have some of the canvas covers he had seen in use at Ardencaple when the castle there was being repaired.

John, 4th Duke of Argyll, had bought Ardencaple Castle, a building with its origins in the 12th century. The architect Robert Adam modernised and developed the castle during the 1760s and '70s. George, 6th Duke of Argyll, would die in October 1839 leaving no heirs. Lord John succeeded him and, of course, had been running the estate for some time. In August, just two months ahead of the Duke's death, it does sound as though Robert Campbell and Lord John were picking over the spoils but a canvas cover is just a canvas cover and the men sorting the ore at Craignure needed shelter. As Campbell pointed out, '[T]hey would answer well and be cheaper than anything else we could get as in the meantime they must be moveable. If they can be had they could be sent out by one of the steamers from Greenock on Wednesday first.' It is worth noting that, since the advent of Clyde steamers in 1812, this mode of transport had transformed the speed of travel.

At the beginning of September, there was some hard thinking to be done. It was estimated that it would cost £108 for six men to drive the new adit to and through the lode – a distance of 18 fathoms (36 yards). The cost of ten men driving the adit on the course of the lode was estimated at £180. Labour, stores and so on would cost £480. The man who would carry tools to and from the smithy at Furnace would be paid one shilling a day. It seems these costs were considered a sensible investment because, when Petherick came on 7 September, the men had progressed well with the tunnel and he intended to put three of them to proceed with that work. However, Robert Campbell pointed out that the weather had been so wet (typical of Argyll) that work had been held up. As we have seen elsewhere, too much rain would have meant burns overflowing and underground water rising and there were no pumps in this rudimentary mine. There was also the increasingly hard rock to contend with and Campbell suggested paying the men a daily wage to encourage them to push the work on.

Petherick seems to have stayed at Inveraray for most of September and on the 28th, when he reached Greenock on the next stage of his working round, he wrote to Lord John to say that the ground had been so hard to cut through that just 14 feet had been driven from 31 August to 27 September. By 24 September, there had been flooding in the mine, true to Campbell's weather alert. The men were now cutting just over 4 feet of tunnel in a week. This may sound completely cost-ineffective to our 21st-century ears but this was commonplace. Men with picks were hacking through a seam of granite and the only way to make this more effective would have been to employ more men. Those men would not only have had to be paid but would probably have fallen over each other in this confined space. Our machine-oriented minds have to accept that the past was indeed another country where things were done very differently.

In an effort to speed things up, Petherick adopted a very mid-19th-century mining tactic. He renewed a monthly contract with a worker named Malcolm Munro, who was paid £6 a foot – 'a gratuity to be paid if clear exertion was shown'. Just like the system described by the men at Strontian, this amount was for the team of workers, with Munro given the responsibility of achieving the task. Petherick had expert miners from Strontian lined up to work with Munro because the local men had not yet been trained to the work – and Petherick wasn't too pleased with local labour. 'It appears that there is not much reliance to be placed on the statistics of the Highland labourers,' he wrote to Lord John, who he was still pushing for a formal lease on the mine. Petherick certainly had mining expertise but his human resource skills may have been lacking. The good news on 2 October was that the men had progressed with the tunnel and were 'within 50 feet of where they should get the ore'. The bad news was that Petherick's instructions 'had not been understood' and some men 'gave up work'. Campbell had given them a pep talk and now they promised 'to go on regularly'. Petherick perhaps failed to grasp that the local men were Gaelic speakers and perhaps there was a real language gap when it came to instructions.

There were six men working on the tunnel and another two on the surface making trenches south-west of where the ore was to be found. East of a burn they found a good deal of ore and Campbell sent off a sample box the following Monday by steamer. The analysis came back from Edinburgh University's laboratory on 14 October showing the following percentages contained in the ore:

Iron – 56%

Sulphur – 32%

Copper – 5%

Silica – 6%

Antimony – 1%

The report suggested that some portions of the same ore contained less iron and copper and a greater portion of silica. Robert Campbell had been very careful to deal with this sample forensically. It had come from the east side of the burn at the Craignure mine and a piece (which was rolled up in grey paper) was 'got in one of the new cut trenches 15 yards south west of where we were quarrying the ore'.

The experienced miners who came from Strontian would only work for wages until they could satisfy themselves 'of the nature of the ground'. This, of course, was a more expensive way of hiring labour and these four men certainly were aware of their status as miners rather than simply men digging a tunnel or a shaft. It was clear that they would only stay if the house near the mine were to be finished for them. It was, and they and Petherick were in residence by mid November 1839. The 6th Duke had passed away on 22 October and now Robert Campbell was sending a note of cash payments to the new Duke – John, who had no catching up to do in terms of Craignure because as Lord John, he had been so intimately concerned with the mine. This cash flow account from 1 May to 1 November amounted to £168 18s 1d. For labour, the Inveraray smith Robert Buntain's costs and outlay for the Strontian men, payments amounting to £14 had been disbursed. Malcolm Munro 'and others' had been paid £15 for driving 15 feet of tunnel at 20 shillings per foot. The 'English miners' were paid £10 for five weeks' work. The team listed as working at this time included Archibald Campbell, Alex McGougan, John McCallum, Malcolm Munro, John McFarlane, Duncan Sinclair, Neil Bain, John Sinclair, Neil Campbell, Peter McCallum, Duncan McFarlane, John McNicol and Archibald Gillies. Many of these men's names would appear in the Inveraray mine accounts over a number of years, suggesting that the working conditions and pay were acceptable. But, as they entered a new decade, there were new social problems to face, including the potato famine that first of all brought a tidal wave of Irish families, their men vying for work, and then created destitution throughout the Highlands. Those who had jobs, like the Sinclairs, Malcolm Munro and the McCallums, would have been wary of trying their luck elsewhere under such circumstances.

Although the wet weather of November 1839 prevented work in the mine, Robert Campbell kept the project going by repairing the road from Auchindrain to Brenchollie. A track went from Brenchollie to the mine. Today, the new Forestry Commission tracks make the route to work that the miners would have taken difficult to trace but at the side of the new track that leads over to Loch Awe is a fenced-off area with 'danger' signs where at least two entrances to the mine can be seen. This is just yards from dense forest and mine buildings must be buried deep in the trees under a century and more of Argyll moss. Robert Campbell took along the military road surveyor when he improved the original track. This man suggested that it would cost 1s 6d a foot to 'put it in good order'. The plan was to broaden it to 11 feet and to give it a good basis of gravel or broken metal. He intended to seek a contribution from the county authorities because this road would not only be an access to Argyll estate farms and the Craignure mine, it was an important route along which all the cattle from Kilmichael market (then still the most important in Argyll) were driven on their way to Falkirk via Loch Fyne ferries.

When the rain allowed, the Strontian miners got back to work and Robert Campbell underlined in his report to the Duke that these men were working well. He was recommending that the Duke would make them a present over and above their regular wage and had told the Strontian men this to keep at bay their requests for more money. One shaft had been sunk six feet and Alexander Campbell was to be paid £9 to sink to a second fathom. This was a high price but, because of the hardness of the rock, the contractor had been 'dispirited' at the results of the previous contract. And, indeed, that word 'dispirited' must have applied to all of the men as each day they trudged up the hill to the mine only to be met by flooding or a wall of rock so hard as to defy normal mining tools. Cold, wet, aching and with little to look forward to at the end of their long day, what was there to raise their spirits? Perhaps Petherick's identification of 'good copper in the south part of the bottom of the shaft' would have given some purpose to their hard labour.

There was clearly underlying trouble. Archibald Campbell and his brothers had been offered a contract to sink the shaft and he turned it down. Instead, during the two possible days of work one week at the end of November, he undertook to complete the footpath from the road to the mine. And that, he told them, was that. His employment at the mine had ceased. This caused problems because, not only had Archibald Campbell been one of those involved in tunnelling and sinking the shaft, he was also in charge of the stores of gunpowder, candles and other necessities for the job. Thomas Petherick arranged for a man named Murray to take charge of the team. This resulted in the adit being extended 21 feet, the depth of the shaft increased 11 feet and the vein exposed. Although there was not much ore to be had in the shaft, the Strontian men were estimating in late December that the two shafts would be joined in a matter of ten weeks. When rain filled the shafts with water, the labourers were deployed on the Brenchollie road repairs but, by 21 December, the copper ore was becoming 'more plentiful', the rock was less hard and contractor Alex Campbell had 'agreed to sink another fathom at the price of £9'.

The good news was always interspersed with bad and, between the evening of Saturday 21 December, when progress seemed so good, and the Monday morning, someone had taken 17 new boring tools (called 'jumpers') out of the adit and no trace of them could be found. Petherick bitterly suggested they must have been thrown in a bog 'from sheer malice'. One of the shepherds told him that, on the Sunday, he had 'met a certain person lately in your employ . . . coming from the direction of the mine'. Petherick wanted the Duke to appoint Robert Campbell in a role 'calculated to show them that such outrages will not be lightly passed over'. Clearly there were suspicions about Archie Campbell because he had walked off the job but appointing Robert Campbell as Inspector Morse on top of all his other duties seems inconsiderate.

And the Duke had more on his mind – he was considering not only the presence of copper at Craignure but elsewhere on the Inveraray lands and he wanted Petherick to advise on whether it would be possible to establish a smelting furnace at the Argyll Furnace – just down the road, on the loch side. Creating a product ready to sail to market would surely be more profitable than shipping out the raw material. The Duke had clearly heard that copper could be smelted with wood charcoal and that this process might be preferable to coal. He also wondered if 'proper mining tools' could be made in Glasgow. Even though this Duke had been born in London and spent much of his time there as a politician, it was in his best interests and those of Scotland to generate such industry on Scottish soil rather than importing from Cornwall.

As the year and the decade drew to a close, heavy snow stopped most outdoor work as well as Robert Campbell's search for the missing jumpers. Petherick was now naming names and Archibald Campbell was very definitely in the frame. The incident had soured his opinion of local labour and he told the Duke, 'I felt so disappointed at the neglect, and slow performance of the native labourers in their work, and so much at a loss for an adequate supply on moderate terms of steady labourers, if the mine should open favourably, that I felt quite unprepared to come to any conclusion on the subject.' Petherick had personal as well as professional misgivings. His wife and family had travelled to Inveraray from Greenock (where they had moved from Cornwall) and they were all ill 'because of the change to so moist a climate'. Those of us who live in 'so moist a climate' know that it gets into your bones and our hearts must go out to the poor Cornish-raised Pethericks huddled round a coal (or perhaps peat) fire in early January in the mid 19th century, without the benefits of double-glazing and central heating. Petherick confessed to the Duke that 'settling might be liable to serious objections'. He had hopes that the family would 'become seasoned to the climate' but he must have been suffering the cries of the children and the complaints of his wife. By May 1840, he still hadn't convinced the family that living in the west of Scotland could be their permanent future, and had moved back into lodgings at 15 Cathcart Street from West Blackhall Street, in Greenock, while minds were made up (and that had to include the Duke's mind as to the future of this venture).

Petherick was also on the receiving end of complaints from the Strontian miners, who 'would prefer to be at home'. He could only think that miners from Leadhills (reputed to be rough and ready but also used to being exposed to the extreme weather of the moors of Lanarkshire) might be recruited for the Inveraray mine but warned the Duke that the rate would have to be good 'to induce them to migrate'.

The weather and the family and miners who would rather have been elsewhere perhaps were irritants enough but there was one other 'Argyll' problem that Petherick had to get off his chest. 'The drinking and idleness of this place is quite disgusting,' he wrote on 2 January 1840. He had perhaps been soured by New Year celebrations. The many configurations of standing stones in Argyll demonstrate a devotion to the solstices. The ancient tribes built these to line up with the sunrise on the longest and shortest days of the year. The Vikings introduced their own winter celebrations in the 8th and 9th centuries and while the word 'Hogmanay' was not recorded until 1604, some form of riotous behaviour had always lightened this dark time of year when the days shrink to around six gloomy hours of light. With the advent of the Reformation in Scotland came a denial of any celebration of Christmas (which continued until the 1960s) and the New Year, officially celebrated on 12 January but surely often extended either side of that date, continued as the time of revelry. Petherick must have been exposed to some of the Hogmanay excesses but there had evidently been a history of alcohol consumption at Craignure mine and he had experience of it elsewhere. He wrote, 'Whether the temperance society will break down the whisky drinking or not is a doubtful but interesting point.' He went on to explain that, in a Waterford mine in Ireland, the men had been fined if they were caught drinking.

In England, the temperance movement began with Joseph Livesey and seven Preston miners signing a pledge in 1832 that they would never again drink alcohol. In Scotland, a similar movement in the 1830s was inspired by temperance societies in America and, by 1844, the Scottish Temperance League, preaching total abstinence, was formed in Falkirk.

As Petherick pointed out, alcohol had unwelcome effects on safety, family life and society. In *Alcohol and Temperance in Modern History: An International Encyclopaedia*, Jack S. Blocker wrote that a parliamentary report on drink-related arrests between 1831 and 1851 found that 'Glasgow was three times more drunken than Edinburgh and five times more drunken than London'. How the West Highland mining community would have fared in such a survey is hard to estimate. The arrests would not have been so numerous, simply because the mines were too remote to police efficiently, but that is not to say that the alcohol was not consumed. For mine managers, the difficulties were not just the 'idleness' that ensued – the incident with the jumpers was probably whisky-fuelled – and any workplace where gunpowder and candles were kept in close proximity was quite literally dynamite in terms of safety. Those missing jumpers were found in the bottom of the old shaft in early January and Robert Campbell suggested that it would still be possible to find the culprit. A drunken prank? An act of revenge fuelled by alcohol? Neither Petherick nor Campbell could have been absolutely certain but they had their suspicions.

In Neil Munro's novel *John Splendid*, the miner on trial at Inveraray for stabbing a man from Strathlachlan, on the other side of Loch Fyne, confessed, 'We had a little too much to drink, or these MacLachlan gentlemen and I had never come to variance.' Witnesses testify to the unruliness of the Strathlachlan men. Munro may have been writing fiction, but as in his *Tales of Para Handy*, there was fact in the detail.

However bad the alcohol situation may have been and however reluctant the Pethericks may have been to migrate to Scotland, work did get underway and Petherick himself seemed more determined than ever to chase the Craignure dream. The tunnel was now just days away from joining the two shafts and the 'metaliferous' part of the vein was in touching distance. Petherick had been in Ireland and had discussed the mine with his brother, who was working there. That conversation led him to tell the Duke, 'If the prosperity at Craignure, when further developed, shall induce Your Grace to extend the operations there, I believe that a peculiar system, in respect of the underground labour, must be introduced to meet the peculiar circumstances of the case, and at the same time to tender the labour of the native population available, which I shall be ready to explain to Your Grace.'

In the coming weeks, however, there was little to encourage His Grace to extend the Craignure operations. 'No appearances of ore' was a regular phrase in Robert Campbell's reports to the Duke but the Temperance Society did make an appearance in Inveraray and set up shop. Campbell commented that it was doing well and 'I hope that it will do much good.' Perhaps the men all sobered up because, by the beginning of March, there was a bit of a breakthrough. Petherick was on his way back to Craignure (travelling from Greenock via the fish steamer to Lochgoilhead and then across Loch Fyne by ferry) and there was copper to welcome him. He was able to confirm a vein of copper on 7 March and he now planned to use labourers from Furnace to do the donkeywork while the Strontian men went home 'to till their farm crops'. They would be away for about six weeks and Petherick would also hire a miner for the work 'capable of sharpening the tools, by which means the work will be performed both cheaper and more conveniently than at present'. Robert Campbell's own report to the Duke on the same situation was at variance with Petherick's – he thought the work would have to be given up while the Strontian men were away and he wasn't too convinced about the quality of the copper ore that had been reached.

As it turned out, the copper vein was vertical, rather than the more usual horizontal seams, and Petherick gave orders how to deal with this phenomenon, despite being confined to bed with a bilious attack and inflamed throat. By the time he had recovered, he had to tell the Duke on 20 March that they had indeed found a larger proportion of copper ore than was near the surface but it was probably not enough to 'pay the expenses of working unless there should be a large body of it, so as to justify the erection of machinery for cleaning it'. In the absence of the Strontian men, he put another four on the job to check out the quantity of this ore. Robert Campbell, whose voice often tempered the optimism of Petherick, complained to the Duke that six of their own men were not working but Petherick had 'procured another two' and the appearances were 'not good' on the copper ore front.

At this time, sketches were flying daily to the Duke from Petherick's pen depicting the shafts and adits and all the changes up and down and in between. Even so, the Duke was unclear on the progress. Petherick sent a relatively technical explanation about the 'plurality of veins' that may or may not have satisfied the former soldier, parliamentarian and peer of the realm. It is interesting that he was now asking Petherick to clarify his travelling expenses – was he losing faith in the man who was pushing so hard to make Craignure a success? Petherick for his part said he had no idea of the going rate for such expenses (although as he was responding from Limerick and had frequently traipsed around the rest of Britain, he should have at least known the price of a steamer ticket) and wanted the Duke to name a ballpark figure. He eventually invoiced for 60 guineas, excluding travel expenses, for the year ending December 1839.

Robert Campbell was certainly a little disillusioned. The men had followed Petherick's instructions and there was no ore forthcoming. He wrote to the Duke on 2 May 1840, 'I think it is throwing away money for them to continue it longer in that direction and I have stopped them in the meantime until Mr Petherick sees it again.'

His other duties – including the creation of a new drive up to the castle and the overseeing of plantations on the estate – may have made his patience with the Craignure work a little thin. Petherick, however, was planning to meet the Duke at Craignure to show him all the possibilities. Copper ore was being extracted but not in sufficient quantities to make this a viable proposition. At the end of June 1840, the Strontian miners returned from their crofts and uncovered the face of the rock in the bottom of the open excavation near a new shaft that had been sunk. Here, Petherick said, 'copper may be found more plentiful'. The men were hoping to be paid 16 shillings a week from the time of their arrival from Strontian and they were claiming expenses. Local man Malcolm Munro had also been contracted and contingency plans were drawn up in case no vein was to be found in this new excavation.

Petherick left Campbell and the miners to it. He had been asked to present the Duke with a report on the Drumlemble coal mine but had not been able to complete this because his children were again ill and his connections with mines in Swansea called him on urgent business. Swansea's population had almost tripled since the start of the century and the Industrial Revolution had moved in with a vengeance. In the 1700s, Swansea became known as the Copperopolis because of its huge copper output and then coal became an important part of the economy. But, in the 1840s, unemployed miners and discontented people from the rural areas of Wales contributed to civil unrest. Swansea was being bypassed as a coal port when a new railway and port took traffic to Cardiff instead. Riots and strikes because of low wages and even wage cuts became the norm. It was to this that Petherick was called in July 1840 to face workers calling for 3s 9d a day (considerably more than the Strontian men were holding out for).

Robert Campbell had to take on the day-to-day overseeing of Craignure and, despite following Petherick's instructions, no ore was found. He decided to follow his own instincts and go back to working in the adit where copper ore had been found in the earlier explorations. On the evening of Saturday 22 August, Campbell sent a note from Craignure to the Duke saying that Archibald Campbell (back in favour) and his son had collected 2cwt 59lbs of ore, the labour of nine days and at a wage cost of £1 7s. Campbell estimated that, at this rate, it would cost around £11 a ton to collect the ore after being quarried. He reckoned that it would take three 32-gallon barrels to hold the tons of ore. Meanwhile, the six men digging the ore that Archibald Campbell and his son were collecting had adopted Robert Campbell's scattergun approach, following the veins where they could find them.

Were they now distancing themselves from Petherick? Towards the end of September, cash was transferred to settle up Petherick's travelling expenses from 1839, the cost of the 40 coils of fuse from Smith and Davey in Cornwall and the dumping tools, bucking plate and so on from James Thomas in Cornwall. But still the work went on. Towards the end of December, over two tons of ore had been sent to Liverpool by the steamer *Commodore* to the British and Foreign Copper

Company, who sent back that the bulk of the 10 casks of 'copper ore' was in fact iron and sulphur. The wages and expenses for the first half of the year at Craignure had not been cheap. The second half of the year could not have proved any cheaper.

Petherick had, in fact, been dealing with the 'turbulent times' in which he had found himself embroiled in Swansea, from whence he wrote with apologies for the long delay in communication on 14 February 1841. Whatever the sensitivities of the day, by modern standards, Petherick's reaction to the striking Welsh miners, who had stopped all mine operations in the October and November of 1840, was politically incorrect. Now the colliers had entered into a contract to last for the following 12 months but the struggle to achieve that had been violent and acrimonious. Petherick had received 'diabolical' threats and 'large pieces of ore' had been thrown at his house by what he termed Welsh Nationalists. He wrote that the 'lower classes of the people here have as strong a dislike to the Sassenachs as any of the Irish. In politics they are Chartists.'

Clearly, Petherick wanted to get back into the Duke's employ as a mining consultant, being 'very desirous to know what has been done since I left Scotland, at Craignure, and the results and prospects'. He told the Duke he would be very happy to be of any service. He had analysed coal from Drumlemble but it was the copper mine that was drawing him back to Scotland because copper was clearly what he saw as his field of expertise. The Duke, however, was seeking advice elsewhere. At first, the news that came back was better. Feedback from the British and Foreign Copper Company on analysis of Craignure ore suggested it contained 13.44 per cent copper. Stanley Walton wrote from 2 North Court, Royal Exchange, Glasgow, that this might not have been as rich as the Duke had anticipated but 'it is very good and ought to be lucrative to your Grace'. The Royal Institution told the Duke in March 1841 that the specimens of ore that had been left with their metallurgists for analysis were copper pyrites, a 'compound of sulphur and copper', and the specimens contained 'about 22 per cent copper, analogous with copper ore of Cornwall'.

Walton wrote to explain an 'improved method of manufacturing copper direct from the ore' that his brother had invented. It was a chemical process that was an immense saving on the conventional methods, according to Walton, and it had the advantage that a 'marketable commodity' – sulphate of zinc – was a by-product. It used an electro-galvanic process that had already been applied successfully to the assaying of ores. Walton offered to introduce the ore to the principal copper smelters and the bad news was that this would cost the Duke £100 in the first year, with a commission of 1 per cent on the sales. After that, Walton explained, 'should Your Grace think proper, other terms can be decided as one year will show Your Grace with what success your mines are likely to meet'.

While there was no guarantee of such success, things seemed at last to be moving in a positive direction. Analysis of two samples by Anderson's University put the copper content at 9.7 per cent in one and 13.44 per cent in the second. Also known as the Andersonian Institution, this university in Glasgow was founded in 1796 under the will of John Anderson, Professor of Natural Philosophy at the University of Glasgow (and, in the 20th century, the institution became the University of Strathclyde). There were courses in chemistry, natural philosophy, mathematics and other scientific subjects, as well as English, rhetoric, music and art. Analysis of metal ore was on offer. All in all, three separate analyses by different institutions suggested there was some substance to the idea that the Craignure mine could produce a decent quality of copper. It would have been tempting to consider Walton's brother's galvanic action – Walton pointed out that the present method of getting the copper from the ore was wasteful and expensive, requiring a huge amount of coal and high wages to go through eight separate processes. The new method, Walton stressed, would require 'a mere trifle in the outlay of capital' and the copper extracted would be pure.

Just as the Duke was considering all of this, Robert Campbell wrote on 27 February with what seemed like bad news: 'The vein on the northeast side where the two joined has nearly run out.' There was, however, still a 'good appearance of ore' where the Strontian men were working and Campbell had sent two of the men working on the dwindling vein to work with them. An Englishman working at Craignure had also been deployed to work on a more productive area. Indeed, Archibald Campbell now had two other men working with him to collect the ore. There were 25 men working at the trenching and, although it was a 'great deal of work', Campbell was sure that the Duke would be pleased with it when it was done.

But then there came really bad news. These extreme swings from negative to positive and back to negative must have been hard on the nerves of the man holding the purse strings. One day it seemed that purse would be filled to overflowing; the next it seemed that the Craignure mine had snipped a hole in the bottom of the purse and the cash was sifting out swifter than the sands of time. A man named John Barratt sent a report to the Duke on 1 July 1841 saying that, while appearance at Craignure had been favourable two years previously, now things had gone too far and too much money had been spent. Barratt wrote, 'As Your Grace authorised me to give instructions to Mr Campbell . . . and as there did not appear to me the most distant hope of a chance of success attending any further attempts that might be made, I advised him to stop all proceedings and to put an end to all expenses at once . . . I have taken samples of the site of ore lying on the surface and as soon as I have seen our assay master I will inform Mr Campbell of the results.'

Copper had been worked at Craignure since 1799. In 1842, the search for the all-too-often illusive metal was brought to an end. It was not, however, the end of the Craignure mine. The Swedish mineralogist and mining expert Axel Fredrik Cronstedt had identified nickel as a chemical element in 1751 – and we should not be too harsh on the likes of Thomas Petherick for not recognising it because even Cronstedt mistook the ore for copper. It had, of course, been in use since around 3500 BC and the ancients seem to have been aware of its usefulness as an ingredient in metal alloys. However, it wasn't until the early 19th century, with the developments emerging from the industrial revolution, that it began to be sought for its own sake. Large scale smelting of nickel only began in the 1840s so the fact that Petherick ignored its presence at Craignure is not surprising. It would be another 40 years before the demand for nickel really took off when it was introduced into steel production.

When nickel was found among the copper ore being extracted at the two mines nearer to Inveraray, the abandoned Craignure was revisited and nickel was found in the spoil heaps. This spoil was wrangled over for £700 and, when the Craignure Mining Company began working the mine (without ever signing a lease, as neither the Duke nor the company could agree on terms), it extracted 320 tons of ore.

There was something of an expansion in the mid 1850s, when a smithy, a large shed to shelter the workers, a shed for tools, a magazine and shop were built. The nickel ore was shipped to Liverpool and Edward MacCallum from Auchindrain carted the ore. Eventually the company walked away from the mine, leaving the door open for such interesting characters as John Whitburn, the Cornish prospector who stood up the Duke's lawyer then demanded all the Craignure mine's details from Mr Robertson in 1863. The mine was worked for nickel until 1873 by the management of the Coille Bhraghad mine and the men, under their foreman Neill McGougan, worked part of the week there and part of the week seven miles up the road at Coille Bhraghad.

The nickel era begins at Coille Bhraghad and Craignure

So much effort had been poured into the Craignure mine, with so little return despite the apparently good quality of the copper to be found there, that it is surprising the Argyll Estates even considered further exploration for minerals. However, with a new Duke in charge – John, the 7th Duke, died in 1847 and was succeeded by his second son, George, who, like his friend Prince Albert, was something of a scientist – the mines nearest Inveraray Castle were reinvigorated.

There had been mining in the vicinity of Inveraray since at least the late 18th century but copper had proved no more profitable there than at Craignure. The Coille Bhraghad mine was re-opened in 1851 when it was found to contain nickel and, as a result, the Craignure mine was re-examined after its decade in wraps and was also found to have between 10 and 12 per cent nickel content in the ore. Chamberlain James

Robertson told the Duke on 28 November 1851 that he had gone that Friday to Brenchoille (the Craignure mine) only to find that the men were 'picking too minutely' among small bits of ore and so had not made much progress. The idea was to pick out the best pieces of ore to get a good price from the spoil heap.

That same week's report written for the Duke recorded the 'most encouraging' appearances of a 13-inch thick vein of ore at Coille Bhraghad, which was being explored near the Cromalt Burn, about a mile and a half south of Inveraray. Robertson said he was 'delighted to find so fine a mass quite pure and hard so near the surface'. The seams were not all so conveniently placed, however, because, according to the Joiners' and Wrights' Time Records of 1851–54, the miners descended the shafts by ladders. Once the mine was in operation for nickel extraction, the pick men worked by candlelight and the air was kept circulating by windmills and air pipes. As with all of the Argyll mines, water was a constant problem and pumps operated round the clock to keep the workings water free.

Having already advised the Duke on the Coille Bhraghad mine on 24 January 1853, J. Arthur Phillips of 8 Upper Stamford Street, Blackfriars, London, sought management of the Craignure mine. It was already being described as a 'nickel mine' rather than a copper mine. By the following year, Cumberland man John Cain was in charge at Coille Bhraghad and, while legal wrangling over boundaries and legalities went on at a higher level, Cain showed his thoroughly professional mining background by organising the labour force in teams working under 'bargains' or contracts. These teams were listed in 'Bargain Books' (still in existence in the Inveraray archives) and names such as those of John

Forbes 'and party', John Macfarlane and partner, Alexander Bain and partner, John Bell and partner, crop up over several years – many well into the 1860s. Sometimes, one man would sign the bargain for another (James Forbes for John Forbes and party), which could suggest that the signatory was the literate member of the group or simply that this was the man present the day the bargain book entry was made.

One such bargain signed by Robert McKenzie on 4 September 1855 'for self and partners' reads 'Agreed to draw all the work out of the mine at 10 shillings per fathom measured off to workmen – this bargain to continue to 30 September next'. On 30 September, the team was paid £14 15s. Another, dated 3 August 1855, was agreed by John Forbes and four partners 'to work a heading cast of the engine shaft three feet high, at the rate of £3.5 shillings per fathom of six feet long and six feet high, so far as may be required by the agent'. And on 30 September, Alex Bain signed for John Forbes and partners, having measured off five fathoms, and took £16 5s back to the men – the princely sum of £3 5s each for two months' hard labour. But it must have sufficed because Forbes and four partners were still there in 1857, driving into a vein at different rates for the different ground they had to dig through – £5 10s per fathom through slate, £7 10s per fathom through rock and £14 per fathom 'for driving in solid quartz from roof to sole of level'. Samples of the slate, rock and quartz were kept in the chamberlain's offices to be checked against. Over the years, there was complex documentation of the way that men were to be paid. One such agreement signed on 10 November 1865 read: 'Agreed with James Munro and John Livingstone to drive a level six feet high with the usual breadth, commencing at the base of the bank on the south side of the vein or as far as the agent may think proper, the price per fathom to be £6, if their wages reach 16 shillings per week, if not, the price shall be £7 per fathom.' On 31 December 1865, Munro and Livingston were paid £12 for a measure of two fathoms at 120 shillings.

Sadly, although Mr Cain's management of the day-to-day working of the mines was very efficient, the business of leasing the mines never seemed to go smoothly. The Duke wrote from London to lawyer James Dalglish at W.T. Rutt in Edinburgh about Crown leases and charters. His claim to be 'more and more' puzzled to understand the state of the law and the facts' in relation to Crown leases of minerals suggests more that the Duke thought the law to be an ass, rather than that he was unable to grasp the detail. By his understanding, the Crown had the right to 'one tenth of all the enumerated metals found in Scotland'. The proprietor of lands where such minerals were found had the right to work them, subject to the Crown royalty. The Argyll Estates had already been granted a Crown charter conferring these rights to work such minerals. He assumed this allowed him to work the minerals and 'appropriate the remaining nine-tenths' and that this would apply to all lands over which the charter extended, meaning that he had no need to apply for a lease from the Crown. However, 'the language of these leases' was at variance with the understanding of the documentation and rights the Duke assumed he already had. Signing a lease would, it seemed to him, 'imply a power on the part of the Crown at the end of the 31 years [of such a lease] to resume possession of a right over these minerals, which by right belong to [him], and would abandon altogether the benefit of that charter'.

If, for centuries, one has held charters granting certain rights over vast tracts of land (in this case the Argyll Estates), this need for legal nit-picking was essential but it did mean that, for the duration of the working of the Inveraray mines, leases to companies were never completed and it seems fortunate that a man such as John Cain was actually managing the mines or what profits there were and what royalties had to be paid would have been in jeopardy. The Duke did not let the matter rest with lawyers. He also asked Thomas Sopwith FRS, the English mining engineer, geologist and historian, for advice. Sopwith wrote from Allenheads, Northumberland, on 24 March 1854 explaining that 'lot ore' and 'duty ore' were subject to different dues but that nickel and cobalt were not yet under the same scrutiny as lead. Quoting from a book dated 1694, ore subject to dues was that which had been made fit for smelting, melting and refining – the washed and dressed ore, in other words, with the earth and rubble removed. He asked what was known of former mines in the area and suggested that John Cain, with whom he had spoken on the subject, should explore that particular issue. Cain, with his mining expertise, had thought the draft lease was 'carefully done'. Sopwith felt its provisions were very favourable for the lessor. The complication was over who would owe one-tenth to the Crown – the Duke as lessor or the lessee who worked the mine. Sopwith suggested regular reviews of lease terms.

By May, accountant Thomas Nettleship of Palmer and Nettleship, 14 Trafalgar Square and 33 Mark Lane, London, was involved in attempts to formalise a contract for the Craignure nickel mine between the Duke and a couple of adventurers recommended by J. Arthur Phillips, the metallurgic chemist from London who had negotiated over the Craignure mine from February 1853. Phillips wanted to buy the spoil of the old workings for £700 and take a 21-year lease on the mine. Now his colleagues were pushing for a lease, which they said would have to 'be prepared in the Scotch form'. In July of that year, the Duke signed an agreement for a lease of the Craignure mine. The signatures on the agreement (not an actual lease) were those of Richard Cook Manuel, Charles Wakefield and George Andrews, and the company also comprised a Mr Webster, a Mr Humfrays and a Mr Braithwaite. The following month Webster and Humfrays took over Manuel and Company. This disparate crew visited the mine with their 'eminent' engineer Frederick Braithwaite. There were 30,000 shares available in this company at £1 a share. They appointed an agent, purchased tools and barrows and set 20 men and boys to work. They began making a new road and acquired timber to build cottages and a smithy. Impressive though this flurry of activity sounds, it didn't really bode well that they had talked with 'capitalists' in the city about forming a company 'as the best possible way of developing and working the mine properly'; or that their solicitor was telling the Duke that, despite 'property of this description' being 'very much depressed', they were 'quite prepared to pay the Duke the amount agreed upon and fairly and with energy work the mine and merely wish for the lease as soon as possible'.

The Duke had been wise when he signed an agreement for a lease rather than an actual lease. The intended lease (to follow when all clauses were agreed to by all parties) would have been for 21 years and the lessees were to pay £21 a ton to the Duke and a royalty of one 13th part of the gross value of the minerals extracted. The problems that arose in connection with the potential lessees, however, were clearly ringing alarm bells. Nettleship advised, 'It is so much the practice of the present day for individuals to take leases of mines, and then either to get up a company to work them, or to sell the lease to an existing company, that I think it probable that such is the intention of the parties in the present case. But whoever may come into possession of the mines there will be the means of exploring an efficient working of them.' He suggested various clauses in any lease that would force the lessee to work the mines efficiently. Correspondence dragged on over the next couple of years and the problems relating to the price of nickel of course applied to the other Inveraray mines as well as to Craignure. The difference was that the Duke retained the other mines as his own responsibility rather than leasing them. His fellow landowners throughout Argyll shared the Craignure problem. In that middle period of the 19th century, the flames of these ephemeral companies briefly flared and then were snuffed out, frequently leaving behind the destruction of property and of lives dependent on the work they so momentarily provided – not to mention the losses borne by those who invested in such transient set-ups. Perhaps knowing what the landowners didn't – that they would move on almost before the ink on any agreement had dried – some of the correspondence is at best flippant, at worst as impudent as our friend Mr Whitburn.

In his correspondence with the Duke, the London accountant Mr Nettleship aimed to be protective but, in reality, had no choice but to pass on correspondence that was rarely couched in respectful terms. One letter from Richard Cattarns of the Craignure Mining Company (how it must have irked the Duke that these adventurers had registered this name) dated 29 April 1856 reads, 'I am desired by the committee of management of this company to inform you that after many months of successive working and expending a large sum of money with no good result whatever it has now been determined to dissolve the company forthwith and that in all probability all the people at the mine will be discharged on Saturday next and whatever property may remain at the mine will be sold to pay the company's liabilities so far as it will extend unless the Duke should wish to take what there is by valuation if it should be of any use to His Grace, in which case I would be glad to be informed thereof.'

This was as a result of the protracted correspondence over various clauses in the lease that the Duke has been advised to insert and which the Craignure Mining Company objected to – or indeed simply failed to respond to. Nettleship had to advise the Duke that the company's right to 'throw up their contract' depended on whether they had used 'fair and reasonable exertions, and expended such an amount of capital' to test whether or not the mine could be worked for profit. But perhaps an even better get-out clause for the duke was that the people who came together as the company were not the people the Duke originally contracted. He was in his rights to suggest that those original 'parties' should be asked to take up the contract. And then there was the small matter of the company's accounts. Nettleship suggested that they were not satisfactory but that, if they were correct, 'it will account for the company not being so anxious on the subject of the lease heretofore'. There was more correspondence, more arguments about royalties. The company did pay two instalments of £350 to the Duke, suggesting these were for the lease but, in view of the fact that the lease had not been signed, this amount computes with the £700 offered for the nickel ore to be recovered from the spoil from the original mine. It was all too messy and, in May 1856, the Duke rescinded any contract with the Craignure Mining Company and Nettleship advised that the workings should be securely fenced off to prevent accidents.

We need to remember that such companies made their money not through any actual mining done but from the investment in shares made by members of the public. Some of those investors would be members of the clergy, widows left some small capital and members of the newly emerging middle class who were earning enough to part with £5 for a share in a 'foolproof' nickel mine. Many would be innocent enough to be shocked by project failures that perhaps plunged them into debt, but such an outcome would not have come as a huge surprise to one Craignure Mining Company investor, Lewis Thompson, described as an eminent chemist and geologist. In 1854, he had raised concerns on several occasions. In July of that year, he noted that the saleable value of the ore recently sampled from Craignure by a Birmingham assay company was 'so close upon the actual cost of raising and transporting the ore that it would not be worthwhile to carry on the mine provided we find that no improvement can be made upon the state of things'. He had pointed out that 'a great rogue' ran one particular smelting plant and he was 'not in any way to be trusted'. By the November, he couldn't have expressed his anxiety more clearly – more than £3,300 had been spent and only £1,260 made from the ore. Imagine the losses had the company built a smelting plant planned by Braithwaite. This company 'executive' had dismissed the old charcoal iron works at Furnace as outdated and suggested that new buildings be erected on Loch Fyne. He wasn't too impressed by the mine itself, saying, in January 1854, that it was 'impossible for the miner to follow the ore in any degree of certainty as with regular veins'. Investor Lewis Thompson, who took the trouble to visit the mine, reported to the company directors that it was 'one great disruption of "fault" and cannot be treated as a regular mine'. With hindsight, we know the directors probably didn't care one jot about such expert advice.

Almost 50 men and boys were employed at Craignure in 1854 but their output didn't always reach its destination on time – through no fault of theirs. The weather, as always, was not on the side of the endeavour. A steamer didn't arrive to pick up ten tons of nickel ore on 11 January, for example, and, while 'Weather permitting' is an almost unspoken phrase when it comes to ferries and steamers in the winter months in Argyll, a report concerning this particular no-show led to a fierce underlining of the word 'expected' in reference to the next steamer that could take the cargo. This was not a company that understood local conditions. The wages bill for April at Craignure was £124 and tradesmen's bills came to £46. In modern terms, this equates to £84,935.40 – clearly the cash was draining away and, if the ore didn't reach its destination, the Craignure Mining Company could only find itself deeply in the red.

Knowing all of this, the company still carried on regardless. The company records showed no capital (but the records were questionable), there were no estimates for future operations and by November 1854 Lewis Thompson advised them that 'with winter approaching we must ca' cannie, and reduce outgoings as much as possible'. Over the brief life of the venture, he had wisely attended Craignure Mining Company committee meetings and knew that there was a struggle finding a market for 'Scotch ores', which were considered 'sulphural' and therefore more difficult to process than the foreign ores that were by then being imported in quantity. Thompson confessed he had 'been led to believe that the deposit of ore was "illimitable" and that we had nothing to do but howk it out like whinstanes'. His eyes were now open to the reality and he confessed, 'I feel that I have been very foolish in muddling with such matters.'

Although the Craignure Mining Company moved out of Craignure, the business was not finished. Thomas Nettleship wrote to James Robertson on 1 October 1858 to say, 'I very much fear that the claims against the Craignure Company are irrecoverable.' He had chased the band of adventurers for more than two years and resorting to the law courts to force the company to complete the lease and 'then fulfil the terms of it' proved prohibitively expensive. He reminded Robertson (if reminder was needed) that even the expenses connected with the preparation of the lease had not been paid. The terms the Duke required were never agreed to and the lease was never completed 'but it was to have taken effect from the 11th of July 1853'.

John Cain's opinion of the Craignure Mining Company was that 'they are not miners, but a set of adventurers – not mining adventurers but of that class that will job in mining or anything else if they can make money without considering the means employed in making it. This astute class of men generally injure the mining industry very much.'

And with the Craignure Mining Company removed from the scene, the efficient John C. Cain, a mineral surveyor from Alston in Cumberland, could get on with the job of integrating the work at Craignure with that at Coille Bhraghad. Sketches of this mine signed and dated December 1851 suggested that there was far greater promise at Coille Bhraghad (also known as Essichossen Mine). A team of Cornish miners organised by J. Arthur Phillips (who had been involved in the setting up some of the science demonstrations in the Great Exhibition masterminded by Prince Albert in 1851) had got the output underway in 1852. In a report written in February 1852 from

2 Kent Villas, East Greenwich, Phillips explained that he had made inquiries about getting one or more Cornish miners to superintend the work at the nickel mines at Inveraray. He said there was no difficulty in getting 'two respectable and industrious men who would be willing to work for the sum of £5 each per month' but he recommended that their travelling expenses would also have to be paid as the distance between Cornwall and Inveraray was 'considerable'. The alternative was to make an agreement for a definite period or they would be reluctant to leave their work and travel so far for just a few weeks or months. It was also advisable to employ two men as miners were used to working in pairs and would work together at Coille Bhraghad. If only one were to be taken on, it would be preferable that he would be well educated, know the 'most minute details of mining and ore dressing' and would direct the men rather than work himself. In this case, he should be paid £4 a month. The decision was for two Cornishmen to come north.

The Duke of Argyll perhaps felt that Phillips had too many other responsibilities to be able to devote much time to running Coille Bhraghad were he to have a lease on it so, while he was happy to have him get that mine up and running and to seek his advice on the Inveraray mines, he decided to keep it under his own management. Once bitten, twice shy, it seems a wise and cautious move to have put a manager rather than a lessee in place. John Cain commenced work with Cumberland miners in 1852. An overview of the accounts from May 1851 to August 1856 shows that 257 tons of varying qualities of ore were produced during those years. The value of this was £4,659 – around £2.3 million at today's values. The expenses over those years amounted to £3,463 6s 9d, including the excavation of a new adit, labour and analysis of the ore. The profit was £1,197 or almost £600,000 at today's values. Labour levels clearly fluctuated because, from February 1853 to September 1854, the wage bill was £1,310 1s 11d, around half the total expenditure for five years.

Given the geography of the Inveraray mines, it would always have been more profitable had the ore been refined on site and then shipped out for sale. The big profits were always going to go to those who refined the product, in the same way today that Ghana's cocoa bean growers will never make the profits that high-class Belgian chocolatiers achieve when they process those beans. But, however promising (and even successful) the extraction of ore may have been, ploughing profits back into such improvements was never really going to be on the cards.

'Encouraging' and 'promising' are words that occur too many times in the reports and correspondence about the Inveraray mines. But, while James Robertson was the one constant in all the dramas surrounding the mines and these two adjectives were often used in his own weekly reports, he could also be the voice of reason. In February 1852, he told the Duke that the expense of the Essichossen Mine to date amounted to £494 12s 5d and this was because the work was still exploratory rather than productive. The idea of sending off samples of nickel instead of concentrating on copper was beginning to take hold. The Duke was aware that the men were not making much progress and Robertson reminded him that the weather was against them. From 1 January to 27 February, there had been 'only two dry working days'. Another difficulty in the way of getting on with the job, however, was the lack of skilled men and Robertson ha written to the manager at the Tyndrum lead mines 'to se he could recommend two good working miners experienced in shafting' and asking him to state the rate 'per day or per fathom' at which they might employed.

By 14 March 1852, J. Arthur Phillips had engaged Francis and John Webb, father and son, to work in the nickel mines and they were to leave Cornwall at the end of the month and take with them to Inveraray special pattern tools that the Duke had asked for. The men were to receive £10 travelling expenses and were required to keep an account of their spending en route. Phillips himself was paid £40 7s in May of 1852 to cover inspecting the nickel mines, his own travelling expenses, a copy of plans of the mines and reimbursement of the money advanced to the Cornish miners.

Francis Webb seems to have been as little impressed by local workers as others before him. James Robertson told the Duke in May 1852 that 'the Cornish man is quite despondent today' and had asked him to get two more regular miners from Cornwall 'to keep the work going night and day by relays'. The vein in the Coille Bhraghad – or Essichossen as the locals more often referred to it – shaft had come to an abrupt end and water was pouring through the mouth of the shaft. Robertson had no intention of employing more Cornish workers but he did divert six other men to work in the shaft so that sinking it could continue 'night and day'. Four men operated in pairs working eight-hour shifts and the other two removed ore and acted as dogsbodies, one on each of the shifts. With perseverance and a little imaginative thinking, the course of the vein was recovered by the end of May, when two whole days without rain gave cause to celebrate – even if the meagre size of the vein did not. Writing from London, Arthur Phillips said that dislocated ams were common in Cornwall and elsewhere and sent a sketch to suggest where to seek out the next part of the elusive vein.

With patience and hard work, Robertson was able to tell the Duke in September 1852 that 'James Munro and MacArthur have come upon a fine mass of ore about two feet thick in the place where I set them to work between the two east most shafts'. The cobalt sent from Essichossen for analysis contained around 16.5 per cent nickel and Robertson added 'I only hope that a large quantity may be got at Craignure equally rich'. A month later, the McGougans had lifted some two tons of ore at Craignure and Robertson reported that 'nearly seven tons of ore have been broken by the old men and boys and there is about one ton or more of selected ore to break'. The hard-working McGougans had driven their way through a foot of hard rock in the shaft to get at ore that was 'nearly a foot thick'. The analyst was telling Robertson that this ore was rich in nickel and samples of it were being loaded into casks to be transported south. In November 1852, analysis of ore from Craignure was shown to contain 10 per cent peroxide of nickel, which equates with over 6 per cent of metal, and a promising seam ranging between eight and eighteen inches thick had been uncovered at Essichossen, with both copper and nickel being lifted in quantity, and there was an overriding optimism that had been lacking for a decade.

This seam of positivity was of course layered with difficulties. What the Webbs didn't quite understand (like fellow Cornish folk Mr and Mrs Petherick and family before them) was the quantity and quality of the Argyll rain which, even in May, could flood out their place of work overnight. Weather was a constant enemy. That the mines would flood in winter was a given but often James Robertson reported cold wind in April and, in May 1853, he mentions that 'another ch died' when he wrote of unseasonable hail and snow. It wasn't only the weather that remained a constant negative. Misunderstandings between the local labour force and 'foreign' overseers persisted. It may sound as if the McGougans, James Munro and his partner MacArthur and other local men were doing a good job but Francis Webb had a different way of working entirely. James Robertson told the Duke, 'The working hours of the Cornishmen are different from those of the men here, viz, from seven in the morning to three in the afternoon. These eight hours they are <u>constant at work</u> [Robertson's underscore] excepting a few minutes to eat a bite of bread. They breakfast before going out and don't take dinner till they return. Webb seems to be a very sensible quiet man. The son looks too much a boy for heavy work – one would say from 15 to 16 years old, but his father says he is 19 and able in mining to do the work of a full grown man.'

John Cain would bring men from Cumberland, others would come from different mining areas of Scotland and there were Irish workers passing through from time to time. The constant workers in the 'bargain books' were local men or became local men when they married into families in the area. Cain, like Petherick before him, wanted to train local men to do the more complex mining work but was only partially successful in this.

Gossip that there was nickel in the Inveraray mines had reached the columns of the newspapers. The 8th Duke was in correspondence with his friend Lyon Playfair, 1st Baron Playfair of St Andrews, who was a Fellow of the Royal Society, a distinguished chemist (he had lectured on 'Chemistry applied to the Arts and Agriculture' in 1851) and Gentleman Usher to Prince Albert. The Duke had asked for a chemical analysis of ore samples from the Inveraray mines and this, as well as a scientific paper presented by Lord Playfair, attracted the attention of still more speculators, who wanted to be shown around the mines. James Robertson was a reluctant guide but recognised that some of those who came to look did have expertise that could be helpful. One inquiry that was not expected came by letter to Mr Robertson from James Braithwaite, one of the Craignure Mining Company crew. He wrote in September 1853 from 32 Gower Street in London, 'I was very much surprised to hear yesterday that someone has led the Duke to think that the "Craignure Mine" is being, to use the vulgar expression, <u>hawked about</u> [Braithwaite's underscore]. Pray immediately disabuse his Grace's mind for I most solemnly assure you that such is in no way the case and further assure him – I think far too favourably of the property to do anything of the kind.'

The letter ended bizarrely with some almost unintelligible gossip that was prefaced, 'I am not desirous, nor is it my practice to speak against anyone, but . . .'. His 'but' rambled on about those seeking a slice of the Inveraray mines being 'seriously alarmed at the splendid appearance of the Duke's property and they fear a downfall to their monopoly'. James Robertson must have been seriously alarmed himself at the wildness of the correspondence of someone considered competent to analyse nickel ore. The sentence 'They will not succeed for the furnaces shall be again on a blaze before they will be allowed to have it any longer all their own way.' might suggest to a modern recipient of the letter that the writer was under the influence of drink or drugs. Laudanum, that popular Victorian opiate, may have been Mr Braithwaite's drug of choice.

The mines were indeed being 'hawked about' and, as correspondence shows, the Duke was on his guard. He was still the throes of checking what should and shouldn't be included in mine leases and was advised that the usual stipulations for ensuring efficient working included requiring that a certain number of men be kept at work within usual working hours, that a moderate minimum rent should be charged that would be absorbed in the dues or royalties and that there should be conditions regarding the erection of machinery. He was up against some tough and demanding people who pulled no punches. For example, James King of 1 Pensions Gardens, Oxford, had commissioned an examination of the mine with a view to buying the ore and working the mine. When he did not receive a response within two weeks, he told the Duke in no uncertain terms he was 'hindered from making other engagements' and was 'retaining the services of persons practically acquainted with the matter at very considerable expense'. The Duke's response was that the offer made for the ore was 'wholly inadmissible' and that it was not his 'present intention to let the mine' unless certain conditions were met. He added, 'I think it right to inform you that I have been, and will be, in communication with other parties in reference to the same matter.' The Duke made his position more than clear. 'I must myself be free to enter into the arrangement which on comparison may seem most satisfactory or failing to approve of them to decline them altogether.' In other words, don't try to bully a peer of the realm.

7

Life, work and the changing world

The 1847 so-called 'Ten Hour Act' restricted shifts in factories to a ten-hour day. It would seem that the 1842 Mines and Collieries Act was considered a step far enough for those who worked underground and, while the minimum age was raised, the number of hours worked was not legislated for. In November 1853, John Cain was advocating two shifts of eight hours rather than the three shifts that had previously been worked at the Coille Bhraghad mine. He had, according to James Robertson's weekly report to the Duke, brought three working miners with him from Cumberland on 22 November and set two of them to work with 'MacArthur and young McGougan' on the new level of the mine. Other men were working in the shaft. Cain had made it clear that he did not 'approve of the three shifts in working the level'. He considered 'two shifts of eight hours each much more advantageous in as much as there is more cooperation among the men and a greater facility to check on the work done'. Robertson confided in the Duke that Cain had 'much experience in mining and is a modest, judicious man with whom Your Grace will be much satisfied'. The men must also have been 'much satisfied' with a boss who promoted such good working conditions. This was, after all, in the same year th men were being bullied into working long shifts in dangerous conditions for take-it-or-leave-it 'bargains' in the Strontian lead mines. Cain seemed to have his workers' welfare at heart.

Like his predecessors, Cain did not work exclusively at Inveraray and between inspection visits returned to his native Cumberland, where his wife and family lived, or to other mining ventures where he was employed. Over the years, he became close friends with James Robertson, and the whole family visited Inveraray from time to time. Letters and reports always contained greetings to each other's wives and the inquiries about health are intimate and concerned, rather than polite and distant.

Modest, judicious and caring though he was, Cain was not a pushover. His 'bargains', however, which were meticulously recorded, do seem fair to both employee and employer. He was able to negotiate in such a way that the English miners and local Scots would be employed in the most appropriate way without friction – the English miners saw themselves as a cut above the Scots who, to be fair, had still not been given the kind of training that the itinerant miners must have absorbed since they were children down dark tunnels with a candle that would never have lasted a whole shift. After a visit to Coille Bhraghad in early January 1854, when the level had been driven 38 feet underground, Cain reported that he had 'let the two English miners a bargain of 13 fathoms at £5 5s per fathom to find or pay for their own candles, powder and tools, to have the use of your tools but at the end of the bargain, or any other suitable time, to return as many tools or the value of such, to have the privilege of hiring two men to receive 40 shillings per month subsistence money, and have a clear settlement at the end of every three onths commencing 1 January 1854'. By comparison with the Strontian bargains, this seems fair – even generous. Cain explained that '[t]he English miners refuse taking a bargain with the Scotchmen and I could not press them to do so yet, as for want of skill in mining, four Scotchmen will not do more work than two good English miners. I have therefore arranged that the English miners could have a contract of the level or at least a portion of it and hire two of the Scotchmen.'

Cain was also making the mine more efficient and easier to work by installing rails and a wagon in the level to bring out the rubble. He instructed the foreman, Samuel Walton, how the wagon should be built and suggested the wood for both the rails and the wagon could be cut at the Inveraray sawmill. Walton was also to be in charge of the records of the mine. Cain reported that he had left two books. 'The smaller one is for the purpose of keeping an account of every article that goes to the mine and what it is used for.' Walton was to make an inventory of all the materials and tools on the premises and Cain stressed that he aimed to know 'what is at the mine, what goes into it, and whether everything is properly applied without extravagance'. The second book was to be a weekly journal, which he preferred to a daily one. His plans for the mine from his survey made in early January showed the skills of a draughtsman. Although the nickel ore at Craignure was not as rich as that at Coille Bhraghad, Cain's survey suggested it could become a 'rich and profitable mine'. However, and perhaps this was inevitable considering the history of the Craignure Mining Company, Cain did not approve of the 'system of working this mine' and he hoped to be able to advise on a 'better and cheaper plan if they are not conceited in their own views'. He found the cost of living higher by four or five shillings a week per man in the Inveraray area th in the lead mines district of Cumberland but believed th the Scottish mines continued to produce at a profitable level, then proper stores could be established that would bring the cost of living down.

Nationally, income had risen from £18 per annum in 1800 to £25 in 1842 but taxes were rising faster than levels of income and local taxes increased that burden. In the West Highlands of Scotland, the staple diet was potatoes and herring and, in the 1840s, the potato blight led to terrible destitution. Schemes were set up to feed the poor and 'destitution roads' were built to provide employment. Most taxes were imposed on consumer goods and, in Argyll, then as now, the additional costs of transporting everything from food to fuel were responsible for the extra four or five shillings Cain noted on the weekly outlay in the 1850s. Over the years during which the Coille Bhraghad mine successfully produced nickel, national wages rose but the 'bargain' system in the mines makes it difficult to estimate whether individuals were keeping up with that rise. The wages bill for April 1854 for 47 men and boys was £124, which averages at around £2 10s a month each but the miners and the smith would have been paid more than the labourers and the boys. In September 1856, men and boys employed at working and breaking ore at the Coille Bhraghad mine were paid at very different daily rates, ranging from eight pence for Angus Bell and nine pence for George McIntyre, Peter McKellar and Donald Livingston (presumably the 'boys'), through eleven pence for John McCallum and John Livingston, a shilling for Donald Walker, 1s 2d for Angus and James Munro and Duncan McKellar, 1s 4d for Robert McKenzie, Duncan McFarlane and John McNair, 1s 6d for Donald Munro, 4d for William Dewar and 2s 6d for John Munro the smith. A fisherman hired by James Robertson to pilot the yacht of one of the Duke of Argyll's visitors was engaged for one guinea a week (£1 1s) in August 1856 and must have thought his ship had indeed come in. Given that records suggest the average London smith in the 1860s was working a ten-hour day, six days a week and was paid 6s 6d a week and a seaman working on the steamers in the south of England earned around 16s 4d a week, the Argyll wages do not seem too much out of order. But, whatever wages were earned, purchasing power was decreasing throughout the mid 1800s as prices rose and of even greater significance was that the days worked by Duncan McKellar for 1s 2d might have been few – the effects of the weather and the nature of the work meant that employment was sporadic. Most of the workers in Argyll probably also worked on their crofts to maintain a hand-to-mouth existence.

As we have seen, alcohol was a problem (without doubt home-made and therefore more lethal than any spirit bought over a bar) and, while Petherick could only condemn and hope that the new temperance organisations would work miracles, Cain went for a more direct approach. When Samuel Walton, who managed the Inveraray mines for Cain, abused his trust, he was given the kind of talking-to that would appeal to any man's self esteem. In December 1856, Cain told Robertson that he had found the mine in an unsatisfactory state and, when he took Walton to task, 'he showed an unusual degree of stupidity' and had 'altogether a very silly appearance'. Confessing to having indulged in alcohol, Walton 'begged a thousand pardons'. That didn't wash with Cain, who told Robertson and the Duke of Argyll that the man would have to go if he persisted in drinking. However, he had not dismissed him on the spot but made it clear th he 'would have nothing more to do with him if he allo himself to be turned away for such disgraceful conduct'. Cain then suggested Walton should be made to sign a contract binding him to be at the mine every day at the hours Cain stated and to do the same sort of work as he had previously shown himself capable of. Cain said, 'It is a great pity the man has neither conduct nor principle to guide his actions' and he regretted that some men could be very foolish, even when one tried to help them 'out of the grips of poverty'. This approach (harsh enough as reported to superiors but fair in its directness to the man himself) had positive results – Walton was still manager in later years when the mines had grown and were prospering and he was even offered a job in Northumberland by Cain in the early 1860s.

The Industrial Revolution experienced in England was slower to reach north of the border. One reason men were reluctant to move from Cumberland to Argyll when Cain offered skilled men work was that new steel works and mines were opening on their doorsteps offering permanent and well-paid jobs. In Scotland, textile factories and burgeoning coal and steel works in the Central Belt drew labour there from the Highlands. The small-scale development of mining in Argyll, therefore, was never going to turn the county into an industrial heartland and the coming of the railways only partially helped with the transport of copper and nickel to the real centres of manufacture where they were needed.

Even the mechanisation of the Inveraray mines (just as in the Kintyre coal mines) was slow and it was John Cain who introduced pumps that would allow excavation to continue while water was removed from the base of the Coille Bhraghad mine. Of course, such mechanisation cut the wage ll but put labourers out of a job. On the other hand, small hing machines to clean the ore had to have operators and Cain was pushing for installation of these at both Coille Bhraghad and Craignure in 1855 so that a better product could be marketed and more ore could be extracted from the refuse. His way of working was all about efficiency and the sketches he drew were accompanied by detailed instructions as to which teams would work in which areas. One sketch sent to James Robertson on 21 April 1855 specified two areas where the team 'J and J Forbes and Son' were to proceed in the Coille Bhraghad mine, one where 'Peter McPherson and Partner' were to work on ore four to five inches wide, another where 'Peter Cameron and Partner' would extract ore in a vein up to six inches wide. Precise instructions also related to 'Bell and Partner', 'William Hymers and Partner' and 'Dugald Livingstone and Son'. This was certainly an improvement on the situation complained of back in 1814 by John Bedlington, the colliery viewer in the north of England, who told pit owners that the men sent to inspect the pits knew their layouts so little that accidents and fatalities were bound to occur. Cain was, of course, more than a 'viewer' but it could be imagined that his more senior role would have distanced him further from the intricacies of each mine. Instead, he intimately knew his men, his mines and the developments in his industry.

Cain's logging of every piece of equipment, every candle, every ounce of gunpowder and every pick, alongside his micromanaging of the men to achieve the most favourable results by the most economical means suggest this was the man the Inveraray mines had been waiting for. His April 1855 schedule detailed the bargain he had let to four English miners – Viponds Clementson, Thomas Hymers, Jon Spark and William Craig. As with other bargains, the men wou be paid according to the distance dug and the type of mat being dug through – £12 per fathom through solid quartz where the beds were more than 15 inches thick, 'below this £10 per fathom' and, through slate, £8 10s per fathom. Cain told Robertson, 'This is safer should a change from quartz to slate take place than a fixed price.' By October of that year, this micromanagement was at least revealing that the Craignure mine was poor but what he had planned could lead to a place where the ore was more abundant. Some 12 or 14 tons of ore had been extracted by six pick men and there were three labourers working with them, as well as five men and two boys and 13 women and girls employed at dressing the ore. In the 1851 census, 11,000 women were shown to be working in the mining industry in Britain. Although the 1842 Act had banned women and girls from working below ground, Cain would not have been acting illegally to employ them above ground dressing the ore. At least these women and girls were recorded as working in the industry – many working women were not registered in the 1851 census. The Argyll women would have been accustomed to heavy work that equated with the jobs they were entrusted to do at Coille Bhraghad. Although written a century later, the poet Norman MacCaig's description of his crofting relative in 'Aunt Julia' gives the picture of the kind of tough women bred in Argyll and the Isles – women who 'wore men's boots when she wore any', who could cut peats alongside the men, 'her strong foot stained with peat', and who were well able to carry heavy burdens, including the buckets of water that had to be brought from a well or spring.

The advice that the mining engineer and geologist Thomas Sopwith had given the Duke of Argyll when he was in the throes of battling with the Craignure Mining Company was provide 'tolerably comfortable dwellings and the prospect of moderate but permanent remuneration' if he wanted to keep 'the scale of labour free from fluctuation which I am always anxious to avoid, being as injurious to workmen as it is detrimental to any large concern'. Sopwith had considered Cain to be the very man to achieve stability in the workforce, having among his many other positive qualities 'good tact' in management, both of men and 'unknown' quantities in terms of what the job might hold. Sopwith told the Duke to offer Cain between £100 and £120 for a year, in quarterly payments, suggesting that he would be more likely to spend more time at the mines if the contract was yearly, rather than a daily payment. Cain certainly seems to have examined the mines regularly; his quarterly reports were extensive and his 'good tact' could be successfully used in 21st-century personnel management.

The mines were small-scale and the Industrial Revolution didn't swamp Argyll but the county did have to tap into that revolution in order to reach a suitable market. It is perhaps important to remember that, as a mode of transport, steamers had only existed since the *Comet* was launched in 1812 and, while they were growing in size and increasing in efficiency, they still had their limitations. By the 1850s, that other mode of transport created by the invention of the steam engine, the railway, was in operation in sufficient parts of the country to offer a service to the mines at Inveraray. In December 1853, James Robertson told the Duke of Argyll that a quantity of ore was 'ready barrelled in the cellar, except the putting on of the iron hoops which I shall have immediately done'.

The decision then was whether, once the ore was transported to the Clyde port via Loch Fyne, it should be taken to Liverpool by steamer or sent direct by railway to Birmingham. Sending the ore by steamers in quantities of ten tons at a tir would evidently have saved on the expense of insurance but these niceties of transport were now on the agenda. What is more, it was now possible to arrange transport with the aid of the telegram. After many years in the development stage, the first commercial electrical telegraph was co-developed by Sir William Fothergill Cooke and Charles Wheatstone in 1837. At first, it connected the stations on the developing railway lines and, by the 1850s, these telegraphed messages were common enough to be given the nickname of 'telegrams'. It would take until 1870, however, for the Post Office to launch its telegraph service and, in the intervening decades, messages between companies and individuals had to be sent between railway stations and then passed on to the intended recipient by more conventional means. Mail deliveries at this time were, in the main, very efficient – a letter from the Duke of Argyll written in London one day would be in the hands of his Inveraray chamberlain the next and the chamberlain's response would be back in London the day after that. Local mail would often arrive the day it was sent. In 1856, there was a great toing and froing of letters about transporting ore to Swansea and the insurance that should be paid on the barrels. The *Margaret Wilson* was initially hired at a cost of £50 but the skipper was afraid of Loch Fyne, 'to which he was a stranger'. In early November, the *Mount Stewart* – a steamer that could take a cargo of exactly 100 tons – was hired. She had sailed from Greenock on 7 November and was expected in Inveraray as quickly as the instructions from a William Easton, on behalf of William MacEwing (the shipping and insurance agent) of Glasgow, would reach James Robertson by mail. It was evidently more expensive to insure from Glasgow and so a London insurer had been instructed to cover the 100 tons for a value of £2000 at 1 per cent. After this wrangling, the policy was not sent off to Robertson until 11 November so clearly there were delays to despatching the *Mount Stewart*. Bills of lading then had to be organised and signed and sent to Inveraray which further delayed the actual journey. At last, on 21 November, the *Mount Stewart* was again officially hired for the journey to Swansea. A return trip carrying cargo from Port Talbot to Glasgow was added into the deal to avoid penalties (no different to the freight systems of today) and then on 22 November came the excitement of a telegram from Munro and Sutherland in Greenock to Morris Munro & Company in Glasgow that read: 'MOUNT STEWART HAS GONE TO INVERARAY AND WAS PASSED TODAY AT THE MOUTH OF LOCHFINE BY GILPHEAD STEAMER'.

This most modern of communications, transmitted by the British Electric Telegraph Company and the Submarine Telegraph Company, probably at a cost of one shilling because it was transmitted less than 30 miles, was then enclosed in a letter from William MacEwing at 17 St Vincent Lane, Glasgow, to James Robertson in Inveraray. It is possible that Mr Robertson felt that this new-fangled messaging service would never catch on and certainly there is scant evidence in the Argyll archives that any other telegrams were received at Inveraray before the Post Office became part of the system. Old-fashioned letters continued to inform him that the *Annabella*, the *Halcyon* and the *Maria* had delivered cargoes of ore to Liverpool and Swansea. Even so, the thrill of being part of that exhilarating new age of telecommunication, industrialisation and mechanisation must have touched a nerve even in the stoical Mr Robertson.

If the precursor of the text message excited Mr Robertson, then the predecessor of the 21st-century idea of celebrity pleased the honest, down-to-earth Mr Cain and his wife. In September 1856, John Cain had taken his wife to Inveraray when he went to inspect the mines and write up his quarterly reports. A note at the end of his report tells James Robertson, 'I was glad we came home by Edinburgh as it was lively and gay on account of the Royal visit. Mrs C saw Her Majesty and the other members of the Royal Family twice in open carriages. This was a treat we scarcely expected.'

Queen Victoria and Prince Albert were no doubt on their way to Balmoral Castle, which they renovated between 1853 and 1856. Why the Cains would have detoured via Edinburgh to Cumberland is a different matter. The Scottish engineer Thomas Telford had upgraded the road from Glasgow to Carlisle in 1824 and the railway from Glasgow to Carlisle had been in operation since 1850. Cain doesn't mention in his reports how he made his way to and from Argyll (although he obviously would have travelled by steamer from Greenock to Inveraray as most people did at that time). Travelling for pleasure was beginning to seep down from the upper classes – and perhaps Robertson had whispered to the Cains that the Duke of Argyll's friend Prince Albert would be in Edinburgh with the monarch at just the right time.

Both Cain and Robertson would now commence lengthy relationships with Mr Vivian of the Nickel and Cobalt Works at Hafod Isha in Swansea and with the Rolling Tube and Wire Mills' Soho Works in Spring Hill, Birmingham. In June 1859, Robertson typically received a letter from Hafod Isha to say that the *Maria* of Liverpool had safely discharged a cargo of ore from Inveraray. But not every hiring of a sea-going steamer was straightforward and chartering the *Maria* came about as a result of a bizarre incident. On 21 April 1859, the *Caledonian* had been chartered to load 120 tons of nickel ore from Inveraray to Swansea at nine shillings a ton with an insurance covering £1,800 at 15 shillings per cent. On 4 May 1859, the agent who had set up the charter wrote to James Robertson to say that the master of the *Caledonian* has broken the agreement before the 150 tons were freighted. William MacEwing wrote that the captain, 'having got I suppose an offer of a better freight and seeing the charter lying on the broker's desk, threw it in the fire and refused to go'. This left MacEwing in a pickle and he had been trying since 21 April to find another vessel to do the run. Only now had he secured the *Maria* of Liverpool, which he described as 'a very fine vessel' (but then, he would have had to create a positive from this somewhat negative situation) that could take the 150-ton cargo. He had already transferred the insurance – and in view of the volatile nature of the *Caledonian*'s captain, it was perhaps for the best that the original plan had not come to fruition.

Modern life was firing such a range of new and exciting experiences as well as new complexities at those who found themselves almost inadvertently involved in the Argyll mines. A community just getting to grips with the travel offered by Clyde steamers was now required to work to timetables imposed by seagoing steamers, freight trains and canals linking industrial English cities where the ore they scraped from the ground was refined for use in almost unimaginable new manufacturing and scientific developments. The Duke of Argyll was at home in that world – those who worked for him had to run hard to catch up.

8

Inveraray Metal – a stitch-up and the wind-down of the Inveraray mines

The Crimean War may have seemed very far removed from the daily grind of mining nickel ore from Argyll hillsides but, for a brief moment in the 1850s, the spotlight shone on Inveraray in the struggle to produce efficient arms to fight that war. The conflict lasted from October 1853 to March 1856, coinciding with the discovery that the Inveraray mines were not a great source of copper but did, in fact, promise an abundance of nickel. Like most wars, the cause seemed far removed from the arena of conflict. In this case, the Russian Empire was ostensibly in dispute with the Ottoman-Turkish Empire over the rights of Christian minorities in the Holy Land. The real reasons were territorial. The Ottoman-Turkish Empire was in decline and France and Britain allied themselves with the Ottoman-Turkish Empire because they did not want to see the Russian Empire gain Ottoman territory. The war was bloody and ranged from the Balkans to the Crimean Peninsula. It was one of the first conflicts to use modern technologies such as submarine mines, explosive naval shells, the railways and telegraphy. At the battle of the Alma on 20 September 1854, the British and French used w rifled muskets.

One of the many lessons learned in this new-style conflict, in which the Russian Empire was defeated, was the need for lightweight, super-efficient weaponry. According to a book review in an 1884 edition of the science journal *Nature*, to meet the needs of the Crimean conflict, the former Board of Ordnance was abolished and a newly created Minister of War was put in control of the manufacturing departments at the Royal Arsenal in Woolwich. Colonel F.M. Eardley-Wilmot, R.A., was appointed Superintendent of the Gun Factories in July 1855. Eardley-Wilmot was looking for suitable materials for guns and that was when the Inveraray mines entered the equation. Minerologist Dr Lewis Thompson believed that an alloy using Inveraray nickel could provide the material sought for strong but lightweight artillery.

In September 1855, Thompson wrote to the Duke of Argyll explaining why he thought a British government-backed experiment to produce a wrought-iron gun had failed – he believed that the proportion of iron used would allow it to crystallise when it was repeatedly heated and hammered. He compared this failure to railway carriage axles, which he said were 'notoriously subject to fracture from very slight concussions'. On the other hand, a metal alloy could be more successful and he, of course, was aware that the Duke had an interest in nickel ore. Thompson could have gone to any source of nickel but he knew that the nickel ore found at Inveraray was devoid of arsenic and he suspected an artificial 'meteoric iron' could be produced from this. He explained to the Duke that, when this ore was roasted at a dull red heat, it became a mixture of the oxide of iron and nickel. 'If, therefore, when roasted as common iron ore is roasted, it were thrown into the blast furnace of an iron works with the iron ore, a mixed metal would result, which upon undergoing the usual operation of puddling and refining might be made to contain any required percentage of nickel according to the proportion of nickel ore employed relatively to the iron ore.' He suggested that the additional cost would be 'a mere trifle' and that an alloy of 99 per cent iron and nickel would answer the gun problem perfectly.

He needed to confirm all of this through experiments, of course, and the Duke was evidently drawn to the idea. Not only was the Duke the Lord Privy Seal in Lord Aberdeen's cabinet between 1852 and 1855 and therefore would be in consultations about the war, but he also shared Prince Albert's scientific interests. Thompson's detailed suggestions would have been seen as important on both fronts. In November 1855, Thompson suggested to the Duke that, if '5,000 tons of the alloy could be worked up every year' – a quantity he said was 'by no means large' – then 100 tons of nickel would be required each year. In the state of metal, this would cost £67,000. As ore, the cost would be £25,000, which he rightly said was 'a very considerable saving'. At today's values, this would be around £5.6 million for the metal, £2 million for the ore (recent Ministry of Defence contracts for small arms for the British Army have been worth around £2.7 million). Thompson was confident that 1,000 tons of ore a year could be raised at Inveraray 'without much difficulty'. This would bring the Inveraray mine £20,000 a year profit.

Having raised such hopes, Thompson went off to the South of France to troubleshoot at a lead and silver mine. Airily, he offered to correspond on the subject and to afford the Duke 'all the assistance in his power'. By the beginning of December, Thompson was attempting to use all of his con-nections to set up an experiment at the Woolwich arsenal. He had previously spoken to Colonel Eardley-Wilmot, who had at that time seemed keen to allow him to carry out experiments within the confines of Woolwich – even promising to erect a small cupola furnace and to provide a colleague of Thompson who was prominent in this field of science, Sir William Fairbairn, with experimental bars of alloy. Fairbairn supported Eardley-Wilmot's campaign to modernise Woolwich Arsenal and so Thompson may have felt he had good reason to think he was being taken seriously. However, when Dr Thompson went to Woolwich, supported by a letter from the Duke of Argyll, Eardley-Wilmot refused to meet him. Not totally fazed but certainly deeply offended, Thompson now turned to Benjamin Hawes, the deputy Secretary at War, who told him that the reception he had been given was 'unworthy of the object proposed to be effected'. Eardley-Wilmot was in charge, however, and Thompson graciously gave him the benefit of the doubt, suggesting that he had acted as he did because of 'red tape'. There was, after all, a war going on.

At this point, some very big guns indeed were employed in the attempt to get Lewis Thompson's experiment off the ground. Michael Faraday FRS, the man who discovered the principles of electromagnetic induction, was showing an interest, albeit academic, in the creation and production of alloys, and Isambard Kingdom Brunel, genius in the bridge building world, was also working on improved designs for large guns. He had already designed a floating armoured barge used successfully in 1854 in the Crimean campaign and, in 1855, had been working on a prefabricated hospital building that was shipped to the Crimea in sections and used by Florence Nightingale. In the letter dated 4 December 1855 from Thompson to the Duke in which he bemoaned the reception he had experienced at Woolwich, he added, 'It may perhaps be as well for me to mention that Mr Brunel is able and willing to procure me a cupola furnace in London and to undertake construction of a furnace on no other grounds than those of scientific interest.'

Thompson was a reasonably well-known figure in this field himself. He had previous experience with premature decay of a mix of iron and copper. In 1836, he had been employed as a chemist to analyse some gas mains belonging to a metropolitan gas company that had become rotten and oxidised prematurely. Analysis showed that a percentage of copper in the iron had caused the decay. Now he was worried that any prejudice Eardley-Wilmot might have against him as a person would attach itself to the nickel alloy for guns that he hoped to promote. He told the Duke, 'I could therefore wish it to be known that this is no invention or discovery of mine, but a recognised fact within the reading of every chemist in which I have no part or share of merit whatever.' He could understand that, as an outsider to the military, there could be some suspicion – he admitted this was even 'commendable' – but added that 'as regards the alloy of nickel there ought to be neither surprise nor jealousy. The thing belongs to the world at large.' He believed that an alloy of nickel and iron would prove useful in 'gunnery and many other arts' and hoped that the Woolwich experiments would be undertaken impartially.

Eardley-Wilmot had not really been honest with Thompson, however. When he was persistently turning Thompson away from the arsenal gate, he must have known that decisions had already been taken. Thompson and the Duke of Argyll received copies of an official document from the War Department dated 18 December 1855, documenting the presence of 14 officers, civilians and a professor at an Ordnance Select Committee meeting on 6 December 1855 and confirming what had been agreed at an earlier meeting – that his report of experiments to date were not convincing enough to merit further experimentation 'in order to prepare an artificial meteoric iron'. The committee would, however, 'be glad to receive a small quantity of nickel as offered by His Grace the Duke of Argyll for the purpose of trying experiments with that metal'.

Thompson wasn't daunted. He continued to develop his formula for roasting ore, telling the Duke of Argyll that his experiments showed the advantage of sending the ore to market in a roasted form and that this 'ought to have been the plan practised by the Craignure adventurers'. At the end of December 1855, Colonel Eardley-Wilmot persisted in refusing Thompson and his associates access to a small furnace and told Thompson that the Woolwich committee would carry out experiments themselves, using 'their own way and under their sole management'. Secrecy in the development of arms is nothing new. Thompson left a small sample of the Inveraray ore at Woolwich and told the Duke that he suspected those experiments were being done for alloys 'made with any other metal rather than nickel'. He said that copper seemed to be an especial favourite, 'though I have fully explained its galvanic disadvantages' (and no doubt Michael Faraday would have done so too).

Suspicions were aroused, however, that others might be being favoured in this particular arms race. A lot of parliamentary money would be made available for whichever company won a contract to produce the kind of guns needed for this conflict. On the one hand, there were armament giants such as Sir William Armstrong, who was clearly a frontrunner in any competition. In 1854, Armstrong had offered the Secretary of State for War a rifled breech-loading 3-pounder gun for trial and he was currently developing this weapon. On the other hand, there were men like Dr Lewis Thompson who saw the potential of metal alloys and wanted to develop them for queen and country, regardless of personal gain (or so he insisted to the Duke of Argyll in several letters). The battle was between a speedy defence solution and an interesting industrial development. It may have seemed like a fix that Armstrong got the £2-million contract and Thompson was left out in the cold but men were dying at the front and Armstrong was already well ahead in the arms trade.

The Ordnance Select Committee that had dismissed Thompson's findings said there was no argument in favour of a special superiority of this alloy for the manufacture of ordnance. They were also dubious about the very existence of meteoric iron consisting only of nickel and iron. The report said, 'Our practical knowledge of the properties of meteoric iron is so meagre, and the composition of the substance itself is so uncertain that to attempt, with the data we possess, to manufacture meteoric iron would be to enter upon a most extensive subject of research with a very uncertain object in view . . . [T]he arguments brought forward by Mr Thompson are certainly not sufficiently correct and conclusive to induce the committee to recommend a series of experiments with a view to prepare artificial meteoric iron.' This ignored the fact that the nickel from Inveraray had been shown to consist only of nickel and iron. It perhaps wasn't only that Armstrong was already in the frame to produce the required weapons but that other sources were already favoured for the raw materials from which to make them.

In his paper 'The Woolwich Arsenal and Acadian Mines', Kenneth Pryke of the University of Windsor in Canada explained that, in 1856, the Royal Arsenal undertook to locate a British source for high-grade ore to be used for ordnance. Iron was evaluated from Sweden and Nova Scotia, which Eardley-Wilmot said contained 'mountains of this precious material'. Even so, the Canadian ore was rejected and Pryke suggests that the analytical chemistry of the time had 'relatively little to offer the metal trades'. Perhaps Eardley-Wilmot relied too much on that emerging science. In the summer of 1859, it was decided to adopt the Armstrong breech-loading system and, in November 1859, Colonel Eardley-Wilmot was requested to resign his post at the Gun Factories. William Armstrong moved in behind his desk.

Was it all about chemistry? Was it all about sourcing raw materials? Was it about contracts being fixed? Whatever the truth about the development of lightweight ordnance, the Inveraray mines did not benefit in the way that Dr Lewis Thompson had foreseen in his enthusiasm. Even so, neither Thompson's nor the Duke's interest in developing an alloy with the Inveraray nickel was diminished. In January 1856, Thompson was asked to bring his ideas before the French government. Both Brunel and Fairbairn were experimenting with the Inveraray ore to create an alloy in early 1856 and, on 12 January, Thompson wrote to the Duke from 3 Parliament Street, London, to say that he 'had the honour to enclose a sample of the mixed metal resulting from the sulphite fusion of the roasted ore, with a portion of lime and charcoal – the silica of the crucible supplying the place of sand'. This was the first incarnation of 'Inveraray Metal' or, as Thompson described it, 'This metal is therefore the true Inveraray Metal without admixture and it has been made or reduced in the precise manner proposed to the authorities at Woolwich. The farther operation with this is merely to melt it with sufficient cast iron to realise the proportion of 98 iron to 2 nickel'.

Thompson's sample had already been subjected to rigorous tests. He told the Duke, 'As you may perceive by examining this button, very violent attempts have been made to break or bend it, so as to show its fracture – but these have failed. Your Grace may therefore cause experiments to be repeated with this view.' The 'button' had a silvery lustre, a malleability and ductility, or ability to be shaped as required. This was all down to the scientific knowledge of Mr Brunel, who had carried out the experiments to Thompson's evident delight. Brunel had accepted the challenge and was willing (as Thompson was) to give the project his 'warmest support' on 'public grounds alone'. He and Brunel had agreed that the experience at Woolwich had been unfortunate but Thompson found that Brunel's 'influence in other directions' was more than sufficient to 'carry this project to a final and decisive experiment'. In February 1856, Thompson told the Duke that operations had gone ahead at Battersea and that Mr Brunel wanted to repeat the experiment to 'test uniformity'.

Thompson had sensibly given up on any involvement with producing guns. Every obstacle had been put in his way and, with hindsight, we can perhaps see that the dice were loaded against this idea from the start. A Captain Vandeleur, who was overseeing experiments with wrought iron in 1856, had told Thompson that no experiment was worth making 'upon a canon less that 56cwt'. From this, both Thompson and Fairbairn concluded that there was 'no real intention of making a canon at Woolwich' and Fairbairn was 'upset at the inertia of the arsenal authorities'. However, Thompson was more than sure that his alloy – Inveraray Metal – was a very valuable substance. Brunel and other engineers were convinced by its strength and Thompson was now anxious to promote it as a 'public utility'. With a view to that, he wanted to set up a private interview between Brunel and the Duke.

By March of 1856, Thompson was negotiating with nickel refiners in Staffordshire and elsewhere and Fairbairn had sent a copy of his report on the alloy bars produced at Battersea under Brunel's expertise. The results were not perfect but Fairbairn had offered to continue with the project. The next steps would be crucial – would the Duke be involved only in experiments, in which case, Thompson could provide the equipment or would he be interested in creating a company for which building an appropriate furnace would be essential? Thompson claimed to have no pecuniary interest in the venture whatsoever and wanted only to produce a product 'useful in developing this industrial interest of the country'.

It certainly captured the public imagination. The alloy was exhibited at Newcastle in Staffordshire, caught the eye of Alfred Crosskill, an agricultural implement maker from East Yorkshire, and he wrote to ask for the price of the Inveraray nickel ore. He hoped to make lighter farm implements, carts and wagons from the alloy and wanted to try it on a practical basis. It was possible that, even though the Inveraray Metal would not reach the Crimean War in the form of artillery, it might get there in the form of carts and railway tracks manufactured for the war effort by the ambitious Crosskills.

The process was seen as important by the journal *The Engineer* which, in the edition of 18 July 1856, drew attention to the idea that 'wherever mechanical strength is desired, an alloy is preferred to a pure metal'. Iron's tendency to 'crystallise' had to be addressed and the use of artificial meteoric iron would have to be considered. 'Meteoric iron' (its name, the journal explained, 'based on supposition that these masses have fallen from the atmosphere') was composed of iron and nickel, the nickel varying from 2 to 10 per cent with small quantities of cobalt and chromium. 'Science has made artificial meteoric iron,' the journal reminded its audience, 'and it has been tested. Its qualities have proved identical with those of the native compound. In addition it is more ductile and has more tenacity than pure iron and it is not so liable to rust or oxidise. Possessing such qualities, meteoric iron is certain to become a branch of national industry. A mixture of 98 parts of iron and 2 of nickel has all the peculiarities of best meteoric iron.'

This clear endorsement of the alloy was followed by this very positive report on Inveraray Metal: 'A few years ago an ore or sulphur of nickel, devoid of arsenic, was found in Inveraray, in Scotland, and by its means meteoric iron has been made of the best quality. The mine exists on the estate of his grace the Duke of Argyll, and its produce may be easily converted into meteoric iron at a very small outlay. In no great while hence, nickel and iron will be made together to supply the world with instruments that possess increased strength and a greatly diminished tendency to rust and tarnish. Happy will it be for this district if its manufacturers are the first to extensively use this very desirable compound.'

William Fairbairn had told the Duke that experiments with the new metal could lead to 'important and most satisfactory results'. This was certainly the start of the most productive period in the Coille Bhraghad mine's history. Between 1854 and 1867, more than 400 tons of nickel ore, comprising pyrrhotite, chalcopyrite, pyrite and pentlandite, were produced. Over £1000 a year was spent on development and production continued successfully into the mid 1880s.

Of course, during that time there were fluctuations in demand and price, which both James Robertson and John Cain had to learn to ride. In August 1862, for example, the Swansea smelters wrote to James Robertson to say that, while he might well have had 50 tons of nickel ore ready for shipment, they were sorry to say that 'the nickel trade is very bad and we have large stocks of both ore and refined nickel'. They would therefore be glad not to receive the 50 tons 'just at present'. In June 1864, the Rolling Tube and Wire Mills at Aston Road in Birmingham was seeking to do 'some business in nickel ore', the Swansea company asked for 70 tons in October 1864 and, in March 1865, business continued between Robertson and the Nickel and Cobalt Works at Hafod Isha in Swansea, albeit with occasional errors in invoices. Samples of ore were still required and were sent by steamer to Liverpool to the associated company there. Lewis Thompson continued to seek samples of the ore too – by the 1860s mainly 'as a source of amusement' as he was 'no longer under the necessity of "earning [his] bread"'. He thought there might be gold in the Inveraray deposits and was happy to analyse as little as three ounces of ore in his 'little laboratory'.

Reports in the press in April 1865 – in both *The Daily Telegraph* and *The Mining Journal* – that a rich seam of nickel ore had been found near Inveraray attracted the attention of several mining speculators and nickel refiners. The Duke told Mr Williamson of the Goldenhill Cobalt, Nickel, Colour and Chemical Works that, although the quality of the new vein of nickel had not yet been 'fully ascertained', he had reason to believe it was richer than the old one. He passed Mr Williamson on to the faithful Mr Robertson for samples. Mr Williamson sent £10 for half a ton of nickel ore. By June of 1865, he was looking for more, which suggests it was of a good quality. In December 1865, he asked for five tons of ore from the Ballantyre seam 'before the frost closes the canals'.

This Ballantyre seam, discovered on the boundary of the Achnagoul land to the south-west of Inveraray was also publicised in *The Mechanics Magazine* in April 1865 and, as this was read by a different type of audience, it sparked another round of requests for information and samples. The seam had been uncovered in March of that year when the ridge where it was situated was still filled with snow. A young man, son of McNeill of Ballantyre, had told Robertson and Walton that there was a 'string of ore in a rock near the Achnagoul march'. Walton took the bearings and a measurement for the Duke but, by now, James Robertson had enough experience of mineral mines to know that, while this 'promised well on the surface, . . . how it may turn out when opened up no one can tell'.

The lad who found the ore had not just stumbled upon it. He was a shepherd, had lost his brother in a drowning accident the previous year and had been neglecting his duties with the flock because he had developed 'an extraordinary craze', according to James Robertson, for seeking out metal ore. To some degree, there must have been a bit of mining fever in the area that put the boy up to this. Robertson described him as 'half witted' and said he had dreamed he would find ore in the very burn where it, in fact, was discovered. The place was called 'calves' precipice' and the Duke's memory was jogged on the exact place by its description as a 'granite perpendicular face'.

This find came at an appropriate moment. Samuel Walton's final report on 8 April 1865 announced solemnly, 'I beg to report that all the nickel ore in the Coillivraid (*sic*) Mine which will pay is now worked out and John Forbes, Neil McGougan (*sic*), John McNicol, Robert McKenzie are withdrawn from working in the Mine.' He added that the men – James Munro, Donald Munro, John Livingston, Donald

McCall, John McCallum 'and a boy Duncan Munro' – who were formerly employed at washing ore would now wash and dress the ore stuff brought out of the mine the previous winter. 'When this is finished,' Walton said, 'there will be no more work for them to do at the mine.'

Meanwhile, battling against snow, sleet and rain, Walton and others had been trying to get at the newly found Ballantyre ore. There was a vein divided into two seams, which Walton suggested would 'each emerge six inches thick of good ore from the granite to the east as far as the vein can be seen and the section to the westward is also divided into two seams not far from the same thickness'. This lay near the top of the Ballantyre ridge 'looking towards Loch Fyne, in a northerly direction from Coille Bhraghad'. The McNeill boy, of course, had not been aware of these seams of ore – he was attracted by a lump of ore that Walton believed must have dropped from the top of the vein and that lump suggested to the experienced Samuel Walton that there was no doubt that the vein 'must be large where it came from'. Folk memory, however, may have prompted that dream about the ore. On 5 July 1766, Charles Freebairn the tacksman of the lead mines in Islay and elsewhere, wrote to the Duke of Argyll of the day to say that, having been shown a sample of ore that was said to have been found in the Waters of Aray, he had gone with a miner to the place where it had been found – about three miles from Inveraray, 'near a place called Ballantyre'. Freebairn had examined the bed of the river and found 'two small strings . . .with good lead ore from one quarter to three-quarters of an inch lying in a very hard sort of granite and stretching across the river in the direction of north east and south west'. In the deepest part of the river, the string appeared to be about four inches wide. He described the land as level for 300–400

yards before it rose 'very quickly to nearly 80 fathoms perpendicular to which place if the vein could be traced by open
cast across her course and followed into the hills, she may
possibly form into a workable vein and the ore of the best
quality'. This expedition would no doubt have been accompanied by at least a handful of local people, particularly folk
from Ballantyre itself. The findings may well have lived on
in the stories told around the peat fires of Ballantyre, until a
disturbed lad decided to look for himself 99 years later.

Charles Freebairn found lead. McNeill's find seemed to
suggest nickel, just as the Coille Bhraghad nickel was running out. The analyses made over the next few years suggest
that what was left of the minerals was not worth following
through. By the 1870s, however, it was sulphur, rather than
lead, copper or nickel, which was seen as the 'must-have'
material from mines. As the Industrial Revolution gathered
momentum, sulphur was converted into sulphuric acid for
use in the creation of steel and rubber. It was also used in the
production of inorganic chemicals, matches, fumigants and
glass, explosives, cement and fertilisers. In July 1870, Edward
Stanford of the British Seaweed Company Ltd, manufacturing
chemists based at Whitecrook, Dalmuir, wrote to the Duke
about analysis carried out on Coille Bhraghad nickel ore.
The composition was 27.84 per cent sulphur, 46.60 per cent
iron, no copper, a trace of nickel, 6.56 per cent arsenic and
19 per cent 'insoluble'. He asked the Duke for more samples,
as this analysis seemed to show an 'irregularity in composition'. Knowing the Duke's interest in the science of it all,
he explained that the ore gave off only around 10 per cent
of sulphur, even after very prolonged heating, although he
had continued to the 'point of fusing'. This, he said, would
render it valueless as a source of sulphur.

As a reliable method of isolating sulphur was not discovered until 1887 (although a cruder method was used from 1875), this suggests that some interesting work was being carried out in the Glasgow area that was ahead of its time. Whatever the chemists in Glasgow were looking for, they were still interested in nickel and even copper and all three Inveraray mines – the new Ballantyre seam, good old Coille Bhraghad and even the apparently defunct Craignure – were still limping along into the 1870s. The same metals were to be found in all three mines, according to the Dalmuir analyses, and, while the Coille Bhraghad vein may have been lost, it could no doubt be followed up again. Copper was found where there was no nickel. Both copper and nickel were found in the samples from Ballantyre. As these samples had been taken from outcrops, the supposition was that better quality metals were to be found at lower levels. This could have aided the Dalmuir company enormously. Most sulphur at the time came from Sicily and they had been importing some 1,200 tons of copper pyrites each year from Spain to make vitriol. While the Spanish ore contained around 48 per cent of sulphur compared with between 23 and 31 per cent found in the Inveraray samples, a local source would surely have reduced their costs.

Mining continued into the 1880s and was then revived again in the early 1900s. By then, the chamberlain in Inveraray was Thomas Maclean and he facilitated a visit to what were being described now as 'the old Inveraray mines' by A. Knox Brown of 18 Walbrook, London. Mr Knox Brown had taken samples from Craignure, Coille Bhraghad and Sallachry, to the north-west of Inveraray and probably the site of the Ballantyre findings, in 1902 with 'excellent results'. When he visited Inveraray, he 'found that the old workings . . . had not been opened for twenty-five years'. They were consequently 'now closed at the surface or full of water so that it was impossible to see the ore body'. He had taken samples from the rubbish dump and had found veins of 'rich ore' running from a few inches to six feet in width or so he learned 'from an old man named D. McGougan, 79 years of age and who worked in the mines 50 years ago and again 25 years ago'. At the castle there were papers, plans, reports, accounts and sales figures but he had not been able to examine these without the Duke's permission. With that permission and with analysis of the ore samples, Knox Brown believed that new technologies in the treatment of compound ores, together with the accessibility to Loch Fyne 'where the ore could either be refined or dressed and shipped to the most favourable market' would make these mines pay 'even with low grade ore'.

Knox Brown pursued his interest in the Inveraray mines into September of 1902, when he stayed at the Ferry Inn at Rosneath and communicated with the then Duke of Argyll's chamberlain Alfred Lowis at Rosneath Castle, sending missives back and forth with corrections to a possible lease on the mines. The old story of royalties, ground rents, length of lease and the right to erect machinery were inserted, crossed out and reinserted. More modern (and ambitious) requests to build jetties and to make roads and tramlines were also picked over. All of this was written on the Ferry Inn's notepaper and, perhaps unbeknown to him, read and acted upon by the Duke and not just his chamberlain. John 9th Duke of Argyll had inherited the title just two years previously. He had spent five years as Governor General of Canada from 1878 to 1883, before which he had travelled in the Americas writing travel literature and poetry. He had a brief spell as

Member of Parliament for Argyllshire and he was married to Princess Louise, Queen Victoria's fourth daughter. He was far more interested in the arts than industry and science and, with Knox Brown down the road in the Ferry Inn, he telegrammed the Duchy of Cornwall's office in London for advice on how to proceed with this request to reopen the Inveraray mines.

Walter Peacock at the Duchy of Cornwall's office telegrammed back (and of course, by now, there was no need for this to be sent on in a letter from Glasgow to the castle on the Gare Loch – it would have been delivered by a local postman) to say, 'Any answer must be unsatisfactory as the rents and rates of royalty vary with each particular mine, according to the difficulty and expense likely to be incurred in working and winning the ores and to the special circumstances of each case. In Cornwall generally the average rate of ores is probably ¼th small ores and the dead rents perhaps £20.'

Eleven days later, with A. Knox Brown back in London, lawyers Lindsay Howe and Co wrote to Lowis from Edinburgh to say that the agreement would need 'careful adjusting'. Knox Brown left for Constantinople at the beginning of October, leaving that most modern of communication aids, a telephone number. If he didn't get the lease before he left, the matter would have to go on hold until the following spring. He left the matter in the hands of his own lawyer and Lowis but the changes and counter-changes to the proposed lease led nowhere. Another attempt to mine was made when the Inveraray Mining Company Ltd was incorporated in 1910 but that too was dissolved before 1916 – the timing could not have been worse.

The Inveraray mines may have been remote and there is no doubt that their output could never compare with the thousands of tons of copper and then nickel ore that were produced elsewhere – particularly from parts of the developing British Empire. But these mines made a significant contribution to science, to the industrial revolution, and of course, to the local economy. The dedication of a succession of Inveraray chamberlains, the personal interest of some of the Dukes and the skills of men like Petherick and particularly John Cain put three small mines on the national map. They, of course, could have achieved nothing without the contribution of the men, women and children who worked the Inveraray mines for almost half a century. And, during that half century, the succession of dukes were a plack the richer as a result – and perhaps by considerably more than that very small copper coin known as a plack.

9

The men behind the Islay mines

The history of the Islay lead mines is well documented, not least by R.M. Callender and J. Macaulay in their publication *The Ancient Metal Mines of the Isle of Islay, Argyll.* Callender and Macaulay concentrate on the technicalities of mining in this southernmost of the Western Isles but the history of those who facilitated the industry and those who included the island in their tours of the Hebrides because of the industry is equally fascinating.

Charles Freebairn, whom we last met examining the Ballantyre mine to the south of Inveraray for the Duke of Argyll, spent most of his mining career on Islay. But mining was not Mr Freebairn's original profession – he was, by training, an architect. The son of an Edinburgh French teacher, he did practise his profession for a while in the 1750s. In 1755, he designed a new dining room at Abercairny Castle in Perthshire, home of the Moray family. In 1758, he was commissioned by Robert Hay Drummond to design and build a new library at Innerpeffray. This was to replace the original building – the first free public lending library in Scotland which had been founded in the 1680s by David Drummond 3rd Lord Madertie. This library still stands – a testament to Freebairn, whatever else befell him. He also designed buildings in Cant's Close in Edinburgh and all seemed to be going well for him. He was elected a member of the Royal Company of Archers in 1756 and admitted as a burgess of Edinburgh in 1761. It was then that he became involved in mining – first of all in the Ochil Hills, forming a partnership with James Wright in 1762 to exploit the Logie mines. James Wright was the Laird of Loss and, among his family's extensive properties and interests, there had been quite a history of mining in the Ochils. Freebairn was said to have a technical knowledge of the industry and he invested his own money in this venture – presumably the money he had earned from designing beautiful dining rooms and libraries.

Freebairn's relationship with Wright was at first cordial and Freebairn seems to have been more practically involved – although the partnership in Logie was evidently an equal one – engaging people to work in the mine according to his own plans. The work on the Logie mine lasted for five years, dwindling in success in 1766 and coming to a halt at the end of 1767. By that time, Freebairn was already involved with the mines in Islay. He had written to Wright from Islay in May 1763 about the success of the work there and, in the July of that year, he was invited on the basis of his expertise to examine the Silvercraigs and Inverneill mines on Loch Fyne. He was able to claim in 1764 – perhaps tactlessly as the Logie mine was certainly proving less successful – that the Islay mines 'go better that any other in Scotland except Leadhills'. In 1766, when as we have seen, Freebairn had been consulted by the Duke of Argyll about a potential mine near Inveraray, he was writing that the 'furnace is going here [Islay] and bars mounting in piles like the pyramids in the plain'.

By the early 1770s, he was tacksman of the mines in Islay and was visited there by a succession of 'celebrities'. The

Welsh naturalist and traveller Thomas Pennant recalled in his account of his Scottish tour in 1772 that Mr Freebairn of Freeport showed him around Islay. They visited the mines, of course, and Pennant wrote, 'The ore is of lead, much mixed with copper which occasions expense and trouble in the separation.' He saw that 'the veins rise to the surface, [and] have been worked at intervals for ages'. This was almost an understatement on Pennant's part. While there is no evidence to suggest that the Vikings mined in Islay during their tenure of the island in the latter centuries of the first millennium of the Christian era, they did perhaps profit from it and, in the 16th and 17th centuries, lead mining was already a thriving industry there. Pennant, whose scientific pursuits were wide, had visited Cornwall in the late 1740s. The minerals and fossils he encountered there led to these becoming his main interest during the 1750s. He had opened a mine of his own, based on his geological knowledge, and this was successful enough to finance the small Welsh estate he inherited from his father in 1763 – and, presumably, his travels, too. This mining know-how suggests that we can trust Pennant's judgement, therefore, when he said of the Islay mines, 'The lead-ore is good; the copper yields thirty-three pounds per hundred; and forty ounces of silver from the ton of metal. The lead-ore is smelted in the air-furnace, near Freeport.'

A very different visitor was David Loch, whose expertise was in trade, commerce, manufactures and fisheries – or so his essays based on his tour of Scotland in 1777 suggest. Loch had sailed round the Mull of Kintyre on 28 April of that year and, on Wednesday 29 April, he entered the Sound of Islay, 'abreast of Mr Charles Freebairn's house and lead mines', but could not land because of the strong wind and tides. The next day he was able to visit Freebairn, getting a 'cordial reception' at his house and receiving much information about the 'fisheries and manufactures of this country, and the situation of the coast'. Loch gives an interesting insight into the domestic life of this architect turned mining expert: 'Mr Freebairn, by a prudent choice of a very sensible and frugal woman, has himself and family clothes from the wool of his own sheep. Better cloth, stocking-pieces, and stockings, and indeed, all kinds of woollen goods for the use of the family, need not be wished for, or desired. His worsted, of which he has a good store, of different grists, is equal to any I ever saw for evenness and strength.'

Of course, Loch also inspected the lead mines, which he said were 'succeeding very well', adding that 'the whole of his [Freebairn's] machinery is constructed upon plain, rational principles'. Perhaps not rational enough – or perhaps Freebairn had just come too late to the feast, as the mines had been well worked in relatively modern ways for at least 150 years before his arrival in Islay. And, just like the Duke of Argyll, one of the main issues surrounding the mining activities was the payment of royalties on the minerals to the Crown.

The records of such payments go back a long way. On 22 May 1616, according to the Register of the Privy Council, a patent was passed to Archibald Primrose, Clerk of His Majesty's Taxations, of the copper and lead mines in Islay, Mull, Skye and Lewis. The mines were inspected and, in 1619, Primrose's colleague, James Mowat, wrote to the Laird of Calder (Cawdor) in the Nairn area of north-east Scotland, who was then very interested in the lands of Islay, explaining to him that Crown Duties for the Islay mines would have to be paid. The mines had been examined and Archibald Primrose had returned from the island with a letter declaring that the 'fellow who was in Islay did say little of the lead in

Islay'. Mr Mowat suggested that this fellow was 'a knave'. By August of 1619, Mowat was suggesting to the Laird of Cawdor that there was money to be made from the mines and, in 1626, a report by Thomas Knox, Bishop of the Isles, writing about the state of his diocese, noted that '[t]here are many lead mines here [in Islay]'. The Laird of Cawdor was convinced enough that there was sufficient valuable lead to offer 15,000 merks on 8 October 1620 for a 19-year tack of the island's mines. There were 12 Scots pounds to the English pound. The merk was two thirds of a Scottish pound or 13 shillings and 4 pence. The price paid for this tack was therefore around £1,000. It is difficult to equate this to modern currency but clearly Cawdor was expecting much more than the plack – the four-penny piece – that his fictional contemporary said was his profit from Inveraray's silver mines.

His descendant Sir Hugh Campbell, 15th Thane of Cawdor, was investing in Islay and Jura by the 1670s. He built Islay House around 1677, which was completed by his successor Alexander Campbell. The baillie in the islands (Hugh's uncle, James), reported on stock, horse breeding, lime, timber, iron, whinstone, deer and rabbits, lambs and, of course, the lead ore. Even in the late 17th century, when civil wars were disrupting Scotland, Ireland and England, there were those who wanted to speculate in mining and one John Mackay was bold enough to make an offer to lease the Islay mines on behalf of himself and his partners in 1680. The £1,369 per annum that he offered for the lease in the October of that year was laughed out of court and, instead, a Squire Dobs and his partners made an offer that was preferred. Sir John Campbell, Sir Hugh's cousin, who conducted the interviews, supported Dobs's offer because it concentrated on improving agriculture and 'civilising' the country people. He suggested

that Dobs and his partners be given the tack and that, during
it, they were welcome to 'make the best use they can for their
own behalf of any iron mines, lead ore, copper, brass, or any
other manner of minerals, were it coal or what other ores . . .
which they can find in any places of the island, freely and
without payment of anything therefore, except a discretion,
as they commonly call it'.

On 13 November 1688, the year of the 'glorious revolution', when William and Mary were invited to take on
the throne of these turbulent islands, Sir Hugh resigned the
islands of Islay and Jura to his heir Alexander and his wife
Elizabeth Lort. Sadly, by 1717, after a number of difficult
years not helped by the Union of the Parliaments in 1707,
the Campbells met with financial disaster and had to sell up.
Daniel Campbell of Shawfield, a politician and wealthy merchant, bought Islay for £12,000 and managed to turn around
the economic situation, improving life considerably for the
impoverished islanders. Indeed, these Campbells actually
moved to the island. Daniel set about modernising the island's
agriculture and introduced the flax industry to the island. His
grandson, also named Daniel, succeeded in 1753. This was a
thoroughly modern man, who not only continued his grand-
father's improvements but also introduced a ferry service to
the mainland, built schools and developed both the fishing
and linen industries. By 1772, there were around 700 men
employed in fishing and mining and, at this time, there were
seven lead mines – at Mulrees, Portnealon, Shenegart, North
and South Ardachie, Ballygrant and Gartness – which would
soon be joined by seven more. There was also a copper mine
at Kilslaven. It was during this period that Charles Freebairn
became tacksman and he seems to have helped to create the
wealth that transformed lives in Islay.

It had been slow work to bring about that transformation. An account of mining in Islay between 1720 and 1760, found in the Kildalton charter chest, suggests that a Glasgow company had the lease of the mines from the Laird of Calder and into the early years of the Shawfield ownership of the island. As the tack had almost expired, the company set the miners to washing wastes and slags. There was 'plenty of ore' at that time so the miners 'undertook to deliver them clean washed ore at 20 shillings the bing'. The work was hard and the men were only paid for what they delivered so, without 'regard to rule or order', the men simply broke new ground to get at the ore in less time and with less expense – as Pennant would point out in the 1770s, the ore was close to the surface. This account adds that the best-experienced miners left the country and, soon afterwards, Sir Alexander Murray of Stanhope (from the Strontian mines) took a lease from Shawfield and 'promised to keep a certain number of miners constantly at work and carry on the work in a regular mineral order'. Murray had never visited Islay himself and simply followed his questionable practices from the Strontian mines, letting 'bargains' to the local people who had 'little skill and little encouragement'. This went on for two or three years until Shawfield saw how the island was being abused and ended Sir Alexander Murray's involvement. The next tack went to a man named Hailey and it too went badly, ending in tears with the smelt mill closed down and tools removed. In 1745, the military moved in under Captain William Thyne, who ordered the employment of a dozen skilled men to go out into the hills and glens of both Islay and Jura to make new discoveries. When the rebellion broke out, the Captain and his company were dispatched to England and he wrote to stop this exploratory work. Any ore excavated during that time was sent, in April 1746, to a furnace on Clydeside and the Captain was paid for his investment the rather meagre sum of £51.

Those with good and bad intentions continued to offer their 'expertise' in Islay, each one with an eye on the spoils that mining always promises. Alexander Sherriff was asked for a report on the mines in July 1770. Sherriff was a Leith merchant who had become heavily involved in the Scottish mining industry and had been consulted by the owners of the Ochil Hills mines, which is how Freebairn would have known him. His detailed examination of each of the Islay lead mines and the copper mine was very positive. He reported that, on the whole, the veins showed that, with some investment in machinery and exploration at lower levels, these mines 'might become at length profitable and lasting . . . with considerable profit to the proprietor and undertaker'. This was no Raspe-style blarney — as Callender and Macaulay have pointed out, the Islay mines (at the height of the industry, the 14 Ballygrant lead mines and the Kilslaven copper mine) were possibly Scotland's second most productive location.

Charles Freebairn was the man undertaking the work at the time of Sherriff's report. His own opinion in October 1770 was that, having examined some of the old mine workings, he too found all of them had good ore. He started work on what he saw as one of the 'most promising'. Freebairn continued to be involved in the Islay mines and their success story but, having invested his own money in the Ochil Hills venture, he had to seek funding elsewhere for the Islay project and he had borrowed heavily to buy into that involvement from William Hogg, banker in Edinburgh. Hogg then left Freebairn high and dry, stopping advances, and Freebairn's creditors began knocking on his door. Freebairn now had to explore ways of paying off the creditors. His income came from the mine tack – but that income went straight out again to pay his debts. Between a rock and a hard place, he had to find a way to sell on the tack by way of shares. He was not the first to fail in a mining venture, having boasted very publicly of its success, and he most certainly would not be the last.

The mines were undoubtedly a good investment and Freebairn had spent his borrowed cash on expanding them, building furnaces and houses for the miners. The sum he asked was fair, considering the trouble he had taken to put the work on 'such a respectable and promising footing'. He wrote that 'the mines of Isla (*sic*) enjoy their great advantages over any other mines in this kingdom: first, for mineral soils and multiplicity of veins contiguous to one another, perhaps never heard of in any country, and, according to the nature of metallic veins, as Mr Sherriff observes, will enlarge downward when properly carried on'. He added that 'for the cheapness of working of the lead, there being none in Britain its equal'.

This really does not appear to be an exaggeration. In an extract from the Campbeltown Records in the Kildalton charter chest, the total amount of lead exported from Islay between 2 February 1769 and 3 October 1774 was recorded as 260 tons 1 cwt in bars, 72 tons 6 cwt ore, and 90 tons of slags of lead. Some of this was exported from the island on the *Lady Largy* of Islay which, of course, was a pre-steam vessel. The cost of transporting the Islay ore always made it almost twice as expensive to produce as that from Leadhills but it was a very viable industry that helped to maintain the island's populace when other areas of Argyll saw populations drastically depleted. It may have cost Charles Freebairn dearly but his contribution to the island's fortunes cannot be dismissed. The records suggest that Freebairn died in 1780. A meeting of the creditors of 'the deceased Charles Freebairn, late architect in Edinburgh was called in January 1782. He may have overreached but that was typical of that age of Renaissance men.

The Shawfield family owned the island until 1852. Many improvements, including the construction of model villages and a good infrastructure, had been made by then but, in some ways, the island was a victim of its own success at times in the 19th century. The increasing population – it reached 15,000 in the early 1820s and emigration was offered as a solution – could not be supported even by improved agricultural methods or a healthy mineral mining industry. The laird, in the mid 1800s, had great sympathy for the working man. He scuppered his own finances by trying to instigate a support scheme for the destitute during the potato famine of 1846, investing in a new mining venture. He also asked the Duke of Argyll if employment could be found on the Crinan Canal for Tiree men who had been sent to work on 'destitution roads' in Galloway, where they were not understood because they were Gaelic speakers. Sadly, the mining venture didn't take off and workers had already been laid off from the Crinan Canal. And, just as sadly, this altruistic laird lost out. No one could pay their rents, he had overspent trying to help and he now faced bankruptcy. The Islay estate was sold in 1852 and that included what Callender and Macaulay call 'a cautious reference to "a great variety of minerals"'.

Lead mining in an industrial sense came to an end in Islay in 1880 with the production of 38 tons of lead and 1,214 ounces of silver. The hundreds of 'strings' of lead that can still be found in the island were exposed in the days when the lairds encouraged the crofters to dig up ore for a given price. Naturally, with the lure of payment, the crofters dug haphazard trenches across the 10-mile area of the lead deposits. Callender and Macaulay suggest that there may still be enough ore in Islay to merit more scientific exploration than that which the inexpert crofters exposed. The island has the most visible remains in Argyll and the Isles of a mining industry. The island's other industry, the production of whisky, has roots almost as old as those of the lead mines. After a change in excise laws made distilling a legal possibility, the pure peaty waters of this beautiful island have produced some of Scotland best spirits and the distilleries and mine remains only serve to enhance the enthralling history of Islay.

10

Lochaline and Strontian –
mines for the future

There is, as we have seen, gold in these Argyll hills. To date, that most revered of metals has made no one a fortune, although it is more likely to happen today than ever before. Today, Tyndrum officially stands in the local authority area of Stirling but the village was historically part of Argyll and it deserves a place in the story of our mining past – if for no other reason than that experienced miners were sought from Tyndrum to work in both the Inveraray and Strontian mines. Like the island of Islay, Tyndrum has a very long mining history dating back six centuries. As long ago as 1424, James I of Scotland received silver from the Tyndrum mines.

Sir Robert Clifton, 5th Baronet Clifton from Nottinghamshire, may seem an unlikely candidate to take on a lease of mineral mines on the edge of Rannoch Moor. This gentleman had been imprisoned during the first Jacobite uprising, was imprisoned again for debt and seems to have been as much an adventurer as many of the other speculators of his era. The Earl of Breadalbane, the Duke of Argyll's cousin, leased him the Tyndrum mining rights for 38 years in 1730. Some eleven years later a rich lead mine was found and Clifton had this

worked until 1745 when his debts caught up with him and he
was back in prison. He had to surrender the lease, which was
taken on by the Company of Mine Adventurers of England
– a name that might have set alarm bells ringing, but Clifton's
record was worse in Breadalbane's eyes. Correspondence in
the Earl's estate papers for 1746 suggests that the devil with
some amount of mining knowledge was better than the devil
who lands himself in debt: 'I am sure it will be upon the
whole more beneficial and much safer to do with a known
reputable company than with people who upon trial may be
perhaps too late found unequal to the undertaking.'

The company had a history of mining in England and they
worked Tyndrum until 1760. The pattern then follows that
which is found throughout the mines of Argyll – and no
doubt of all Scotland – with small companies dabbling for
short periods and then walking away to leave the way open
for other 'adventurers'. The Scots Mining Company took on
the lease from 1768 to 1790 and their records suggest the old
story for all remote Argyll mines – the transport costs were
higher than the lead was worth. Surprisingly, it was Clifton
who left his mark on the area – the row of miners' cottages
on the other side of the main A82 opposite the Green Welly
service station is, to this day, known as Clifton.

In the 21st century, Tyndrum is a busy tourist hub on a
main Highland artery. Modern hillwalkers and climbers in
their thermal outfits and kitted out with safety equipment
may revel in the challenges of the wind- and snow-swept
mountains but imagine the hardships endured by miners
working the main vein on the northern slope of Sron nan
Colan, where ten levels were driven into the hillside. Some
work was opencast and, if bargains were made with the
miners, it is easy to envisage men seeking to work in dark but

sheltered tunnels rather than on the inhospitable open hill-side. Those who enjoy hillwalking in the area today mingle with the ghosts of men who didn't even wear a hard helmet or steel-toed boots, let alone clothes suited to the biting wind that can whip across these hills.

Just as we have seen in other areas of Argyll, these mines were almost abandoned until the middle of the 19th century, when the then Marquis of Breadalbane picked up the threads and had the mines worked until 1862, the year of his death. During the First World War, Tyndrum Lead and Zinc Mines Ltd took a lease and worked some of the old mines. They also revisited the old spoil heaps but moved out in 1926 when the country's economic situation was in a parlous state. Mining for lead, silver and gold continued at various times in the 20th century and a dressing plant was built after the Second World War. None achieved the success they no doubt hoped for.

Today, the goldmine above Cononish Farm south-west of Tyndrum depends on the fluctuations of the market. Work there began in the 1980s but the project was closed because of the low price of gold. In 2011, the mine was reactivated and there were plans to employ more than 50 people and extract quantities of both gold and silver that would generate an estimated £80 million for the Scottish economy. The Australian-based mining company, Scotgold, which invested in the project, has a licence to prospect for gold in an area covering more than 4,000 square kilometres of the Highlands and, at the end of 2016, it sold its first gold in the form of 11 commemorative coins, raising almost £46,000 that will help fund the ongoing project.

Like Tyndrum, the mines of Strontian were always on the outer fringes of Argyll and today are part of the majestically mountainous district of Lochaber. As part of Argyll's mining history, however, the Strontian mines perhaps best illustrate the hopes and hardships experienced by this industry over the centuries. When Alexander Bruce drew up that 'Plan of Loch Sunart &ct: become famous by the greatest national improvement this age has produced' in 1733, it may have been a marketing ploy but it was a document filled with enthusiasm and hope for a bright future. The drawings show an industry already up and running but hindsight informs us of the many and varied difficulties that had to be overcome before Bruce's 'greatest national improvement' of the age could ever have been achieved. The identification of strontium and its significance could not have been foreseen by Bruce or by Sir Alexander Murray who commissioned the great plan and certainly not by the miners who risked their lives in the dangerous tunnels of the old lead mines.

Scientist Adair Crawford recognised, in 1790, that this new mineral (strontianite) was different from other barium minerals. Humphry Davy completed the task in 1808 when he isolated strontium through electrolysis. It was not, of course, a discovery that led to instant prosperity. Identifying a mineral is one thing; knowing what to do with it is another – Mr Petherick ignoring the nickel at Craignure is a case in point. In the second half of the 19th century, a few hundred tons of lead ore were produced each year until the crash of the lead price in the 1870s. As in so many of the other Argyll mines, interest was rekindled at the start of the 20th century but a 1901 attempt to reopen the Bellsgrove failed before any ore was excavated.

A company named Consolidated Goldfields identified a large deposit of barite and deposits of zinc in the Strontian area in the 1960s. Barite, it was explained, became an essential element for drilling in the new North Sea oil industry in the next decade and a company known as Minworth Ltd developed three opencast sites and a drift between Whitesmith and Bellsgrove mines. As we have seen, it would have made the old Argyll mines so much more profitable had they been able to process ore on site and, in the 1980s, this was Minworth's strategy. The dumps that can be seen from Strontian to Polloch date from the 1980s and the remains of the old Bellsgrove and Middleshop mines were subsumed under the workings of this new industry. But, as with so many previous operations, Minworth also went bankrupt in 1990. Barite is still quarried, however, by a local company.

The mines are no longer active but the area attracts a great many geologists every year and the Steetley Minerals organisation has 're-invented' the location for mineralogists. What would the miners make of the place? The industrial past is belied by Strontian's beautiful setting on Loch Sunart, the local nature reserve, a centre for sailing and hillwalking and the arts and crafts produced and sold in and around the village – but of course, the history of the mines and the very name 'Strontian' are allure enough for many. Perhaps the 'greatest national improvement' of this age has been tourism but, in the same way that we respect the otters and the oakwoods, let us respect the memories of the miners on whose broad backs the hopes for a Highland industry were laden.

The Morvern peninsula reverses the history of mining in Argyll. Never an area of great production, either of lead or low quality coal, the Lochaline silica mine is the big success story of the 21st century. Its product could not provide a greater contrast to that of the lead mines of the past. The chemists of the 1800s spoke of 'meteoric' iron because of a belief that it had come from outside our atmosphere. When Jim Blair of the Lochaber Geopark weighed down my upturned hands with that small lump of lead, I would not have been surprised to be told that it had fallen from a dark planet. When I was privileged to visit the Lochaline mine, the mounds of silica outside the tunnels waiting for transportation felt like the finest silk. Softer and whiter than snow, it has an ethereal quality that is echoed in the mine's labyrinthine tunnels. Of course it is as pitch black underground as in any coal, lead or copper mine. But switch on a head torch and the pristine caverns are more like heaven than the hell of the coal seam. That is not to say the production of Lochaline silica – said to be one of the finest sources in the world – is in any way easy and there have been tragedies as well as triumphs.

This pure white sand was, some 65 million years ago, at the bottom of a clean, clear, shallow sea. When the volcanoes on what today is the island of Mull erupted 60 million years ago, the lava flood covered that sand like a pressure cooker lid. The weight compacted the sand and then acted as a protective cover. There is still a loch underground that contains water as old as the stone itself. Coal was also compacted by that volcanic eruption – something that R.E. Raspe got right when he identified coal in Morvern and Mull, correcting what had previously been thought in the 18th century that such lava flows would destroy rather than protect the minerals it covered.

Interest in Morvern's mining ventures was rekindled in September 1911 when a gentleman named Thorneycroft wrote to the Ardtornish Estate asking for a trial lease of an area where coal might be found. The letter, written from 65 Renfield Street in Glasgow to J. Craig Sellar, said that a recent report by the Geological Survey Department had shown that the outcrop of coal at Inninmore Bay was 'somewhat larger' than had traditionally been imagined. Mr Thorneycroft had 'met one of the staff of the Department while yachting round the coast' in 1910 and now he believed it would be of great scientific interest to locate and measure this seam (and presumably of great pecuniary interest to Mr Thorneycroft, too). His letter was by way of a request to sink a bore at his own expense with the help of 'some friends' and stated that he would 'give the department the benefit of all information derived therefrom'. The real intention came in the next part of the letter, which said, '[O]f course if anything of commercial value were found we should expect to have the right to work it subject to royalty payable to you in the ordinary way.' A plan was enclosed, with an assurance that '[e]ven assuming that workable minerals are found, which is not very likely, I am of the opinion that the sporting rights and the amenity of your property would not be damaged. The boring operations would certainly do no harm.'

These outcrops of coal had, of course, been worked open cast in the previous century without much success and, rather than the black stuff, it was the white stuff that had already proved more important – and would become still more important to the area and to the country. White sandstone had been used in the area historically for gravestones and in chapels. It had been quarried during the 19th century and exported elsewhere – some of the Crinan Canal's locks were constructed from it and it was used in the building of Lismore lighthouse. According to Mary Barnes' account of the mine for Morvern Heritage Society, it had been known that this white sandstone was of a fine enough quality for glassmaking but the old problem of transport upped the cost of it and imports from elsewhere made it the less attractive option.

War, however, changes everything. Just as kelp ash became the must-have commodity from the Hebrides during the Napoleonic Wars when imports from Spain to make glass became scarce, so Lochaline silica became an attractive option when the blockades of the Second World War prevented foreign imports. With the Admiralty crying out for navigational aids and binoculars, Owen Hugh Smith, then owner of the Ardtornish Estate, raised the possibility of using the high quality silica to be found on his estate. This silica had first been identified in 1895, when an 18-foot seam was reported on the Lochaline shore. Later, in 1923, the Edinburgh Geological Survey did an analysis of a Lochaline sand sample. It proved to be one of the purest deposits in the world, largely free from iron and therefore ideal for the production of high-quality glass. As it happened, it turned out to be of a superior quality to the foreign imports that were no longer available when World War II broke out and therefore well worth the investment in a mining venture. Charles Tennants (London) leased the mineral rights from the estate and Charles Tennants (Glasgow) managed production. While plant was installed, the United Glass Bottle Manufacturers Ltd supplied untreated sandstone and the next essential was to find workers in a village of 60 inhabitants.

The government was making decisions on the hoof about which industries to prioritise, and the Ballachulish slate quarries were not ranked as essential to the war effort. Charles Tennants (Glasgow) owned the quarries and their manager, Donald Noel Paton, was deployed to Lochaline in 1940 to manage this essential silica mine. At first, he took a quarry foreman and ten workers with him but, in time, there were 18 Ballachulish men lodging in Lochaline. Huts bought from a roadworks company at Strontian were then converted into a dormitory and the White House, once the village poor house, was turned into a canteen with living space for the catering staff.

Work began in July 1940 to open up the cliff face and, by September, the puffer *Lascar* was loaded with silica. The next month, the workforce rose to 40, including some coalminers deployed by the Ministry of Labour. The history of mining in Argyll has shown that men from different industries and with different skills don't always gel as a team but the Oban branch of the National Union of General and Municipal Workers, according to Mary Barnes, managed to settle disputes. By the end of 1940, 300 tons of silica were being produced each week and the plant at the site was developed. MacBrayne's, the ferry company, and Coast Lines Ltd got together to install the plant at the west pier and tramp ships requisitioned by the War Office shipped the sand. Captured German cargo provided the railway lines from the mine to the pier but, in turn, the Germans were making submarine attacks on UK shipping and so the transport of explosives for the mine was dangerous. Vaughan Russell, managing director of Charles Tennants (Glasgow), bought a cabin cruiser to do the job and for ten years, the *Nivag* brought explosives from Oban.

By July 1941, with the help of a lot of new machinery and a conveyor belt, Lochaline was providing all the silica needed by the country for optical glassmaking and domestic glassware. Barr and Stroud of Glasgow used Lochaline silica sand throughout the Second World War to make binocular and periscope lenses. At first, the 19th-century miners of Strontian and Inveraray would have felt quite at home in the mine. The sandstone was taken out at first in wheelbarrows, then by horse and cart. The only ventilation was natural air. There were rockfalls and water in the tunnels caused the same problems that had been experienced in every Argyll mine, whatever its product, throughout the centuries. Eventually it was a diesel 'puggy' that pulled the wagons inside the mine and to and from the processing plant at the pier. In 1942, a powerhouse was built that took electricity (and a ventilation system) into the mine.

There was a team of around 30 men working at the mine throughout the war, all of them living in the dormitory hut. Another hut was used for dances and concerts and the whole village came to these events. The Tennants took over the local hotel, which was 'dry'. The temperance movement that had begun in Scotland in 1830, to the delight and relief of mining managers and consultants like Petherick and Cain, left many towns in Scotland alcohol free until the 1970s and many individual hotels chose to be classed as 'temperance', even though the movement was seen as increasingly irrelevant. Certainly, during World War II, the government did not impose the same bans on alcohol as had rather ineffectually been in place in the First World War. Now Donald Noel Paton (who continued to manage the mine until 1962) went to live in this 'dry' hotel.

The Admiralty acknowledged the contribution of the Lochaline mine to the war effort. Production rose from 15,600 tons a year in 1940 to 35,000 tons a year at the end of the war. That production would rise to 52,000 tons between 1946 and 1949 but, by then, foreign competitors were back in business and able to compete with the Lochaline mine. Quality and production had to be improved at Lochaline – and while the quality of the sand was unquestionable, the production methods and the workers' conditions had to be improved. Who outwith war conditions, for example, would continue to work there if bunking with 29 other men were to be the long-term accommodation? The local council and the

Ministry of Works built 25 temporary houses and followed through with 36 permanent dwellings, still there today. The ventilation system had to be improved when two workers contracted the lung disease pneumoconiosis – a beautiful product does not ensure perfect working conditions.

When the Edinburgh mining engineering company John and G.H. Geddes made an initial report on Lochaline white sandstone in July 1940, they suggested that '[i]f the crushing plant be properly screened and storage bins covered, we see no reason why this should be unduly disturbed, or nuisance caused by wind-borne silica dust, except when a strong N.E. wind in dry weather prevails'. They drew attention to the Coal Mines General Regulations for the working of gan-ister (rock used in furnaces) or material containing not less that 80 per cent of silica, pointing out that 'these rules lay down the conditions of working so as to minimise the effects of harmful dust'. There was also a compulsory insurance scheme that had to be adhered to in the working of a silica sand mine or quarry against workers developing silicosis. 'All sandstone mine and quarry owners have to contribute so much to the central fund which then pays out compensation as it is required,' the Geddes report stressed. Lack of safety equipment for the men working in the mines meant that these schemes became an issue of closing the stable door after the horse had bolted.

The post-war era was troubled. Ballachulish workers went back to the slate quarries and those who had been deployed in the mine from other areas on the orders of the govern-ment also went home – just as the troops did. Because of the competition, the management was trying to keep costs low and that meant low wages. Unofficial strikes in 1953 closed the mine but a new workforce comprising former employees and Irish miners took the mine forward. Working conditions were part of the deal and that included providing a social club with a licence so that the men didn't have to travel 18 miles to the nearest pub. The management was struggling to survive, replacing lost contracts with one that would provide lower quality sand for Colgate Palmolive's scouring powders, such as Ajax. A fire is never fortuitous but, when the compressor house was destroyed by fire in November 1953, it did mean that more efficient generators and a new compressor had to be installed which improved productivity. A range of new equipment pushed production capacity up to 65,000 tons a year. By 1957, Lochaline sand was being used in the nuclear power industry and, by the 1960s, the Colgate contract was asking for 45,000 tons a year, allowing Donald Noel Paton to retire in 1962 with the mine making a huge contribution not only to the local but the national economy.

A subsidiary of Charles Tennants (Glasgow) took over in 1962. Tennant Loch Aline Ltd moved with the times in terms of technology and when Tilcon took over the lease in 1972, further investment meant that not only the mine but also the village itself could expand. There were now 70 houses and a population of 250. There were children in the village and a new road made life easier than it had ever been in history. Throughout the 1980s and '90s, production increased with the modernisation of the plant. Tarmac took over in 2001 and, with a smaller workforce, the output was maintained at around 100,000 tons, mainly sold to make glassware in the UK and abrasives in Norway. It was the economic downturn in 2008 that led to the closure of the mine and the loss of the remaining 11 jobs.

But this is where the story of Argyll's mines is reversed. Instead of the death of an industry, in June 2011, Lochaline

Quartz Sand Ltd, the name of a new joint venture involving the Italian-based company Minerali Industriali and NSG/Pilkington, came into being and, on Friday 14 September 2012, Lochaline Sand Mine was officially re-opened by the local MSP. Today, the mine's main product is a high-quality silica sand with low iron content and exceptional whiteness that is unique among UK sand sources. Known in the trade as 'Low Iron Sand', it is used in the production of high-quality flint glass and has other uses in which a consistent white colour and low iron content are required. The new company has also developed an additional sand grade with the iron content controlled at a slightly higher level. This high-purity silica sand is used in clear glass production. The layer of white sandstone that is currently being worked at the mine is up to 40 feet thick. The mine itself is the only underground silica sand mine in the UK (other sand sources use a quarrying method) and a 'room and pillar' system is used – pillars of the sandstone are left in place to hold the roof. The sandstone is drilled and blasted, loaded into dump trucks and taken to the surface plant, where it is crushed, washed, screened, scrubbed and spiralled to remove impurities. Most of the sand is transported by ship from a special pier. To reduce the moisture, the sand is stocked under cover and there is a drainage and pump system in place. This is one of the major improvements that the old Inveraray mine managements would have been glad to tap into. The number of letters written by and to James Robertson, the Inveraray chamberlain in the mid 19th century, complaining that the weight of the ore was not as stated on the invoice because of the additional moisture or the loss of moisture en route to Liverpool, Swansea or Birmingham, reminds us that this was one of mining's major problems before technology could offer a solution, as it has today at Lochaline.

Records of the 17th-, 18th- and 19th-century mines of Argyll come to us down the centuries from the pens of those in charge. From the Dukes of Argyll and their privileged associates, through the ranks of the chamberlains and men who managed the mines and kept the day books, it was only when something went very drastically wrong – such as that court case heard in Mull about the fatality in the Strontian mine – that we hear the voices of the men who bore the burden of the work. Film-maker Jan Nimmo has given us an opportunity to hear from those who worked in the coal mines of Kintyre, and Veronique Walraven, who now works at Lochaline Quartz Sand Ltd, made a film to commemorate the re-opening of the mine with Ansgar Hoeckh and Kenn Musso that gives a voice to those who worked in the silica mine.

There are still people living in the Lochaline community whose memories are a far richer source of history than the dry reports of managers and mineralogists. Men like Alistair Scoular, who is now in his early 90s, and George King, born in 1947 and, like Alistair, rooted in Lochaline because of his parents' wartime past, conserve between them a wealth of social history. Alistair's parents were originally from Lochaline but had moved to Loch Etive. He went to Oban High School, cycling six miles to catch a train from Ballachulish. When his grandmother fell ill, the family moved back to Lochaline in 1945 as the war ended. His parents ran the Lochaline Hotel where Donald Noel Paton stayed. Alistair remembered Paton coming out of the hotel 'in his dressing gown and slippers to see why the men had not started work at 8 a.m.'. With a wry smile he added, 'He was dedicated to work.' The men he expected to see at work were bedded down in the long wooden hut next to the White House, where the meals for the men were made. Alistair said there were 40 men in the hut, while 10 men were living locally.

The mine remained a restricted area and people over the age of 18 had to carry a green passport with their photograph. There were, of course, no photographs taken in or around the mine during the war years. Alistair was called up to do his national service – the compulsory three-years' service in one of the UK armed forces that lasted from 1939 to 1960 – just after the family moved back to Morvern. When he returned in 1948, he ran a taxi business for a couple of years until, as he explained, 'people started buying cars, so locally there was no place to work except the mine'. That's where Alistair went to work from 1951 until 1958. The work, he said, was with a pick and shovel in his earliest days at the mine and the sand was conveyed by horse and cart to the quay. When blasting was carried out, the sand blasted 'half way across the water'. This job was usually carried out at the end of the afternoon shift, allowing the sand to settle before the next workers went into the tunnel.

Alistair had been conscripted into the Royal Mechanical Engineers and so he had hoped to work as a mechanic in the mine. When there were no jobs in that field, he was sent underground for four years. He recalled, 'I hated underground. It was black and dismal and I kept inhaling diesel smoke.' He became the spare 'pug' driver – driving the 'wee diesel machines that carried the sand up to the entrance of the mine'. Alistair did most of that driving inside the underground tunnels so, when he got the odd shift driving the pug to the pier, he remembered that 'it was great when I got out into the fresh air'. He also took a turn at drilling with compressed air drills and working the scraper – the big bucket-like machine that tipped the sandstone into the trucks that were then driven out on wagons by the pug up an incline of 45 degrees. Alistair said, 'My final job inside was driving the eight haulage wagons. The empty ones came back from the pier and the full ones were pulled back up again. Every second Sunday, you had to clean out the pug's smoke box.' His prayers were answered when he got an outside job. The warnings that the mining safety codes had to be adhered to and insurance taken out against men suffering from lung disease was very far from 'health and safety gone mad' as some today would suggest. The Ballachulish men seemed particularly prone to silicosis and Alistair Scoular confirmed that the 'ventilation was very bad' in those days. The men were sent to Oban for X-rays and that threat of the dust clogging up their lungs was horribly real. Alistair said, 'Nobody enjoyed it but it was the only local work.'

No wonder there was a call for a social club with alcohol. Alistair said that when the club opened in 1954, the men were allowed two bottles of beer each and no spirits. He claimed that, as a founder member, he had the first drink. In the 1950s, the men used to sail by ferry to Craignure on Mull because the boat sold the very powerful Carlsberg Special (not available in either Lochaline or on Mull itself) from the top shelf. However, the temperance ethic was still strong – the only whisky to be found in most homes was opened at New Year, which of course was still the mid-winter holiday, and people worked on Christmas Day.

The strike of 1953 caused fairly major problems for the company and for the workers. It took place just before the coronation of Queen Elizabeth in the June of that year. Alistair said that while no one was dismissed, two or three workers left for jobs elsewhere. Three Irish workers were brought in from Tipperary and two of them married local girls. Alistair said that workers with particular skills were often brought in from elsewhere, especially in the 1960s and early 1970s when there was expansion and 60 people were employed. Those like George King who grew up in the area were given apprenticeships. Alda Grace, a local woman who married one of the miners, said that for the specialised jobs men were sent away to train (at last, the ideas of Petherick and Cain were being put into action to train local men for the work). But of course, with mechanisation, Alistair recalled, 'the numbers went down'. He explained that the plant that crushed the sandstone had at first been at the West Pier. 'In 1974 it moved here [to the mouth of the mine] and that reduced the number of jobs. The pug driver was done away with.'

There was only one fatal accident at the Lochaline mine and it remains an emotional wound in this small community. Today, every health and safety measure required of a modern mine is in place, as I witnessed during my visit into the tunnels and around the external plant. But, in the first decades of the mine's operation, there were no such measures to enforce. There are photographs of men holding lighted cigarettes in confined spaces where explosives were being planted for blasting. Hard hats and appropriate boots were as absent as they were in the Bellsgrove mine when Duncan Cameron lost his life to a rockfall and at Drumlemble when young John McGechie died under a roof collapse. Veronique Walraven said the records show no water was used to dull the effects of the fine dust, and blasting, rather than today's drilling, was the accepted method of producing the white sandstone rock.

In Veronique's documentary, former miner Cubby Ives said, 'We were living over on the other side of the loch and we would hear the whistle – they were blowing the whistle after all the men came out at five o'clock and to begin with you would see them lighting the fuse and see the fuse going up into the hole and then there would be the blast and the debris was blown half way across the loch. But that gradually stopped. The deeper they went, the less effect on the people outside. They always made sure everybody was out before the blast and they always blew this whistle before they set them [the fuses] off.'

In the mornings after such a blast, the men, according to pug driver Neil Mackechnie, 'just had to go ahead and hike [their] way through the smog from the diesel engines. There was no purification at all with them. That was life then. Health and safety? There wasn't any.' Not only was there the smog created by the diesel engines but also the soft drift of dust from the previous evening's explosion. And, as the whole point of the exercise was to loosen the rock, it was perhaps little wonder that one rock above the main entrance would become unstable. At a meeting I had in 2017 with of a number of the Lochaline residents who have personal recollections of the past workings of the mine, the memory of the vibration felt throughout the area was still vivid. Alistair Scoular said that when blasting took place on Sunday evenings, a tremor could be felt during the church service. After a blast, the main remainder was sand but there would be big lumps of rock too and these would go through one of the two big crushers. The situation in which a miner named Gerry Ryan died was an accident that seems inconceivable today. George King explained that it had been a very frosty night and, on the morning of the accident, the rock above the entrance to the tunnel was loosened. Gerry, 'just a young man', according to George, went up a ladder to clear the loosened material. The rock fell on the ladder and Gerry was crushed to death. Alistair Scoular's recollection was that

Gerry thought that only a small amount of the debris had to be cleared but 'a much larger part came down'. In trying to make the area safer for his colleagues, Gerry lost his life.

Alda, Alistair and George agreed that, in the early days, no boots or hard hats were supplied and George King said that, later, the only safety equipment offered was Welly boots and a hard hat. While masks and earmuffs are regulation issue today, they hadn't even been considered when these people were youngsters. Yet Alda said there was enough awareness of the dangers that the doctor thought even the women could be susceptible to pneumoconiosis because they were washing the men's work clothes impregnated with the silica dust. The men worked a long shift, from 8 a.m. to 5.30 p.m., with three-quarters of an hour for lunch. The lights went out ten minutes before blasting at the end of the shift to let people know they should be leaving.

Alda Grace, whose late husband Patrick was one of the three men who came from Ireland to work in the mine, was brought up in the area, living at Ardtornish. Transport in the early years of the mine was Shanks's pony or a cycle if one could be afforded. Alda met Patrick at a dance in Kinlochaline hall below the castle. There were also dances at Lochaline. Michael Quigley, another of the Irish miners, married a local girl, too. The social life in the early years was very lively. There was a dance every fortnight with 'very good local musicians', according to Alda, George and Alistair. There was also film once a week, with two showings because of the number of people who came – far better service than that provided today. The Screen Machine (the Highlands and Islands mobile cinema) visits just once every six weeks these days. Most of the Ballachulish men were over 40 and married, so when a younger man came from the islands or from Ireland he was very welcome. Most lived in what were known as 'the cubicles' – the building erected in 1946 that today is the Scout hut. In those days, there was a sitting room and the men all ate in the White House. Alistair Scoular said the men were given 2s 6d a week to help with their accommodation if they had to stay in lodgings away from the 18 'cubicles' but the quality of the food in the White House was 'the very best', with venison and rabbit featuring on the menu regularly and vegetables grown locally by Tommy McCrone especially for the canteen. Tommy's wife Pat had moved to Lochaline as cook in the White House after being invalided out of the ATS at end of war. The men were very well looked after during the war and that continued long after the war was over, with cooks Chrissie Cameron and Anne Brown making the most of the ingredients available. Over the years, a number of girls came from the islands to cook at the canteen and some married locally, such as the Uist girl who married the Mull man who worked in the mine.

Since the re-opening in 2012, the mine has seen only improvements. The villagers of Lochaline are determined the place will not only survive but flourish. When the mine closed in 2008 with a loss of eleven jobs, it was devastating. Local resident Kathleen Cruikshank said in Veronique Walraven's documentary that 'in a small place like this, the mine was really the focus of work and employment'. In the 1970s, the number of people working in the mine pushed the school figures up to over 70 children. Since then, three schools on the peninsula have been amalgamated and now there are just 17 children at the Lochaline school. Its future is secure because it would be too far to travel to the nearest school elsewhere but, as Alda Grace explained, 'If the school goes down to one teacher, it puts people off coming.' But, on the positive side, at the time of writing, there are 18 jobs at the mine and mine manager Diego Zurolo is positive about the future for the apprentices who are training there. There are careers to be had that weren't even thought of when the Ministry of Defence decided it would be a good idea to start excavating this high-quality sand in 1940 – let alone when men were mining throughout Argyll in the 18th and 19th centuries. Such careers include that of Ian MacLean, a former fish farmer, who studied for an HND in chemistry and trained for work in the Lochaline mine's laboratory. It is his job to make the kind of tests that the Duke of Argyll's chamberlain James Robertson would have given his eyeteeth for – ensuring the moisture content of the sand. Mechanisation, chemistry, health and safety – these are life changers for an industry that is keeping a village alive.

Like Strontian, Inveraray, and the Kintyre peninsula, Lochaline has a stunning beauty that should make tourism a major industry alongside this modern and prospering mine. Perhaps, when the mine museum planned by Lochaline Quartz Sand Ltd, Lochaber Geopark and Morvern Heritage Society is up and running, the visitors will come as they do to Strontian and Campbeltown to learn about the past and, in Lochaline's case, explore the present. The accidents of geology that have given Argyll the mineral deposits that have shaped our landscapes and our social history are part of our rich heritage – and part of our future.

Epilogue

Neil Munro's fictional Marquis of Argyll said the 'damned silver mines' on his patch made him not a plack the richer. A plack was worth four pence in 16th-century Scotland and, while many of those who invested in Argyll's mining ventures made considerably more than this paltry little silver coin, the odds were always going to be stacked against the county becoming part of the real industrial revolution.

In earlier centuries, the playing field was more equitable. Argyll's remotest spots were reached by boat but, then, that was also the situation for those who lived in political or industrial centres. Canals were built in the 18th and early 19th centuries to link burgeoning industry with its raw materials. Almost before they were completed, these were overtaken by the age of steam, which brought with it the magic of the railways. Argyll's Crinan Canal was criticised in the planning for being too wide but, before this safe route to the islands and the fishing grounds was opened, it was seen to be too small for the new steam boats that took to the water in 1812.

Such progress put Argyll's mines at a disadvantage in that copper could be brought from the new world more cheaply and almost more speedily than it could be transported from a mine in Morvern. The discovery of a mineral unique to Inveraray may have contributed hugely to the development of lightweight ships, reliable rail tracks and manoeuvrable weaponry but manufacturers sought alternatives when its extraction and transportation added too much cost to the end product to make it a viable proposition.

The quality of the ores mined in Argyll wasn't always competitive. When it was, the ores seem to have been discovered ahead of their time. Raking through the spoils of lead mines to recover the copper and then the copper spoils to recover the nickel could never have been cost-effective. When the planets aligned and the demand was there for the right ore at the right time, the labour and transport costs put even top-quality raw materials at a disadvantage.

The weather would always be against mining ventures until modern equipment could be employed to keep underground conditions safe and dry. Argyll is a very green and very pleasant land but it is green and lush because the rainfall is so high. Tourists in the 21st century are rightly in awe of the cataracts cascading down our mountains. Those cascades put 18th- and 19th-century miners at risk – not only could they lose wages because rain stopped play, they could also lose their lives if flash floods swept through underground tunnels. The county's geology is fascinating but it never helped in the development of any industry ahead of modern rock-cutting machinery. The men who could only get through seven yards of hard granite in as many weeks were working miracles with their picks, shovels and primitive gunpowder. And, so often, they had to climb steep hillsides to reach their workplaces – as at the copper mine on the Malcolm estate visited by both Petherick and Raspe. Today, the remains of one of the mine buildings sit alongside a spoil heap overgrown with moss and overlaid with fallen trees from a recent forestry venture. From the outskirts of Kilmartin village, the climb to this building takes you high enough to look westward at the level of the Jura snowline. To reach the two adits to the mine itself is a rough scramble up a steep incline – an exhilarating walk for today's visitors to Mid Argyll but, for the miners, an exhausting trek before starting a 10-hour shift.

We must not forget the successes but these were usually wrought because a landowner such as the Duke of Argyll had a financial and, perhaps a scientific, interest in developing a mining project. There could be little stability of investment, however, if the death of a duke passionate about developing the resources of the estates gave way to a duke who preferred to squander the proceeds of his properties – or even one whose time was taken up with politics and didn't make local industry a priority.

The unfortunate development of company law in the mid 19th century did the Argyll mining industry no favours, opening up, as it did, the possibilities for fly-by-night companies to make a fast buck by selling shares in uncertain mining ventures to an emerging middle class looking for apparently fail-safe investment opportunities. These adventurers could wreck a previously functional mine then disappear leaving both landowner and investor high and dry.

The real professionals who did develop mines to the best of their ability were not, however, impressed by local labour and communities, in the main, did not flourish because copper or nickel was discovered in the vicinity. The itinerant miners who learned their skills in the Leadhills, Cornwall, Cumberland, Northumberland or Ireland were the ones who made the money (unimpressive though the wages or 'bargains' sound to our ears) while the local workers – men, women and children – were given the most menial of tasks. Only in the Kintyre coalmines, Strontian and, eventually, the silica mine in Morvern was local labour either trained or paid well. Even then, we learn of the Strontian men needing to go home to tend their crofts. The land came first for the Argyll men.

Our main industries today are forestry and tourism and, in the forests, the paths and cycle tracks take us for pleasure to places where miners struggled for survival. The views over lochs and mountains are superb when we have time to stop and stare. A ten-mile hike is exhilarating when we don't then have to put in a ten-hour shift underground hewing rock or copper ore. The silica mine at Lochaline is a success story and it has been developed in such a way that the picture-postcard village is not marred by the scars of industry. The history of the mining industry in Argyll is part of our rich heritage. By some miracle, it enriches our story but doesn't detract from the scenic beauty we offer as part of our 21st century industry.

Acknowledgements

The research for this book has been fascinating but never simple. Many records about mining in Argyll are often, like Sir Winston Churchill's unwillingness to comment on Russia's plans in 1939, a 'riddle wrapped in a mystery, inside an enigma'. The correspondence and figures are often to be found wrapped in the minutiae of other records and labelled far more generally than 'mining'.

It was therefore a complete joy to meet Alison Diamond, who has taken over as archivist at the Argyll Estates in Inveraray. Alison went far beyond the call of duty to track down references, bundles and boxes in which the most intriguing information about mines on the Argyll Estates was revealed. Her patience and continued enthusiasm were sustained over many months and I hope she won't run for cover when next I contact her. Alison has a team of volunteers at the Inveraray archives and I am most grateful to that 'Tuesday Gang' who contributed hugely valuable nuggets (and, in the case of Linda Fryer, cake as well). Thank you Linda, Diarmid Campbell, Duncan Beaton and Murdo MacDonald.

Micky J Gibbard, a PhD student who was also doing research at the Inveraray archives, found himself drawn into my mining web and came up with details from the 18th century that would otherwise have been overlooked. I wish Micky well in his future career.

Jackie Davenport, who curates the archives in Lochgilp-head, also dug deep for mining detail.

Eleanor McKay of Argyll Library Services found it as difficult as I sometimes did to track down historical mining illustrations but, as always, her efforts made a welcome addition to the book.

Jan Nimmo, documentary maker and campaigner, has a personal history in the Kintyre mines and generously made available material and illustrations from her own archives.

Jennie Robertson of Morvern Heritage Society, Veronique Walraven, Lochaline Quartz Sand Ltd, Diego Zurolo, mine manager, Lochaline Quartz Sand Ltd, George King, Alistair Scoular and Alda Grace all provided not only information and illustrations but, in the case of Veronique and Diego, an absorbing tour of the Lochaline silica mine that beat hands down any coalmine visit I have experienced. Jennie also gave me a memorable family lunch. Thank you all and the many others in Lochaline whose friendly reception made research there a joy.

Jim Blair, chairman of Lochaber Geopark in Fort William, and Auchindrain Township Museum development director Bob Clark both offered much-needed technical expertise, for which I am most grateful.

Peter Briscoe of Steetley Minerals was also of great help in terms of the update on the Strontian operations.

Rosemary Neagle from Kilmartin generously gave up her time to guide me to the Kilmartin copper mine.

Thanks to editors Andrew Simmons and Patricia Marshall, and to Tom Kirsop, the Duke of Argyll's gamekeeper, for taking the time to show me the remains of the Coillebraid mine above the town of Inveraray. Tom's family moved from Northumberland to work in the mines at Strontian a century and a half ago, so he and I share a bit of history. And to Georgie and Colin McCrae, at Achnagoul, just south of Inveraray, who welcomed me into their home when I turned up on their doorstep just as they were arriving back from a long-haul flight. We pored over maps and Georgie told me where she had walked in the footsteps of 19th-century miners. Forgive my intrusion and thank you so very much. That goes for all the strangers whose doors I've knocked on, fences I've shouted over and roads and hillsides I've trodden in my quest to produce this book. It's good to live in Argyll!

Bibliography

Books, articles and online resources

'Argyll: An inventory of the monuments: volume 7: Mid-Argyll and Cowal: Medieval and later monuments', The Royal Commission on the Ancient and Historical Monuments of Scotland (1992)

Barnes, M., 'The Story of the Lochaline Silica Mine', *Exploring Morvern*, Vol. 1 (Morvern Heritage Society, 2004)

Bell, T., 'The Ancient History of Copper' in *The Balance* (2017). Available online: https://www.thebalance.com/copper-history-pt-i-2340112

Blocker, J.S., Fahey, D.M., and Tyrrell, I.R., *Alcohol and Temperance in Modern History: An International Encyclopaedia* (Santa Barbara, Ca., USA, ABC-Clio Ltd, 2003)

Booth, R., *James MacMurchy*, The Kintyre and Natural History Society, Issue Number 47 (2000) Available online: http://www.ralstongenealogy.com/number47kintmag.htm

Callender, R.M., and Macaulay, J., 'The Ancient Metal Mines of the Isle of Islay, Argyll', *British Mining*, No. 24 (Sheffield: Northern Mine Research Society Publications, 1984). Available online: http://www.nmrs.org.uk/assets/lookinside/bm24lookinside.pdf

Clark, G., and Jacks, D., *Coal and the Industrial Revolution, 1700–1869* Available online: http://gpih.ucdavis.edu/files/Clark_Jacks.pdf

Engels, F., *The Condition of the Working Class in England* (1845). Available online: https://www.marxists.org/archive/marx/works/download/pdf/condition-working-class-england.pdf, p. 201

F. B., 'The Construction of Ordnance', *Nature*, Vol. 30, No. 769, pp. 285–7 (24 July 1884). Available online: http://www.nature.com/nature/journal/v30/n769/abs/030285a0.html

Geological Conservation Review, Vol. 4: British Tertiary Volcanic Province, Ch. 5, Isle of Mull Site: *Transactions of North of England Institute of Mining Engineers*, Vol. XV (1865–66). Available online: https://books.google.co.uk/books?id=3CNHAQAAMAAJ&printsec=frontcover&source=gbs_ge_summary_r&cad=0#v=onepage&q&f=false

King, N., *From the East Port of Inverkeithing to South Beechwood: 'descriptions habile to include . . .'*, 2014 Neil's Legal Stuff. Available online: http://neilslegalstuff.blogspot.co.uk/2014/06/from-east-port-of-inverkeithing-to.html

Landless, J., *A Gazetteer to the Metal Mines in Scotland* (2014). Available online: https://www.aditnow.co.uk/documents/Personal-Album-9870/Mines-latest-pdf-02.pdf

Loch, D., *Essays on the Trade, Commerce, Manufactures and Fisheries of Scotland* (Edinburgh: Walter and Thomas Ruddiman, 1778). Available online: https://books.google.co.uk/books?id=11BJAAAAYAAJ&pg=PA162&lpg=PA162&dq=Charles+Freebairn&source=bl&ots=Pw1IyStRE0&sig=KVpYnkk4AExTVqsx73r0m88amMI&hl=en&sa=

X&ved=0ahUKEwjsvsCLurLPAhUlD8AKHVoEC_
Y4ChDoAQgqMAU#v=onepage&q=Charles%20
Freebairn&f=true

Pryke, K., 'The Woolwich Arsenal and Acadian Mines', *Scientia Canadensis: Canadian Journal of the History of Science, Technology and Medicine*, 34. 25. 10.7202/1006927ar (2011)

Rankine, A.G., 'Mining Enterprises in Mid Argyll, *Kist* (Magazine of the Natural History & Antiquarian Society of Mid-Argyll), Vol. 34, pp. 17–22

Seaman, D.M., 'Coal Mining in Kintyre'. Available online: http://www.jannimmo.com/COAL%20MINING%20 IN%20KINTYRE.pdf

Sykes, J., *Local Records or Historical Register of Remarkable Events* (1833). Available online: http://www.dmm.org.uk/ individ0/i00909.htm

The Engineer, 18 July 1856, p. 389.

Tindal Kareem, S., *Eighteenth-Century Fiction and the Reinvention of Wonder* (Oxford: OUP, 2014)

Websites

Ardtun (GCR ID: 18) http://www.jncc.gov.uk/page-2731 © JNCC 1980–2007

Durham Mining Museum website. http://www.dmm.org. uk/individ0/i00909.htm

Hansard: Scotland – Lead Miners in the Isle of Islay – The Truck Act (HC Deb, 21 July 1884, Vol. 290, c.1742). http://hansard.millbanksystems.com/commons/1884/ jul/21/scotland-lead-miners-in-the-isle-of

https://www.thebalance.com/copper-history-pt-i-2340112

http://www.bbc.co.uk/news/science-environment-18674655

Kilfinichen and Kilviceuen, County of Argyle (1791–99). http://stat-acc-scot.edina.ac.uk/link/1791-99/Argyle/ Kilfinichen%20and%20Kilviceuen/

Lismore and Appin, County of Argyle (1791–99): http:// stat-acc-scot.edina.ac.uk/link/1791-99/Argyle/ Lismore%20and%20Appin/

Morvern, County of Argyle (1791–99). http://stat-acc-scot. edina.ac.uk/link/1791-99/Argyle/Morvern/

Morvern, County of Argyle (1834–45). http://stat-acc-scot. edina.ac.uk/link/1834-45/Argyle/Morvern/

Films

Nimmo, J., *The Road to Drumleman*. Available online: http:// www.jannimmo.com/TRTD.html

Index

Abercairny Castle 183
Aberdeen, Lord 166
Achahoish 91, 93, 95
Achbraad 91, 93
Achnagoul 176, 221
Acts of Union 15, 60
Adam, William 44
Africa, Africans 2, 5, 14, 24, 90
Alexander, William 72
Allenheads, Northumberland 137
Allt An Doire Dharaich 98
Allt Claigionnaich 91
Allt nan Nathair 93
Allt nan Sae 98
Alma, battle of 164
Alston, Cumberland 143
Altriochan 42, 43, 105
American Civil War 5
An Rudha 91
Anglesey 3, 49
Anyheilt 31
Appin 90, 98, 226
Ardencaple (Castle) 114, 115
Ardnamurchan vii, ix, 6, 8, 11,
    12, 13, 15, 16, 17, 18, 19,
    20, 22, 23, 28, 29, 31, 46,
    54, 62, 103
Ardrishaig 91, 92, 96
Ardtilligan Burn 91, 94, 95
Ardtornish 36, 44, 49, 199, 201,
    212
Ardtun 44, 45, 46

Argyll Coal and Canal [Cannel]
    Company 75, 76, 78
Argyll Railway Company 80
Argyll, Archibald 10th Earl and 1st
    Duke of 14, 83
Argyll, Archibald 3rd Duke of 28,
    60, 61, 63, 64, 104
Argyll, Archibald 9th Earl of 13,
    14, 59
Argyll, George 6th Duke of 68,
    115, 118
Argyll, George 8th Duke of 73,
    74, 75, 76, 78, 79, 80, 81,
    82, 83, 99, 100, 101, 133,
    134, 136, 137, 138, 139, 140,
    143, 144, 145, 146, 147, 148,
    149, 150, 151, 155, 158, 159,
    160, 162, 163, 165, 166, 167,
    168, 169, 170, 171, 172, 174,
    175, 176, 178
Argyll, John 2nd Duke of 16, 20,
    104
Argyll, John 4th Duke 64, 115,
    177
Argyll, John 5th Duke 41, 42, 43,
    44, 45, 46, 47, 48, 49, 50,
    51, 52, 54, 56, 67, 98, 104
Argyll, John 7th Duke 47, 57,
    118, 119, 121, 122, 125,
    126, 127, 128, 129, 130, 131,
    132, 133
Argyll, John 9th Duke 83, 180

Argyll, Marquess of 13
Armstrong, Sir William 169, 170, 171
Aros 43, 44
Arran 9
Auchindrain ix, 105, 113, 119, 133
Auchindrain Township Museum 113, 220
Auvergne 54, 55

Bain, Alexander 135
Bain, Neil 118
Ballachulish 201, 204, 209, 212
Ballantyre 175, 176, 177, 178, 179, 183
Ballygrant Lead Mines 188, 190
Balulive 6
Bank of Scotland 14
Barite 197, 198
Barnes, Mary 200, 202
Barr and Stroud 202
Barratt, John 131, 132
Barrett, James 31
Beamish xi, xii, xiii
Beaton, Duncan 219
Bedford Hotel, Glasgow 100, 101
Bedlington, John xii, xiii, 157
Bein-an-Ini 45, 46
Beinn Bheag 98
Bell, Angus 154
Bell, John 135
Bellsgrove 29, 30, 31, 99, 113, 197, 198, 210
Birmingham x, 39, 90, 141, 159, 162, 175, 206
Blackbraes Colliery 74
Blair, Jim 11, 36, 198
Blairmore (Cowal) 98
Blocker, Jack S. 124
Boulton, Matthew 12, 39, 50
Braithwaite, Frederick 138, 141

Braithwaite, James 149
Breadalbane, 2nd Marquis 196
Breadalbane, John Campbell, 2nd Earl of 194, 195
Brenachoile 106
Bristow, Colin 40
British and Foreign Copper Company 107, 129
British Electric Telegraph Company 161
British Geological Survey 79
British Seaweed Company Ltd 178
Brown Anne 213
Brown, Mary xi
Bruce, Alexander ix, 6, 21, 22, 23, 25, 27, 50, 197
Bruce, Robert 59
Brunel, Isambard Kingdom 167, 168, 171, 172, 173
Buchanan, John 111
Buntain, Robert (Inveraray smith) 112, 118

Cain, John 134, 136, 137, 143, 144, 148, 151, 152, 153, 154, 155, 156, 157, 158, 159, 162, 174, 182, 203, 210
Caithness 40, 41, 51
Calder (Cawdor), Laird of 186, 187
Callender, R.M. & Macaulay, J. 6, 183, 190, 192, 193
Cameron, Chrissie 213
Cameron, Duncan 30, 31, 32, 33, 34, 210
Cameron, Peter 157
Campbell Alexander (blacksmith/mine worker) 111, 119, 120, 122, 128, 131
Campbell, Alexander and Elizabeth 188

Campbell, Daniel of Shawfield 188, 189

Campbell, Dugald (Kintyre chamberlain) 67

Campbell, Lord John (future Duke of Argyll) 106, 107, 108, 109, 110, 112, 114, 115, 116, 118

Campbell, Neil 118

Campbell, Rev. Mr Dugal 45

Campbell, Rev. Mr Lauchlan 16

Campbell, Robert 106, 107, 108, 109, 111, 112, 114, 115, 117, 118, 119, 121, 124, 125, 126, 127, 128, 131

Campbell, Sir Archibald 92, 93

Campbell, Sir Hugh, 15th Thane of Cawdor 187, 188

Campbell, Sir John 187

Campbeltown 60, 61, 62, 64, 65, 66, 67, 73, 75, 76, 78, 79, 82, 84, 191, 214

Campbeltown and Machrihanish Light Railway Company 80, 81, 85

Campbeltown Coal Company 78, 79, 80, 83, 85

Cant's Close, Edinburgh 184

Carmichael, James 96

Carron Company 65

Carsaig 47

Carswell, John 41

Cassel Spectator, The 54

Castle Tioram 26

Castleton x, 93, 94, 96

Castleton and Silvercraigs Mining Company 94, 95

Cattarns, Richard 139

Caxton, (William) 2

Charles II 13

Charles Tennants (Glasgow) 201, 202, 205

Charles Tennants (London) 201

Chinese 2

Chiskan Water 66, 75

Clachan Beag 91

Clan Ranald 26

Clanny, Dr William Reid xiii

Clark, Bob (manager, Auchindrain Township Museum) 113

Clark, Malcolm 112

Clark, Martin 112

Clean Air Act 1956 86

Clean Air Act 1968 87

Clemenston, Viponds 157

Clerk, Duncan 6, 13

Clifton Company 93

Clifton, Sir Robert, 5th Baronet Clifton 194, 195

coal vii, ix, xii, xiv, xv, xvi, 5, 6, 7, 8, 24, 28, 31, 35, 36, 37, 42, 44, 45, 46, 47, 48, 54, 57, 58, 59, 60, 61, 62, 63, 64, 65, 66, 67, 68, 69, 71, 72, 73, 74, 75, 76, 77, 78, 79, 80, 83, 84, 85, 86, 87, 88, 103, 104, 121, 122, 127, 128, 129, 131, 156, 188, 198, 199, 200, 202, 204, 207, 217

Coal Carbonisation Trust 85

Coal Mines Inspection Act 1850 77

Coal Mines Regulation Act 1860 77, 78

Coal Mines Regulation Act 1872 78

Coal Mines Regulation Act 1881 78

Coalhill 70

Coillebhraid [Coille-Bhraghad/ Coillebraid] x, 9, 10, 43, 105

Coire Mhaim 91

Coire Thoin 98

Colgate Palmolive 205

Cononish 98, 196

Consolidated Goldfields 197
Constantinople 181
Cook, Captain James 40, 41
Cooke, William Fothergill 160
copper ix, x, xiv, xvi, 2, 3, 4, 5, 6,
    7, 10, 26, 29, 36, 37, 43, 48,
    49, 51, 57, 63, 89, 90, 91,
    92, 93, 94, 95, 96, 97, 98,
    105, 106, 107, 108, 109, 110,
    111, 113, 117, 120, 121, 125,
    126, 127, 128, 129, 130, 131,
    132, 133, 134, 145, 147, 156,
    164, 168, 169, 178, 179, 182,
    185, 186, 188, 190, 199, 215,
    216, 217, 218
Corran, Loch Linnhe 98
Corrantee 29
Craig, William 157
Craignure ix, 100, 101, 103, 105,
    106, 107, 108, 109, 110, 111,
    113, 114, 115, 118, 119, 121,
    123, 124, 125, 126, 127, 128,
    129, 131, 132, 133, 134, 137,
    138, 139, 140, 141, 142, 143,
    147, 149, 153, 157, 158, 169,
    179, 197
Craignure Mining Company 132,
    139, 140, 141, 142, 143, 149,
    153, 158
Craignure, Mull 209
Crawford, Dr Adair 7, 34, 197
Creag Madaidh Mor 97
Crimean War 5, 164, 173
Crinan Canal 48, 63, 66, 97, 192,
    200, 215
Croggan, Mull 98
Crom Allt 98
Cromalt Burn 134
Cronstedt, Axel 5, 132
Crossapol, Coll 98
Crosskill, Alfred 173
Cruach Brenfield 91

Cruach Mheadhonach 91
Cruikshank, Kathleen 213
Cruikshank, William 7
CS Wind 87

Dalglish, James 136, 100, 101
Dalglish, James (lawyer) 100, 101,
    136
Darien Scheme 14, 15, 20, 88
Davenport, Jackie 220
Davidson, John 59
Davy, Sir Humphry xiii, 7, 35, 197
Denny's (shipbuilders) 80
Desmarest, Nicolas 54, 55
Dewar, William 154
Diamond, Alison 219
Dobs, Squire 187, 188
Dolcoath Mine, Cornwall 39, 56
Doran, Patrick 95
Douglass, John (mine worker) 111
Drumlemble (Drumleman) ix, xv,
    5, 59, 62, 63, 65, 66, 67, 68,
    69, 71, 72, 75, 76, 78, 127,
    128, 210
Drummond, David 3rd Lord
    Madertie 183
Drummond, Robert Hay 183
Duchy of Cornwall 181
Duke of Monmouth 13
Dumbarton 59
Dunardry 97
Dunaverty 59
Dunollie Museum 12

Eardley-Wilmot, Colonel F.M.
    165, 166, 167, 168, 169, 171
Easdale 41, 43
Easton, William 160
Edinburgh 7, 15, 36, 44, 89, 92,
    101, 117, 124, 136, 162,
    181, 183, 184, 190, 192,
    201, 204

Edinburgh and Glasgow Railway 89
Edinburgh Geological Survey 7, 201
Egyptians 2
Eileach an Naoimh 43
Engels, Friedrich 71, 77, 224
Erskine, George 82
Essichossen [Allt Eas A' Chosain] 42, 43, 105, 143, 145, 146, 147
Excise Act 1823 60

Fairbairn, Sir William 167, 171, 172, 173, 174
Falkirk 65, 75, 119, 123
Faraday, Michael 167, 169
First Statistical Account of Scotland 35, 40, 45, 67
First World War 83, 196, 203
Floyd, James 30, 31, 34
Forbes, John and James 134, 135, 157, 176
Forestry Commission 119
Fort Augustus 17
Fort George 17
Fort William 11, 17, 44, 49
Franco British Company 85
Franklin, Benjamin 54
Frazer, Robert 12, 21
Frederick II of Hesse-Kassel 39, 40, 55
Freebairn, Charles 177, 178, 183, 184, 185, 186, 188, 190, 191, 192
Freeman, Martin 93, 97, 98
Fryer, Linda 219
Furnace 106, 115, 121, 125, 141

Galloway, J. & L. 78, 80
Garvellachs 43
Geddes, John and G.H. 204

General Strike, 1926 84, 85
Geological Conservation Review 46, 224
George II 22, 55,
Giant's Causeway 54
Gilliam, Terry 38
Gillies, Archibald 118
Glasgow Iron and Steel Company 85
Glasgow Stock Exchange 89
Glasgow, University of 35, 130
Gleann Beag 91
Glen Aray 42, 104
Glen Creran 98
Glen Orchy 98
Glen Shira 104
Glencaple 106
Glendon [Glendhu] 25, 26, 28, 29, 35, 50
Glensanda Castle 35
Goethe, Johann Wolfgang von 55
Gold xiv, xvi, 5, 9, 26, 40, 41, 51, 89, 91, 92, 96, 97, 98, 105, 175, 194, 196
Goldenhill Cobalt, Nickel, Colour and Chemical Works 175
Gorton Farm 66
Gottingen, University of 39
Grace, Alda 210, 212, 213
Graham-Campbell, John 93, 96
Greeks 3
Greenock 65, 67, 114, 115, 116, 122, 125, 160, 161, 162
Guest, Sir John (MP for Merthyr Tydfil) 110

Hamilton, Robert 86
Hanoverian monarchy 16, 17, 18
Hansard xv, 85, 225
Happy-Union Mine, St Austell 40
Hawes, Benjamin 167
Helensburgh 106

Herder, Johann Gottfried 54
Highland and Agricultural Society
    of Scotland 6
Highlands and Islands Enterprise
    87
Hillside Farm 66
Hodges, Frank 85
Hoeckh (Ansgar) and Musso
    (Kenn) 207
Hogg, William 190
Hooke, Robert 53, 54
Hope, Professor Thomas 35
Howie, John 68
Hume, David 44
Huskar Colliery, Yorkshire 77
Hymers, Thomas 157
Hymers, William 157

Inglis, George Erskine 82
Inninmore Bay 8, 36, 199
International Lead Association 1
Inveraray vii, x, xv, 9, 16, 38, 41,
    42, 43, 44, 51, 60, 90, 100,
    102, 103, 104, 106, 108, 109,
    112, 113, 114, 116, 118, 121,
    122, 124, 125, 132, 133, 134,
    137, 139, 144, 148, 146, 145,
    149, 152, 153, 155, 156, 157,
    159, 160, 161, 162, 163, 164,
    166, 169, 170, 171, 172, 173,
    174, 175, 176, 177, 179, 180,
    181, 182, 183, 184, 187, 194,
    202, 206, 214, 215
Inveraray Metal vii, 171, 172,
    173, 174,
Inveraray Mining Company Ltd.
    181
Inverneil 90, 91, 92, 93, 94, 97,
    184
Inverness 17
Inverscaddle 98
Iona 41, 44

Islay vii, xv, 2, 6, 36, 93, 177,
    183, 184, 185, 186, 187, 188,
    189, 190, 191, 192, 193, 194
Islay House 187
Ives, Cubby 210

James (VII of Scotland, II of
    England) 14, 83
James I of Scotland 194
James IV 59
Joiners' and Wrights' Time
    Records 134
Jura 43, 187, 188, 189, 217

Kentucky xiv
Keppel, Admiral 4
Kerr, Alexander 72
Kerr, Donald 72
Kildalton charter chest 189, 191
Kilfinan, Cowal 98
Kilfinichen and Kilviceuen
    [Kilvickeon] Parish 45
Kilkerran 59
Kilkevan 62, 63
Killarney, Herbert Estate 51
Kilmartin x, 90, 97, 108, 216
Kilmichael 119
Kilslaven 188, 190
King, George 207, 210, 211, 212
King, James 150
Kintyre (Cantyre) vii, ix, xv, 5,
    57, 59, 60, 61, 62, 63, 64,
    65, 69, 71, 75, 81, 84, 85,
    86, 87, 88, 92, 103, 156,
    185, 207, 214, 217
Kip Hill xi
Kirkudbright 31
Klondike xiv, 38, 92
Knockeenahone 109
Knox Brown, A 179, 180, 181
Knox, Thomas, Bishop of the Isles
    187

Landless, Jeremy 91, 224
Langlands, George 41, 105, 106
lead ix, xiv, xv, xvi, 1, 2, 3, 4, 5,
    6, 7, 9, 11, 12, 13, 17, 18,
    20, 21, 23, 24, 25, 26, 28,
    29, 30, 31, 32, 35, 36, 37,
    43, 44, 48, 49, 50, 51, 57,
    58, 63, 89, 90, 91, 92, 93,
    94, 95, 97, 98, 104, 105,
    107, 137, 145, 152, 153,
    166, 177, 178, 183, 185,
    186, 187, 188, 190, 191,
    192, 193, 194, 195, 196,
    197, 198, 199, 216
Leadhills 31, 113, 122, 184, 191,
    217
Leonard, Ann xi
Liedgesdale [Liddesdale/Lithsdale]
    ix, 26, 28, 35, 51
Lindsay Howe & Co. 79, 80, 81,
    82, 83, 181
Lisbon 53
Lithgow, Sir James and Lady 85
Liverpool 90, 114, 128, 133, 159,
    161, 162, 163, 175, 206
Livesey, Joseph 123
Livingston, Dugald 157
Livingston, John 176
Livingstone, Archibald 82
Livingstone, David 23
Livingstone, Donald 154
Livingstone, John 135, 136, 154
Loch Awe 104, 105, 119
Loch Craignish (Barbreck Estate)
    97
Loch Errol (Arail) 91, 95
Loch Fyne 42, 65, 91, 98, 106,
    119, 124, 125, 141, 159, 160,
    177, 180, 184
Loch Sanish 65
Loch Scrivan 44
Loch Shiel 26

Loch Sunart [Swinort] ix, 6, 7,
    22, 23, 25, 27, 28, 35, 41,
    50, 197, 198
Loch Tearnait 98
Loch Ternate 49
Loch, David 65, 66, 185, 186
Lochaber 11, 197
Lochaber Geopark 11, 36, 199,
    214
Lochaline vii, x, xiv, 7, 8, 35, 36,
    194, 199, 201, 203, 204, 205,
    206, 207, 209, 210, 211, 212,
    213, 214, 218
Lochaline Hotel 207
Lochaline Quartz Sand Ltd 205,
    206, 207, 214
Lochaline Quartz Sand Ltd 206,
    207, 214
Lockhart, George, MP 18, 19
Logie Mines 184
London 20, 21, 24, 36, 39, 44,
    58, 82, 90, 96, 109, 110,
    121, 124, 134, 136, 137, 139,
    146, 149, 155, 160, 168, 171,
    179, 181, 201
London and Westminster Bank
    109
London Magazine, The 4
London Metal Exchange 90
Lord Advocate v Wemyss 1899 83
Lossit Park Estate 82
Lowis, Alfred E. 80, 83, 180, 181
Lowrie, Alexander 31, 32, 33,
    34, 113
Lurga Mine [Lurgbhuidh] 35, 36

MacCaig, Norman 57, 158
MacCallum, Edward 133
MacDonald, Murdo 219
MacEwing, William 160, 161,
    163
Macfarlane, John 135

Macfarlane, Sir Donald xv
Macgilvray of Bennigoil 47
MacGregor, Rob Roy 104
Machrihanish ix, 59, 60, 62, 64, 66, 79, 80, 82, 83, 87
MacIntyre, Peter 112
Mackay, John 187
Mackechnie, Neil 211
MacLachlan, John 16
Maclean, Allan of Drimnin 48
MacLean, Ian 214
MacLean, James 112
Maclean, Thomas 179
MacLeans of Duart 13
MacLeod, Rev. Norman 35, 36
MacMurchy, James 69, 72, 86
MacNeal, Hector 82
Maisel's Petroleum Trust Company 85
Malcolm Estate 97, 108
Manuel and Company 138
McCall, Donald 177
McCallum, John 118, 119, 154, 177
McCallum, John 118, 119, 154, 177
McCallum, Peter (mine worker) 111, 118
McCrone, Pat and Tommy 213
McDonald, John 112
McDonald, Ronald of Sanda 59
McDowall, Charles of Crichen 64, 65, 66, 67
McFarlane, Duncan 118, 154
McFarlane, John 118
McGechie, John 72, 210
McGougan, Alex 118
McGougan, D 180
McGougan, Neill 133, 147, 148, 176
McIntyre George 154
McKay, Eleanor 220

McKellar, Duncan 154, 155
McKellar, Peter 154
McKenzie, Robert 135, 154, 176
McLarty, Neil 92
McLean, Captain, of Kinlochalvin 46
McLeod, Rev. John 36
McMaster, Alexander 31, 32, 33
McNair, John 154
McNeil, Torquell of Ballegregar 63
McNeill, James 82
McNicol, John 118
McPhail, Daniel ix, 68
McPhail, Donald ix, 68, 71
McPhail, Hugh and Mary 68
McPhee, Alexander 31, 33
McPherson, Duncan 34
McPherson, Peter 157
Meall Mor 91
Mesopotamians 2, 3
Middleshop Mine 198
Millar, William xi, xiii
Minerali Industriali 206
Miners' Federation 85
Mines and Collieries Act, 1842 71, 77, 151, 158
Minworth Ltd 198
Moidart 16, 28
Moody, Robert xi, xii, xiii, xvi
Morris Munro & Company 161
Morvern vii, ix, x, xiv, 4, 6, 7, 8, 11, 12, 13, 14, 16, 17, 20, 22, 25, 26, 35, 45, 46, 47, 48, 58, 60, 62, 90, 103, 198, 199, 200, 208, 214, 215, 218
Morvern Company ix, 26, 35
Morvern Heritage Society 200, 214
Mount Erins Mining Company 94
Mowat, James 186, 187

Mull Coal Company 47
Mull, Island of 8, 9, 30, 36, 43, 44, 45, 46, 47, 54, 57, 98, 99, 103, 185, 186, 199, 207, 209, 213
Munchausen, Baron von vii, 38, 52
Munro, Angus 154
Munro, Donald 154, 176
Munro, Duncan 177
Munro, James 135, 136, 147, 148, 154, 176
Munro, John 154
Munro, Malcolm (mine worker) 111, 112, 116, 118, 119, 127
Munro, Neil 9, 124, 215
Murray, Sir Alexander 13, 17, 18, 19, 20, 21, 22, 23, 25, 27, 28, 35, 36, 46, 189, 197
Mylne, Robert 44

Napoleonic Wars 29, 48, 201
National Coal Board ix, 85, 86, 87
National Union of General and Municipal Workers 202
Nettleship, Thomas (Palmer and Nettleship) 137, 138, 139, 140, 143
New York 22, 24
Newcastle (Northumberland) xiii
Newcastle (Staffordshire) 173
Newcomen, Thomas 12, 58
nickel xiv, xvi, 3, 4, 5, 43, 94, 132, 133, 134, 137, 139, 140, 141, 142, 144, 145, 146, 147, 148, 149, 153, 154, 156, 162, 163, 164, 165, 166, 168, 169, 170, 171, 173, 174, 175, 176, 178, 179, 182, 197, 216, 217
Nickel and Cobalt Works, Swansea 162, 175

Nightingale, Florence 167
Nimmo, Jan 69, 85, 207
Nitshill Colliery 73
Norfolk, Edward Duke of 21, 23
Norse[men] 2, 6
Nova Scotia 171
NSG/Pilkington 206

O'Connor, M 28, 29, 35, 60, 62
O'Neill, John (mine worker) 111
Old Poltalloch 97
Old Pretender 17
Ottoman-Turkish Empire 164

Paton, Donald Noel 201, 203, 205, 207
Peacock, Walter 181
Pennant, Thomas 185, 189
Petherick, Thomas 97, 107, 108, 109, 110, 112, 113, 114, 115, 116, 117, 118, 120, 121, 122, 123, 124, 125, 126, 127, 128, 129, 132, 147, 148, 155, 182, 197, 203, 210, 216
Phillips, J. Arthur 134, 137, 143, 144, 146
Playfair, Lyon, 1st Baron Playfair of St Andrews 148, 149
Port Glasgow 113
Pozzolana 48
Preston 123
Preston, Battle of 16
Primrose, Archibald, Clerk of His Majesty's Taxations 186
Prince Albert 133, 143, 148, 162, 166
Princess Louise 181
Pringle, John 54
Privy Council of Scotland 13, 186
Pryke, Kenneth 170, 171

Rankine, A.G. 92, 225
Raspe, Rudolph Erich 37, 38, 39, 40, 41, 42, 43, 44, 45, 46, 47, 48, 49, 50, 51, 52, 53, 54, 55, 56, 97, 104, 105, 107, 190, 199, 216
Redruth, Cornwall 100
Riddell Sir James 29, 30, 31, 36, 46, 107, 109
Robertson, James 99, 101, 143, 145, 146, 147, 148, 149, 151, 152, 154, 157, 159, 160, 161, 162, 163, 174, 175, 176, 206, 214
Robertson, John 111
Roe, Captain Jacob 26
Rolling Tube and Wire Mills, Birmingham x, 162, 175
Romans 1, 2, 3
Rosneath 180
Ross of Mull 45
Royal Arsenal, Woolwich 165, 166, 167, 168, 169, 170, 171, 171
Royal Company of Archers 184
Royal Society 39, 54, 55, 148
Rundle, John, MP for Tavistock 110
Russell, Vaughan 202
Russian Empire 164, 165
Rutt, W.T. 136
Ryan, Gerry 211, 212
Ryburn, James and William 67

St Catherine's, Loch Fyne 42
St Ninian and Ballygrigan 59
St Petersburg 16
Sallachry 179
Saltcoats 64
Scotgold 197
Scott, Sir Walter 52, 53
Scottish Temperance League 123

Scoular, Alistair x, 207, 209, 211, 213
Screen Machine 212
Seaman, D.M. 63
Second Statistical Account 36
Second World War xiv, 7, 85, 196, 201, 202
Sellar, J. Craig 199
Shaftesbury, Anthony Ashley-Cooper, 12 Earl of 77
Shawfield family 192
Sheriffmuir, Battle of 16, 104
Sherriff, Alexander 190, 191
Shirvan 91, 93, 94, 95, 96
Shirvan Copper Mining Company 95
Shirvan Mining Company Ltd 96
Siemens 87
silver xiv, xvi, 5, 6, 9, 10, 26, 40, 89, 105, 166, 185, 187, 192, 194, 196, 215
Silvercraigs Lodge 94, 97, 184
Simpson, Darlington 96, 97
Sinclair, Duncan 118, 119
Sinclair, John (mineworker) 118
Sinclair, Sir John, MP 40, 51, 53
Skye 9, 186,
Smeaton, John 45
Smellie, J. and Son 74, 75, 78
Smith, Adam 44
Smith, Neil 71
Smith, Owen Hugh 201
Smith, William 94, 95
Sopwith, Thomas FRS 137, 158, 159
South Argyle Mining Company 94
South Sea Bubble 88
Spain 3, 90, 96, 179, 201
Spanish Armada 26
Spark, Jon 157
SSE plc 87
Staffa 45

Stanford, Edward 178
Steetley Minerals 198
Stephenson, George xiii
Steven, Peter 73
Stewart and Watson 73, 74
Stewart, J.L. 72, 77, 78
Stewart, Professor Iain 8
Stronachullin 91, 94, 95, 96
Strondoir 93, 94, 97
Strontian vii, ix, 6, 12, 13, 18, 20,
    21, 22, 23, 28, 29, 30, 31,
    34, 35, 49, 107, 109, 110,
    111, 113, 114, 116, 118, 119,
    120, 122, 125, 126, 127, 128,
    131, 152, 153, 189, 194, 196,
    197, 198, 201, 202, 207, 214,
    217, 218
Strontian Mining Company 30
strontium 7, 35, 197
Submarine Telegraph Company
    161
sulphur 61, 105, 117, 129, 130,
    174, 178, 179
Sunderland xiii
Swansea 109, 127, 128, 129, 160,
    161, 162, 163, 175, 206
Sykes, John xi, xii

Tanfield, County Durham xi
Tarbert 6, 57, 59, 65, 91, 92,
    94
Tarmac 205
Telford, Thomas 162
Temperance Society 125
Tennant Loch Aline Ltd 205
Tennant, Sir Charles 96
ternate 36, 49
Tharthis Sulphur and Copper
    Company 96
Thompson, Lewis 141, 142, 165,
    166, 167, 168, 169, 170,171,
    172, 173, 175

Thorneycroft, Mr 199, 200
Thurso Castle 41
Tilcon 205
Tiree 41, 44, 192
Tirfergus 63, 68
Todd, James 71
Torchoillean 59
Travis, Merle xiv, xv
Trewhiddle Ingot 40, 56
Truck Act xiv, xv
Turkey 1, 3
Tyndrum xv, 5, 31, 93, 98, 145,
    194, 195, 196
Tyndrum Lead and Zinc Mines
    Ltd 196

United Glass Bottle Manufacturers
    Ltd 201
Upper Largie 97
Uprising 1715 xvi, 16, 17, 18, 20,
    26, 104
Uprising 1745 xvi, 16, 17, 28, 29,
    97, 104, 189

Vandeleur, Captain 172
Victoria, HM Queen 77, 162,
    181
Vikings 6, 123, 185

Wade, General George 17, 18, 19,
    21, 22, 23, 27
Walker, Donald 154
Wallmoden-Gimborn, General
    Johann Ludwig von 55
Wallmoden, Amalie von 55
Walpole, Horace 39
Walraven, Veronique 207, 210,
    213
Walton, Samuel 153, 155, 156,
    176, 177
Walton, Stanley 129, 130, 131
Watson, Baillie 64, 73

Watt, James 12, 39, 50, 56, 65, 66
Webb, Francis and John 146, 147,
    148
Webster and Humfrays 138
Wheatstone, Charles 160
Whitburn, John 100, 101, 110,
    133, 139
White House, Lochaline 202,
    207, 213
Whitesmith Mine 7, 29, 198
William and Mary of Orange 14
Williams, Tennessee Ernie xiv
Williamson, David 104

Wilson, John 67
Winckelmann, Johann Joachim
    54, 55
Woodcock, Donald 86
Woolwich Arsenal and Arcadian
    Mines 170, 225
Wright, James, Laird of Loss 184

York Buildings Company 20, 21,
    22, 23, 27
Young Pretender 16, 17, 28

Zurolo, Diego 214